ic.

Unsettling

Scores

Unsettling
Scores

German Film, Music, and Ideology

Roger Hillman

INDIANA UNIVERSITY PRESS

Bloomington and Indianapolis

VISUAL & PERFORMING ARTS

This book is a publication of

Indiana University Press

601 North Morton Street

Bloomington, IN 47404-3797 USA

http://iupress.indiana.edu

Telephone orders   800-842-6796

Fax orders   812-855-7931

Orders by e-mail   iuporder@indiana.edu

Manufactured in the United States of America

Library of Congress Cataloging-in-Publication Data

Hillman, Roger.
Unsettling scores : German film, music, and ideology / Roger Hillman.
p. cm.
Includes bibliographical references (p.) and index.
ISBN 0-253-34537-5 (cloth : alk. paper) — ISBN 0-253-21754-7 (pbk. : alk. paper)
1. Motion pictures and music—Germany. 2. Motion picture music—Germany—History and criticism. 3. National socialism and motion pictures. I. Title.
ML2075.H54 2005
791.4302′4—dc22
2004019209

1 2 3 4 5   10 09 08 07 06 05

FOR *Gino*

FOR *Ken*

FOR THE SONG OF THE NIGHT BIRD

Contents

Acknowledgments

This project has evolved over a long time; in its broadest form it has grown over much of a lifetime. The following includes but a few of those who have had some input to reflections on film, music, or German studies. To all, the named and the unnamed, my deepest thanks.

Among university colleagues, Brian Coghlan, Tony Stephens, and Margaret Stoljar spring most readily to mind, though it really started with Jim Woodfield at high school. Then came Michael Noone and—especially—Deborah Crisp from the Canberra School of Music, as well as Robyn Holmes. The Humanities Research Centre at the Australian National University, then headed by Ian Donaldson, first let me loose on film in an academic context, a turning point in life.

The beginnings of the more focused project gained from talks with Professor Wilhelm Vosskamp in Köln. David Roberts responded to chapter 4, Karis Muller and Jeongwon Joe to other sections, Deborah Crisp to the whole manuscript, and a number of conference audiences to reduced versions of different parts. David Boyd was there from the start with film studies input.

Like many, I am indebted to Phil Brophy and his team for the Melbourne Cinesonic conferences, an ideal conjunction of film studies and sound, as well as to their participants, especially Adrian

Martin. Many indirect impulses came from the old Friday night ethnographic film group based on the Canberra house of Judith and David MacDougall. Simone Gigliotti shares all she tracks down of relevance, and has lent encouragement when spirits and perseverance have flagged.

Judith Pickering gathered many materials and was full of ideas while research assistant on the project, and Sandra McColl gave both editorial and more general feedback of great value, when she held a similar position.

Beyond enabling the last two posts, the Australian National University made overseas field trips possible through faculty research grants. I much appreciate a grant from the Publications Subsidy Committee, which enabled the film stills. To library staff, especially at Chifley Library, the Canberra School of Music Library, and the Berlin Filmmuseum, I am very thankful. The Alexander von Humboldt Stiftung enabled me to pursue the early stages of the project in Köln and has enriched acquaintance with Germany over a number of years. In the United States, Professors Tony Kaes, Susan McClary, Robert Rosenstone, and David Neumeyer have been particularly generous with their time and their ideas, while Rosemary and Paul Lloyd have shared the warmth and peace of their home, as well as giving much encouragement.

At the Indiana University Press, special thanks to editor Michael Lundell, as well as to two readers for their thought-provoking reports. Leslie Devereaux and Astara Rose had significant indirect input. Earlier, Christine and Siegfried Wiemer introduced me to much of the culture and many of the identity problems of Germany. Those to whom this book is dedicated have contributed to a degree surpassing acknowledgment.

Other friends and family, even when bemused by a largo tempo at various stages, have kept me going and kept life going. My wife, Vivien, and daughters, Miranda and Kirsten, have had to live with this thing for nearly as long as Kirsten can remember, but they have been ever supportive, and without their good humor this book could not have come to fruition. Mum and Dad cultivated a musical household from the outset, provided the space for films, and encouraged the pursuit of German. I have indeed been fortunate, not least with the unfading thrill of the topic itself.

Acknowledgments

Earlier versions of parts of this manuscript have appeared in a range of sources. My thanks for permission to reproduce these in their revised form to *Slavic and East European Performance*, *Musicology Australia*, *Cinesonic*, and the *Journal of European Studies*.

Unsettling
Scores

Introduction

> Regardless of the words, it seems the melodic contour of
> the song describes the nature of the land over which the
> song passes. So, if the Lizard Man were dragging his
> heels across the salt-pans of Lake Eyre, you could expect
> a succession of long flats, like Chopin's "Funeral March."
> If he were skipping up and down the MacDonnell escarp-
> ments, you'd have a series of arpeggios and glissandos,
> like Liszt's "Hungarian Rhapsodies."
>   Certain phrases, certain combinations of musical
> notes, are thought to describe the action of the Ancestor's
> feet. One phrase would say, "Salt-pan"; another "Creek-
> bed," "Spinifex," "Sand-hill," "Mulga-scrub," "Rock-
> face" and so forth. An expert song-man, by listening to
> their order of succession, would count how many times
> his hero crossed a river or scaled a ridge—and be able to
> calculate where, and how far along, a Songline he was.
>   "He'd be able," said Arkady, "to hear a few bars and
> say, 'This is Middle Bore' or 'That is Oodnadatta'—where
> the Ancestor did X or Y or Z."
>   "So a musical phrase," I said, "is a map of reference?"
>   "Music," said Arkady, "is a memory bank for finding
> one's way about the world."
>   —Bruce Chatwin, *The Songlines*
>   (London: Jonathan Cape, 1987), 108

This study looks at the use of classical music in film, focusing on films of the New German Cinema of the 1970s and early 1980s.[1] Beethoven, Mahler, and others on the soundtrack of German films provide a counterexample to almost every aspect of the classical Hollywood paradigm.[2] Classical Hollywood mainly featured origi-nally composed music that functioned as dramatic mood and narra-tive underpinning. Paradoxically, it was meant to remain invisible/ "unheard," while occupying a significant proportion of a film's duration. The cinema movement explored here, on the other hand, frequently used preexisting music, whose mood and narrative ef-

1

fects were secondary to its cultural weightings. This music consciously called attention to itself, not just as music but as a kind of historical time capsule, except that the intervening years had permeated the capsule. Unlike Hollywood scores, this was music with an independent existence before the film, music which was fragmented (heard on the soundtrack in excerpt form) and part of a grand but problematic cultural tradition. In the group of films treated, this tradition still registered the aftereffects of years of subservience to Nazi cultural politics.

Until fairly recently, any book combining film and music would have had some curiosity value. A literature existed, but some titles were dated, and few exhibited genuine border crossing between film studies and musicology. The historic contribution of Claudia Gorbman in 1987 ushered in a cluster of books appearing in rapid succession, primarily about soundtracks in the classical Hollywood era,[3] though both her work and Brown's also engaged with European cinema, especially French. More recently, quite new directions have been embarked on in works such as Nicholas Cook's *Analysing Musical Multimedia*.[4] At the same time a start has been made on translating literature about soundtracks in different film traditions.[5]

The territory sketched in the first paragraph evokes the disciplinary areas of film studies, musicology, cultural studies, and German studies; the present book draws on all these to approach a subject they have all barely touched.[6]

Let us first dwell briefly on the significance of preexisting versus originally composed music, as the first of a number of contrasts between classical Hollywood and this West German film movement that will emerge from the body of the study.[7] Hollywood, of course, also used existing melodies as an economic means to encompass much else. The function was that of acoustic metonymy. But more typically, Hollywood commissioned original scores, and to great effect. To start at the top, let us consider early entries of David Raksin's theme for Otto Preminger's 1944 film *Laura*. They come from a range of sources, filling out the narrative space. The first, with full orchestra, starts even before the first image and the opening credits, with the camera brought to a standstill by a portrait of Laura herself. This is a standard use of offscreen or nondiegetic music, but what narrative authority this music asserts from the outset. When the detective plays a record in Laura's apartment, where again the portrait dominates visually, the same tune is identified as one of Laura's favorites. And then not long after, a third variation comes with a live performance at a restaurant. A sound bridge links this narrative present and Waldo Lydecker's account (with flashback) of the first time he met Laura; this is also the first time we meet her, at least the Laura of back there. So this music has to sustain a visual absence of the person who is the title figure. It has to keep her alive when she is supposed dead. In doing so, it establishes a strong connection to the enigmatic representation (portrait), ahead of the woman herself. But it does much more—delineating, indeed dominating, this narrative world. It manages that by eclipsing any other world from view, which is possible precisely because it is original music, without prior associations, before it becomes saturated with connotations internal to the film's story.

An altogether different phenomenon is the use of preexisting music, at least when used as purposefully as in the films considered here. Melodies as readily recognizable as the Ode to Joy theme from the fourth movement of Beethoven's Ninth Symphony or the "Deutschlandlied," the German national anthem, instantly evoke a world beyond the film we are watching. It is a world with a history that is likely to have an impact on the story being told and a world independent of narrative control by either the director or the person responsible for the film's soundtrack. The borders of fiction and documentary are instantly challenged by the combination of a story and visuals that are fiction (however heavy the shadow of historical fact) and an audio channel with music created, and above all received by audiences, outside this film. Unlike original film scores, classical music used nondiegetically on a soundtrack works against any sense of the filmic text as an autonomous artifact, precisely the illusion that Raksin's theme (alongside other devices) achieved for *Laura*. To what sort of context might this very different slanting of music be appropriate?

At a time when (West) German films were gaining international attention for the first time for half a century, most directors foregrounded issues of national identity. Beyond themes and recycled images which explored this compelling question, much use was made on the soundtrack of music belonging to the classical canon of the nineteenth century. This reflected a reexamination of the hegemony of German music and of its historical layering for contemporary ears, not least its overtones acquired through exploitation by the Nazi propaganda machine. Composers such as Beethoven, Mahler, and inevitably Wagner offered a degree of continuity amid the discontinuities of twentieth-century German history. But their reception also bore the indelible imprint of the central event of German and world history of the twentieth century.

These and other composers were then used by directors like Fassbinder, Kluge, and Syberberg as cultural markers, a function going far beyond the frequent function of classical soundtracks as high brow mood music. The cultural baggage they brought to a film opened up a further dimension of historical allusion. Contributing to the themes of many of these films, the use of music thus became a very powerful tool, not least in its capacity to suggest a simultaneity of three time frames of reception: (largely) nineteenth-century original context, Nazi appropriation, and a contemporary synthesis of both, which at the same time started to head in the direction of world music. (Throughout, this will be used in the sense of global music, music without strong national overtones.) While the Ode to Joy and the "Deutschlandlied" are widely known, their reception in the context of German films of the 1970s and early 1980s is not. The evolution of the Ode to Joy from national signifier (Hitler's birthday request) to world music (as supranational theme of the European Union) is traced in chapter 3, setting examples from the New German Cinema alongside other European films. The Nazi years still permeate the themes of these films and color the reception of their music. This is most evident in films by Syberberg and Kluge discussed in chapters 4 and 5. The Fassbinder analysis in chapter 6, while more speculative, reinforces the presence of classical music even when this is "hidden," rather like the supposed function of music in classical Hollywood.

Classical music as cultural marker cannot be an absolute claim for the New German Cinema; the far more eclectic approach of Werner Herzog is also analyzed in chapter 7. To indicate that the use of such music from the German tradition is not confined to German cinema, chapter 8 focuses on Bruckner in Visconti's *Senso;* it is also intended as a bridge to further work on other national cinemas. While this book focuses on German examples, which of course include particularities inherent in the German context, the terrain covered is designed to be transferable.

The intersection of film and music is an academic area currently in some ferment. But for a long time, with few exceptions, film criticism was content to identify examples of art music on soundtracks without examining their possible narrative significance or any additional cultural meanings they might bring. Yet a crucial element was thereby overlooked. When art music is employed in film, it is not only any earlier narrative role that is carried across to the new context—e.g., an opera plot whose story mirrors the present one—but also acquired cultural overtones. One has only to think of Beethoven's Ninth as a cultural icon, or of Wagner, Liszt, or Bruckner as case studies of Nazi propaganda.[8]

The particular weight of the German musical tradition requires attention to all sites of its reception, and the use of canonized composers in New German Cinema constitutes such a site. Musicologists have certainly documented music under the Nazis, in work which underpins this project. But their scope has rarely extended to what happens when music thus burdened with associations appears in different contexts. And cultural studies, in querying canonic approaches, has understandably been primarily interested in liberating popular art forms. The present study approaches the question of what, both in and beyond a German context, the amalgam of high art music with *the* art form of the twentieth century might look/sound like. Such interdisciplinary issues point to further clusters where cultural studies has yet to make a fuller impact. Examples cited indicate some of the additional richness and ambiguities to be gained from pursuing the aspect of cultural allusion in an art-house film. Layers of meaning going well beyond the visuals can suggest the politics of culture, and they can simultaneously situate the medium of film (and the art of music) within a broader historical context.

The equivalent U.S. form of national cultural marker would perhaps be the soundtrack of *Woodstock* or, as parody, of *Nashville*, with the Barber Adagio in *Platoon* a rare example of classical music composed on home soil. U.S. deployment of classical music, at least into the 1970s, seems to derive primarily from silent movie use. Certainly the function of Wagner in *Apocalypse Now* is closer to Wagner in *Birth of a Nation* than to anything in Syberberg. Thus the scope of the topic opens out beyond the main case study to suggest a model for approaching classical music in other cinema movements. Verdi, for instance, has both political and musical resonance in Italian cinema, while those U.S. films using music from imported musical traditions provide a very different case.

Alongside fluctuations in the reception history of composers treated here, the sources for recognition of musical quotations changed considerably in the postwar years, and they have continued to change. Since the heyday of the New German Cinema, audiences, and hence cinema audiences, have experienced a proliferation of CDs, television simulcasts, etc., alongside Web site lists of classical compositions used in films (often based, to a greater degree than printed works, on contributors' sometimes erroneous information). The credits of postwar films often did not list noncommissioned music, or they simply named a composer without identifying the work(s). This is a far cry from the effect of current copyright obligations, ensuring that not just music but also its performers are acknowledged in the end credits of films, almost like a concert program purchased after the performance.

In the films treated here, the extensive quoting of the canon assumes a music-literate cinema public and is acknowledged at best in the script (e.g., by Syberberg, Kluge). Identifying the music and its frequent overtones does make a difference to understanding the issues of culture, history, and identity addressed in each film. Tracking it down, wherever possible, is not a trivial pursuit exercise. Nor is it only an attempt to understand the films better, or to locate a new site of reception of German music. It is primarily a search for documentation of cultural identity. And that in a society whose twentieth-century history has ensured a complex and far from stable identity. Forged by the unique nature of the nation's recent history, the German case study sheds much light on other cultures and other identities.

Our own historical perspective sees the films themselves as a second peak of German cinema, a half century after the glory of the 1920s and early 1930s. It finds the music, as used in the films, poised between documenting national reception issues and being absorbed into a new, borderless Europe, beyond which it is consumed by a still broader audience of global citizens. It is a perspective that, with the exception of Caryl Flinn's latest book, has yet to be applied to the New German Cinema, which on this score remains a cultural site for insiders.

N.B.: Except where otherwise acknowledged, translations from German sources are mine.

1

Establishing a Tonal Center

The Material

Even a filmgoer not normally exposed to art music knows its most basic conventions through mainstream Hollywood cinema. Some of its standard devices—such as tonality and cadences—can be manipulated in film, since we seldom expect to hear a complete work on a film soundtrack, but rather extracts. These are linked with an ear to the narrative of the film, an acoustic montage alongside the visual one. And film soundtracks do influence audiences.[1]

This study is primarily about a further feature of art music in film, namely, its cultural resonances, which open up another level of narrative. Going beyond the present focus, and not treated here, is film music commissioned from composers of art music—Bliss, Walton, Prokofiev, and others.

My concern is with musical examples of the Classical and Romantic eras which, in preexisting any film in which they appear, come to the film weighted with cultural associations from a particular tradition. Musical analysis of art music may shed light on dramatic aspects of a film scene, but ultimately the music's reception and iconic status are more relevant to a majority of cases in the present study. At stake is not usually the interrelationship between particular visuals and the harmonic structure of a Beethoven movement. Instead, the question is what happens when music, no longer perceived as "just" music, accompanies visuals that are contemporary not with the music as historic source but with its afterlife in reception.

Michel Chion describes an internal combustion effect when sound and image impact on each other. His coinage *synchresis* (combining *synchronism* with *synthesis*) refers to "the forging of an immediate and necessary relationship between something one sees and something one hears."[2] This relationship can be complicated by preexisting music, precisely because there exists a prior relationship of a similar nature, not between music and screen image but between (familiar) music and mental image or associations. A still richer three-way relationship can emerge from the aspect of historical coding of the soundtrack. If I hear Beethoven in the context of a film, any relationship between it and accompanying images will in turn be colored by associations (personal as well as more generalized) already attaching to the music.

Chion asserts, "Film sound is that which is contained or not contained *in an image;* there is no place of the sounds, no auditory scene already preexisting in the soundtrack—and therefore, properly speaking, *there is no soundtrack*."[3] To rephrase what I take Chion to mean here, with terms which again show the poverty of our language for nonvisual phenomena, there is no acoustic profilmic event. But with preexisting music there is. Just as a film set only becomes one once the cameras roll, the acoustic profilmic event only materializes once activated as such on a film soundtrack, but it is already a historically implied presence, however invisible or unheard. It is not just "contained in an image," and it is certainly not contained by it. Preexisting music used in film is reframed by a different acoustic context as well as a visual accompaniment; in other words, it accrues a context in a different medium. Its power and permeability match what Lawrence Kramer draws from Hitchcock's *Rear Window:* "Another way to describe the musical remainder . . . is to say that it appears when one medium (the imagetext) is no longer allowed to determine the boundaries of another (music)."[4] This is a basic given for preexisting music in film, never being subsumed by the images it accompanies, and for that reason lending weight and authority to the soundtrack itself.

Some preexisting music brings a prior story with it to film: operatic music, with its relation to a libretto, already has a defined narrative function in its original context. A director like Visconti, steeped in European opera, virtuosically blends familiar set pieces from the repertoire with the dramatic situation of his own films. Symphonic music is different in degree, not necessarily in kind. The strongly referential works of Mahler, and especially the role of the human voice in his symphonies, bridge the two genres. It may ultimately be impossible to resolve the crucial issue of whether nonvocal art music per se may have a narrative aspect, though such musicologists as Leo Treitler, Lawrence Kramer, and Susan McClary[5] have made considerable inroads into its hallowed nonrepresentational status. But when transplanted from the concert hall into the cinema (among other contexts), even "absolute music" is pitched toward a cultural memory of other historical contexts, rather than an aesthetic experience alongside other performances. The Haydn *Emperor* Quartet, op. 76, no. 3 in C is primarily a realization of a musical score when heard complete. However, the set of variations in the second movement frequently appears as part of the soundtrack of postwar German films. And in that context, even if played in the string quartet version, this melody cannot fail to evoke what it primarily represented at a particular stage of history, namely, "Deutschland, Deutschland über alles." In an extreme case like this, the private associations of listeners who lived through World War II are almost certain to have been publicly molded, and molded differently, depending on whether living in Germany or in an occupied country. In a case like this, history palpably transcends music history. Film directors can draw on the latter to illustrate the former.

Originally composed film music is bounded by the demands of the dramatic design of the film. An excerpt from preexisting music, on the other hand, forms an arc which at the dramatic level relates to two different hermeneutic circles—the original musical work and the new film score. Between those two sites the intervening reception of the music is strongly present. The suggestiveness of such music and its reception history are crucial factors with the New German Cinema. For a director like Kluge, striving for open-ended films that demand significant "work" by their viewers, unbounded acoustic borders are a decided gain.

Before pursuing the argument further, we need to backtrack through more general territory. An approach to music via its ideological reception history needs to be profiled against the dramatic and narrative potential of art music when used in film. We must remember that, in the context of a particular film, preexisting music functions as film music, though not conceived as such. This then needs to be acknowledged as its dramatic function. The residue it brings to the film in terms of context, historical or ideological associations, and preestablished emotional appeal makes it likely to carry more narrative weight than conventional film music.

To clear the ground for issues of national identity and classical music within a German context, let us first consider some examples from non-German films to try to establish what is at stake. Classical music on the soundtrack is probably the only common feature of *Gallipoli* (Australia, 1981), *Elvira Madigan* (Sweden, 1967), *Platoon* (USA, 1986), *Les roseaux sauvages* (*Wild Reeds:* France, 1994), *Casablanca* (USA, 1942—at least a melody from classical music), *A Clockwork Orange* (UK, 1971), and *Hotel Terminus* (France, 1988).

Classical Music as Drama/Mood, without National Overtones

Peter Weir's *Gallipoli* explores a national myth of glorious defeat. The military campaign of Gallipoli was strategically disastrous, and yet this is the battle which for generations of Australians has embodied much that is worthwhile about Australian-ness. Weir's particular take on the battle suits his long-standing preoccupation with an exploration of national identity via what in his view it was not, namely, a continuation of British tradition. This was seen perhaps most clearly in the vestiges of the Victorian era, poised between two centuries, in *Picnic at Hanging Rock*.

Over the opening credits for *Gallipoli* the audience hears the strains of Albinoni's Adagio in G Minor (arranged by Remo Giazotto). It is not heard again until a scene well into the film when, after an exuberant night's dancing with nurses, the Australian soldiers finally embark for their nation's rite of passage at Gallipoli. The bright lighting, swirling camera movement, and infectious gaiety of the ball scene are abruptly interrupted by a strong edit. As they emerge from darkness and then floating mist, we start to make out the procession of small boats about to land on the coast of Gallipoli, the whole mise-en-scène pointing toward this being a transition from life to death. The music to accompany this Charon-like effect is the Albinoni, and dramatically it is highly effective. Its measured rhythm and sustained minor key lend dignity to these soldiers and lift them into the realm of the mythical. However closely the final scenes match the version of events given by C. W. Bean, the official war historian of the time, this approach is in keeping with Weir's primary concern with a historical myth—and not least how that myth might look after Australia's intervening involvement in Vietnam.

Weir's is far from being the only film soundtrack to use this Albinoni music. A further notable example is Orson Welles's *The Trial*, where it conveys something of the disembodied quality of Kafka's impenetrable Law[6] and the Sisyphus-like task of those who would approach it. The music itself, at least this arrangement by Giazotto employing organ rather than harpsichord, was by the time of Weir's film a kind of world music. It clearly carries none of the national overtones of a Verdi, so often invoked as patriotic icon in postwar Italian films. In that capacity the Albinoni perfectly matches Weir's depiction of these men as universal soldiers, whose fate transcends the battle's historical function as the crucible of Australian national identity. The choice of Italian music for a film exploring Australian national identity would otherwise be bizarre. That said, it may well be that no preexisting Australian music could have combined a similar dramatic mood with recognizably national overtones. If that were the filmmaker's aim, such overtones would seem to be ruled out from all but the most collage-type compilations of originally composed music. The great achievement of Weir's choice is its dramatic inspiration. It both lends his film an art-house tone and consciously forgoes any attempt to historicize the events, either geographically or temporally. The latter quality would be a loss for a differently conceived film, such as *Platoon*.

The defining example of classical music functioning as mood, at least within art-house cinema, is probably the use of the slow movement from Mozart's Piano Concerto no. 21 in C, K. 467, in Bo Widerberg's *Elvira Madigan* (1967). The most evident musical features of the Mozart theme—its light and graceful tread, its high register—accord via conventional associations with the narrative centrality of the tightrope, where Elvira performs her art. In turn, the tightrope reflects the floating happiness of Elvira and her swain, with an increasingly tenuous social anchor. More abstractly, the music provides an undertow of fragile serenity—in this, comparable to Agnès Varda's use of the Mozart Clarinet Quintet in *Le bonheur* (1965), whose lush visuals were no doubt a further precursor to Widerberg's film. It is with the Mozart Concerto as background that Elvira tells how her tightrope act backfired a single time, when she landed in the canal in Venice, but this is in the course of an expression of her love for Italy.

Two sources of counterpoint add to the dramatic effectiveness of the Mozart. The first is the prominent use of silence. On occasions the idyllic setting has natural sounds (e.g., birds or the wind), but on others there is a quite unnatural absence of sound. Nor is Mozart the only classical composer used in this film. Both times Elvira is seen in her tightrope routine (on a washing-line she has strung between trees), we hear Vivaldi. These other examples are complemented by a vigorous extract from his *Four Seasons* (the storm, from Summer) as the lovers flee their idyllic refuge. Vivaldi is likely to evoke Venice, whereas Mozart, especially in a film set entirely in Sweden with occasional mention of Italy, is not linked to Salzburg. The association with Venice carries some significance of location, but purely in relation to the film narrative, not in the ideological sense subsequently explored in this book.[7] There is then a sense at the acoustic level of disaster averted once but ever imminent—*The Postman Always Rings Twice*. These acoustic cues parallel, but exceed in subtlety, visual cues such as the razor in Sixten's hand as he embraces Elvira, or the wine spilt at the first picnic, reddening the tablecloth right next to the knife. This film may sentimentalize the Mozart slow movement, but in a narrative sense there is far more to the choice of music than ethereal strings doubling for soaring hearts. Localizing the musical source in the instance of Vivaldi helps generate the film's narrative tension; in the next example recognition of the music's provenance is crucial to the narrative and historical pattern of the film.

Classical Music as Mood and as National Signifier

Throughout Oliver Stone's *Platoon* one piece of music keeps reappearing, the Samuel Barber Adagio for Strings, an arrangement of the second movement of the String Quartet, op. 11. In terms of the images it accompanies, most memorably the torching of a Vietnamese village, the music functions at one level as a generalized lament, not focusing on the fate of the occupied or the progressive bestialization of the occupiers, but incarnating both. At this level, the soaring strings remain exalted mood music, not stained by the same blood as the U.S. soldiers. In this sense, the production's musical sheen clashes with the more documentary feel of the film's subject matter.

The brevity of the movement itself, now more usually functioning as a free-standing composition, combined with its structure as an ever more broadly developed musical line that keeps recurring, lends it a particular quality as film music. Dramatically the evolving of the single cell of subject matter effectively mirrors a war building up inexorably, spiraling upwards musically and, with the hindsight of Stone's historical perspective, downwards politically. Structurally, too, this choice of music is apt, for most preexisting music in film is far more piecemeal in relation to the original composition it is drawn from, dictated by the editing of visuals. Even brief excerpts from Barber's Adagio function organically as part of a whole.

Stone's "take" does not exhaust different combinations of the same music with very different narratives and visuals. For *The Elephant Man* (1980), David Lynch uses an original score sparingly up until the last five and a half minutes, when an extended passage of the Barber (without the climax in the high strings) accompanies the death of the title figure. The restraint of the music's tempo (and, on this soundtrack, of its volume) is matched by reverential camera movement across the model church he has built. Beyond the dignity assigned to the Elephant Man by the visual and acoustic crafting of this scene, any elegiac quality is confined to the blindness of those still seeing an animal and not a human being, unable to perceive the beauty of this soul expiring.

Postdating Stone's film, George Miller's *Lorenzo's Oil* (1992) has an eclectic and far more prominent soundtrack that ranges from Bellini and Donizetti (seemingly evoking both the unreality of bel canto as well as the ethnicity of the central family) to the Adagietto from Mahler's Fifth Symphony (at one stage over visuals of extremely ripe tomatoes, no doubt an unwanted link, supplementing the musical one, to the overripe strawberries in *Death in Venice*). But it also uses the Barber Adagio, or when the melody first appears, its choral reworking as the *Agnus Dei,* and in so doing possibly draws on the reception of Stone's film for its own. Linked to scenes of mental or physical suffering, the music's dramatic profile and effectiveness are reduced by the richness and scope of other musical examples.

In *Platoon,* the purely dramatic function of the Barber Adagio is similar to that of the Albinoni Adagio in *Gallipoli,* as discussed above. But there is a significant extra element, and that is the overlap between the national identity of film director, composer, and primary subject matter of the narrative. Beyond a more universal lament, this music also resonates at a domestic level. It is after all part of a mid-eighties film that reappraises a turning point in the psyche of the twentieth-century United States, relatively unscathed up until this unlikely watershed of history. It is a rare instance of U.S. classical music used for purposes other than local color (as with much of Copland) in U.S. films. Another is Ives's *The Unanswered Question* in Malick's *The Thin Red Line* (1998), beautifully integrated as a philosophical question mark against warfare itself. Its entry coincides with a point of the film, not the only one, where the burning of a village is reminiscent of visuals and message in *Platoon.* But more frequently, as with that other young national formation, Australia post–European settlement, musical roots are stronger in various directions of popular music. Films like *Woodstock* (1970) or *Nashville* (1975) have telling soundtracks precisely because their narratives explore national identity via nonclassical music.

The argument developed throughout this book is that German classical music used in German film has a cultural validation reserved for very few comparable examples of American music—with the Barber Adagio a notable exception. Furthermore, this status alone provides an impenetrable defense against Americanization. "The Yanks have even colonized our subconscious," observes a figure in Wim Wenders's *Kings of the Road* (1976), but they, or at least they alone, could never colonize the final non-American layer of German classical composers. That conquest was reserved for global music, not an exclusively U.S. phenomenon, to which we shall return later.

The Adagio has the further (but not sole) association of "national funeral music,"[8] most notably in accompanying national mourning for John F. Kennedy. In terms of the reading given above, the work's subsequent exposure through *Platoon* could only have intensified that connection. It works poignantly in a film about the Vietnam War precisely because the latter demarcates the end of Kennedy-era idealism. The later perspective of the film's making is superimposed upon that stage of the war when the outcome, at least toward the beginning of the film, still seemed unimaginable. The musical commentary of the Barber achieves then a synchronicity of a historical verdict, overlaid on the soundtrack upon a fictionalized reconstruction of a historical event.

National music can blend with world music when the eyes of the world are turned to that nation. The 2001 Last Night at the Proms brought the unforeseeable constellation of the first American to preside over this occasion in seventy-three years, freshly appointed as conductor of the BBC Symphony Orchestra (Leonard Slatkin), in a performance of this same Barber work just days after 9/11. The dramatic intensity of work, performance, and cultural overtones fused in unique fashion. Yet for many members of the audience, that power undoubtedly owed much to *Platoon*, which internalized the connotations of the Adagio and then proved to be a major source of their afterlife beyond Stone's film.

André Téchiné's *Wild Reeds* is a particularly complex example in relation to nationalism. The narrative is set at the time of France's painful withdrawal from Algeria at the end of the 1950s. The same Barber piece is used as background to, and seemingly as commentary on, this narrative. On at least four occasions the work appears, functioning dramatically in very much the same way as in *Platoon*, and for an Anglo-American audience undoubtedly evoking the earlier film. The dramatic similarity spills over into a political parallel that the director seems to be inviting. For alongside its own Vietnam involvement earlier in the 1950s, France's agony in withdrawing from Algeria was every bit the equivalent of the United States' with regard to Vietnam. And an attractive thesis crystallizes: that to suggest this further frame of cyclical world history, rather than viewing the Algerian crisis as a purely domestic issue, Téchiné evoked the historical reckoning of Stone's earlier film in his own, whose images are so different.

The Chinese box effect (mise-en-abîme) via the soundtrack is a phenomenon all too rarely treated in film studies. The discipline acknowledges visual allusions to earlier films as a powerful means of creating an additional layer of reference, both to broader history as well as cinema history. But the phenomenon just sketched can be equally powerful, perhaps more so for being "hidden" on the sound-track. In the present case this line of argument is grounded, but not wholly deflated, by claims that the director had never seen *Platoon* when making his own film.[9] This does not invalidate claims above about the likely reception of *Wild Reeds*, but it is a salutary warning against interpretations that are too all-embracing in an area of symbolic signifiers.

To summarize: the Barber Adagio in *Platoon* matches in dramatic intensity the Albinoni in *Gallipoli*, but it introduces a further element with its national dimension. This extra element is not vitiated by the use of the same music to the same dramatic, even narrative ends in a film by a French director, involving a different historical conflict. Even if unintentionally, Téchiné's use of Barber gains much of its own effectiveness for a prior viewer of *Platoon* via that of the film context it evokes. Indeed, it is an illustration of how, once a piece of music comes to be identified with a film, this new combined identity has the capacity to take on a life of its own and to color subsequent uses of the music.

Music as Marker of the Other

In a famous scene in *Casablanca*, the German soldiers in Rick's bar give a lusty rendition of "Die Wacht am Rhein" [The watch on the Rhine]. This briefly threatens the status of Casablanca, set out in Renault's opening gambit with Strasser: "Unoccupied France welcomes you to Casablanca." But then the soundtrack reasserts the true ideological center of the film and national sentiment that has simply gone underground with the local populace. Viktor Laszlo enters the room and starts conducting the orchestra in a musical and political counterpoint to what we have just been hearing, "La Marseillaise." Rick's discarded girlfriend, who on the rebound has taken to fraternizing with a German soldier, suddenly fills the screen in a transfigured close-up, her patriotic pride resurfacing as she joins in the chorus, as do all in the saloon except for the Germans. This proves to be the dramatic turning point of the film, as the hitherto workable coexistence of Casablanca's various elements proves unsustainable, and direct threats are made to the life of Viktor Laszlo. As the Germans stalk menacingly through the saloon, their musical capitulation signaling at least momentary ideological defeat, Max Steiner's score intones a minor key version of "Deutschland, Deutschland über alles."

The whole scene works most effectively through the use of familiar, ideologically weighted music. But in this, like so many other films, it operates as a sort of shorthand, with acoustic stereotyping akin to the visual portrayal in countless postwar Hollywood reductions of German-ness beyond any complexity. This is somebody else's national music, quoted by the ideological and ultimately military victor. The minor key version of the "Deutschlandlied" was understandably to be echoed in films from countries formerly occupied by Germany, and to be found in distorted form in Viktor Ullmann's opera *The Emperor of Atlantis*, composed in a concentration camp.

The intensity is obviously different. The scene from *Casablanca* is highly effective within its own narrative, but equally limited as a more general historical suggestion, such as that achieved by both Stone's and Téchiné's use of the Barber Adagio. In films to be explored in this book, signature tunes like "Die Wacht am Rhein" are largely avoided, except when functioning as the evocation of crowds of the faithful, as in sections of Syberberg's *Hitler: A Film from Germany*. The "Deutschlandlied," however, is factored into German films in its full historical complexity, originating with Haydn, but becoming indelibly associated with Nazi nationalism.[10]

Classical Music as
(Western) Cultural Memory

Kubrick's *A Clockwork Orange* exhibits a wide range of classical music used in various ways. For a start, most examples are filtered via a musical rearrangement for synthesizer, "estranging" the music itself in a Brechtian sense and also fusing high and low culture in a manner typical of the film. Thus alongside Alex's veneration of Ludwig van we are subjected to his violent reworking of "Singin' in the Rain" to accompany his rape of the writer's wife. As a further frame of acoustic mise-en-abîme, the combination of Beethoven's Ninth (again "estranged") and "Singin' in the Rain" is subsequently adopted by *Die Hard* (1988), with this Beethoven work again associated with the aristocratic villain of the piece.[11] The musical references in *Die Hard,* in other words, are filtered via their usage in *Clockwork Orange,* lending them a depth transcending the inherent complexity of citing preexisting music. *Die Hard* is an instance of taking over familiar music, both popularized high art and a highpoint of popular art, as quoted by another film. "Singin' in the Rain" in *Clockwork Orange* also functions as something of an acoustic mise-en-abîme inasmuch as Alex's whistling of the tune in the bath of the writer's home betrays him to his host as the man instrumental in the death of his wife. This narrative detail undoubtedly draws on the giveaway signature tune (from *Peer Gynt*) whistled by the Peter Lorre figure in Fritz Lang's *M,* apprehended by a blind balloon seller while a whole city looks in vain for a murderer. But where Lang had drawn on a set piece from the cue books of silent music days, Kubrick inverts the engaging, harmless quality of virtuosic song and dance within the socially coziest genre (at least pre–*Cabaret* and *Nashville*), the musical.

Music of Rossini and Purcell is employed in *Clockwork Orange* with a high degree of theatricality, the English composer perhaps with some muted sense of nationalism. The latter quality is prominent only in Elgar's *Pomp and Circumstance* Marches 1 and 4, introduced in the scene where Alex and his fellow inmates are inspected. Briefly the state guardians overlay a totally inappropriate sense of Victorian order and the Empire on which the sun never sets on a society whose gaping holes have been exposed by the whole anarchistic approach of the narrative (and soundtrack).

But the most prominent musical example is Alex's adoration of Beethoven's Ninth. We first hear a surrealistically warbled Ode to Joy sung by a "sophisto" lady at the "milk" bar and then a demonically choreographed Scherzo. The "joke" of the movement's tempo designation has become the untamed energy of the droogs, its pounding kettledrum beats almost an antiestablishment gesture. Kubrick's use of Beethoven is closest to Godard's handling of the Rolling Stones. Nonetheless, it is Beethoven's Ninth to which Alex is subjected in the course of his "cure." Its combination with what the script calls concentration camp images he deems a "sin," the first time he has used moral language without satire. In fact, what we the viewers see at the start of the sequence is cinematography

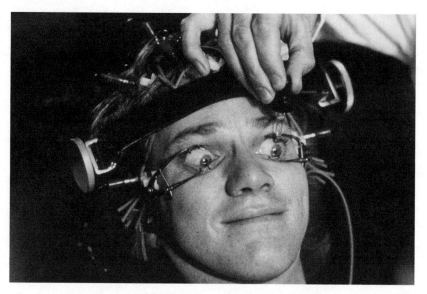

Alex in *A Clockwork Orange*, with no choice but to listen
to Beethoven in a context he's forced to watch.

Courtesy Warner Bros / The Kobal Collection.

akin to Leni Riefenstahl's, not concentration camp images. The
parallel is clear, between the "artistic" documentation that Hitler
preferred to that of a party hack, and the acoustic underscoring by
Beethoven, the rhythm of his music perfectly synchronized with
Hitler and the rally marchers. Alex protests that Beethoven just
wrote music, but with such coordinated choreography the implied
connection, precisely what the Nazis claimed in a nationalistic
sense, is irresistible.

However much the constellation of Beethoven and Riefenstahl is
meant to exemplify Nazi propaganda and the misappropriation of
art, Alex's perspective is certainly not German. Instead, Beethoven's Ninth operates as a sort of generalized cultural memory of the
West, stripping the work of those acquired nationalistic overtones
to which Kubrick is also undoubtedly alluding. Still more complexity is lent by the hovering, never directly invoked sense of the
towering German intellectual heritage debased by camp comman-
dants who required Jewish inmates of concentration camps to perform masterpieces of German music.

This sense is strongly present in the Roman Polanski film *Death and the Maiden* (1994). Although the film has been criticized for "the lack of a specific national context (neither Chile nor Argentina is ever specifically invoked),"[12] this aspect need not be seen as a shortcoming. Certainly a more international tendency gains by the choice of the Schubert, going beyond the aptness of its title. The most beautiful and misused of German music has become something of a blueprint for concentration camp disparities between high culture and low humanity. Such a broadening of the target beyond South America is undoubtedly part of the unstated goal and the European signature of the filmmaker.

At the end of Kubrick's film, a partly neutralized Alex stages a grotesque embrace with the political champion of his curative treatment, now at pains to appease a hungry press. This is caricature even by Kubrick's standards, as Beethoven's setting of Schiller's impassioned verse "Seid umschlungen, Millionen" [Embrace, ye brothers in your millions] is matched to the unbalanced embrace of two, applauded by the crowd of visitors who converge on Alex's hospital ward. Again, the music has attained a quality internal to Kubrick's film, one that divests it of German-ness. This quality is very different from what we shall see in West German films of the 1970s using this final movement of Beethoven's Ninth Symphony as a key to their core quest for identity. Indeed, even had they wanted to essay a film as idiosyncratic as Kubrick's, it is hard to conceive of a freedom such as Kubrick creates being available to their musical signifiers. Kubrick provides an unsettling amalgam of Germanic and generalized Western connotations of the Ninth, all of them championed by an otherwise amoral Englishman on the margins of his own society.

Borders of the Field of Study

In Hitchcock's *Psycho*, there is a cryptic scene toward the end when Marion Crane's sister inspects the Bates mansion. What she finds is an old gramophone with a 78 on it, and the close-up leaves us in no doubt as to the music—the *Eroica* Symphony. The object of our gaze is never played, thereby negating its whole purpose, but functions purely visually as an objet trouvé. Is the choice of the *Eroica* arbitrary, or does it connote something, as the penetrating close-up seems to demand?

In a German context, one might be tempted to think of Beethoven's sense of subsequent betrayal after dedicating the symphony to Napoleon. This could yield a neat, if totally specious, parallel with the betrayal Norman Bates feels when his widowed mother takes a lover. Approaching music as a cultural marker is simply not the appropriate filter for this kind of film. This is the only such cultural reference, and the director's output is not characterized by classical music on the soundtrack. Indeed, the most feasible parallel to the record—which really would make the choice of the *Eroica* arbitrary —are the stuffed birds dominating the mise-en-scène in the motel office, the sense of an originally vital object divested of all life, like Marion herself. Formalistically, the record would seem to be a McGuffin, a visually unexceptional object that is prominent visually, a promise of sound that is never sounded.

But a simple match of European music with European visuals could be equally strained, as Claudia Gorbman illustrates when she imagines various selections, ultimately Beethoven's Fifth, as the music for a scene from *Jules et Jim*. Her commentary, perfectly apt for this film and indeed for most, reads thus: "Since the filmgoer knows this musical warhorse, his/her pleasure in recognizing it in a new context threatens to interfere with 'reading the story' of the film."[13] But with cultural marker references in the New German Cinema, processing the reference is part of "reading the story"— indeed, it is part of the story, of the history behind the fiction level of the film. Furthermore, the vocabulary could lead to the assumption[14] that a story is solely to be read, or comprehended visually, without the acoustic level contributing to (rather than merely underlining) comprehension. Even warhorses, when their resonances are not confined to the concert hall, can function as a further historical, cultural dimension. And the historical dimension, not present in original scores, reinforces music's archaeological siting among the senses, its archaic aspect as a channel of perception.[15]

How different matters are when we come to the work of two non-German connoisseurs of German culture, Jean-Luc Godard and Marcel Ophüls. Ophüls's *Hotel Terminus* is a film dealing with the Gestapo chief in Lyons, Klaus Barbie. Its epic trajectory begins with a number of false starts of the second movement of Beethoven's *Pathétique* Sonata (heard only; no performer is seen). Before we have any further orientation, this acoustic equivalent of an establishing shot dramatically signals gaps in a conventional film sequence, in the pleasurable consumption of music (of music as mood), perhaps even gaps in the German cultural tradition. Some three hours later, after intervening music which has included German folksongs and a Christmas carol, we hear more of the same Beethoven movement and realize that this is a representation of Barbie himself playing. Still later, his daughter reveals in an interview that he played classical and popular music. This unusual use of music by Ophüls demands to be read as a cultural signifier in framing a highly political story. We ultimately are left with the impression of a trespasser on German culture. His rendition of Beethoven confirms him as an amateur, in the sense of Brecht's depiction of the Nazis in *The Resistible Rise of Arturo Ui*, truly an exemplar of the banality of evil.

The most prominent music in Ophüls's film is a recurring German folksong sung with ethereal perfection by the Vienna Boys' Choir. Whenever this meandering film seems to stray too far from its central concern—"The Life and Times of Klaus Barbie" according to the subtitle—this refrain keeps drawing the viewer/listener back to the core atrocity vindicating Barbie's conviction for crimes against humanity, namely, the transporting to Auschwitz of Jewish children sheltered in a French village. These silent victims are lent a voice by the documentarist, their posthumous advocate, in his control of the soundtrack.

The folksong is music that invites generic recognition, whereas the sonata, while free of ideological overtones, evokes in this context the composer perceived in the following terms: "Beethoven as the essence of German music, and this taken to be music full stop."[16] Finally, the historical Barbie is not the pianist playing the faltering notes on the soundtrack. This matches the pattern of the visuals, which rarely show footage of their central subject. But it also shows how issues of documentary representation can be blurred on the soundtrack. A stand-in Barbie would be inconceivable at the visual level. But Ophüls's culturally loaded sound avoids what at the level of documentary veracity is a discord, with another pianist faking Barbie the pianist. The choice of music has a broader allusiveness;

the choice of documentary device has power in its seductiveness. The context of this kind of German music on the soundtrack of a non-German film evokes the tension between high culture and barbarism which is a given for German films of the 1970s, in their reappraisal of national identity issues.

2

Music as Cultural Marker in German Film

New German Cinema and Hollywood

Films discussed in any detail so far, involving ever more complex instances of art music integrated into film soundtracks, all come from outside Germany, the primary object of this study. They have been chosen to illustrate various facets of the relationship between the soundtrack and the rest of each film, while being slanted to develop the notion of music used in film as a cultural marker. This issue, crucial for music in the context of other media, is not confined to it. The notes on the page of a musical manuscript may survive historical flux, but they may also need revision, in the wake of archival discoveries and the like, this alone qualifying any claims for "absoluteness." Their reception, on the other hand, is never above history, and what they "mean" changes. This point is tellingly made by Nicholas Cook when he pleads for meaning to be understood as "the product of an interaction between sound structure and the circumstances of its reception. . . . Discursive content . . . is only negotiated within specific interpretive contexts." Or elsewhere: "Signification becomes a function of context: it is, in a word, performative."[1]

When music is not primarily used as "mood" on the soundtrack, a parallel historical universe can be projected through the earlier origin of the music and/or its subsequent reception. If "the two most 'invisible' contributing arts to the cinema"[2] are montage and music—music of all kinds—then preexisting music foregrounds the cinematic apparatus on both counts (through its standard use in film in excerpt form). Beyond montage as a stylistic device, and of greater importance for the kind of examples to be examined, a further element is created, namely, historical montage, the simultaneous presence of different time layers via the soundtrack. For this phenomenon, West German films of the 1970s and early 1980s prove to be a fertile source, not least through their time frame a generation or more beyond the end of World War II.

Referring no doubt to original film music, Michel Chion finds "nothing analogous to this visual container of the images that is the frame."[3] So, no borders confine the soundtrack. Beyond this inherent mobility, a still more extreme form is achieved when a historical dimension of cultural allusion is also suggested. This use of sound must activate a viewer/listener who responds to it through recognition. Musical chestnuts like the Ode to Joy theme or the "Deutschlandlied" must at the very least evoke subliminal responses. These are likely to vary across German viewers but to be uniformly negative among those from formerly occupied regions of Europe: there is a dramatically effective travesty of the "Deutschlandlied" in Clément's *La bataille du rail* (France, 1946).

Classical Hollywood Cinema relied on a relationship between visuals and sound that Kathryn Kalinak aptly describes as "the transcendent power of the image and the dependence of the soundtrack."[4] But it is conceivable, even likely, that the paradigm might look quite different within another cultural tradition. In Germany, the classical Hollywood relationship between sound and image could be transgressed by the different status as art forms both of film and music. Nineteenth-century music is the reservoir drawn on both by the émigré composers of classical Hollywood, in fashioning their own idiom, and by New German Cinema directors/musical advisors, in directly quoting it. The hegemony of classical music among nineteenth-century arts in Germany ensures in advance a differently weighted balance between sound and image in that nation's films, a balance where there is an inherent temptation to employ music as cultural legitimation[5] in another art form, film, with a highly contested evolution. The same members of the educated bourgeoisie [*Bildungsbürgertum*] who long excluded film from their cultural domain could be addressed and potentially wooed by art music. "Transcendent power" then is more likely in this context to apply to one aspect of the soundtrack, art music, than to the filmic image. By its very nature, as music preexisting the film in which it is used, it turned on its head the standard situation of classical Hollywood, where a film was "virtually complete before it was passed on to the composer for scoring; the composer's job was understood as one of complementing what was already there in the words and pictures."[6]

In the Kalinak quotation above and in other discussions of classical Hollywood aesthetics, the situation envisaged is a cinemagoer who is seeing a film for the first time and is processing both images and sounds that are new. Once preexisting music is used, this balance must alter, as the collective memory of cultural connotations comes into play. This is something quantitatively different from the generalized memory of musical conventions brought to bear on new music composed within old, familiar frameworks.

Royal S. Brown gives examples that are more or less the U.S. equivalents of my primary materials with the evocation of "an entire political mythology"[7] by tunes such as "Dixie" or "The Star-Spangled Banner." But whereas these might embody fairly straightforward instances of "old-southicity" or patriotism, we shall see in chapter 5 how Kluge explores a range of possible associations for a central melody like the "Deutschlandlied," consciously fragmenting cultural myths into historical components that do not necessarily cohere neatly. However much the purveyors of ideology might have liked to impose a particular myth on a piece of music, Kluge as director releases its associations from any unifying interpretation. With him, ideology is not something closed or unambiguous, the product of either a totalitarian regime or a regulating body like a film industry. In their use of loaded art music, directors of the New German Cinema attempted to explode bourgeois myths both in terms of the film's theme (the Ode to Joy had not always served as a banner of humanism) and of the original listening context of the music (transplanted from the halls of high art to the sound systems of cinemas). The way these directors recontextualize German music creates an acoustic equivalent of a negative afterimage.

The notion of a musical soundtrack concealing itself within the larger context is very much a part of the classical Hollywood studio system, while the strong presence of art music in the New German Cinema reinforces the notion of the auteur. Predating both, classical music was used extensively in silent cinema, albeit with particular stereotypical dramatic functions. What Peter Lorre whistles in *M* undoubtedly draws on Ernö Rapée's cue sheets of 1924 in which Grieg's *Hall of the Mountain King* had become one of a number of standard dramatic cues. Thus did the twentieth-century art of cinema draw on a largely nineteenth-century musical repertoire and employ it in a fashion reminiscent of seventeenth- and eighteenth-century aesthetics.[8] Up until recently it was possible to see Hollywood's use of classical music as largely in thrall to this silent tradition, using classical music in a functional sense to create mood. The European traditions, on the other hand, retain the prefilmic use of the musical classics (think of Malle's use of Brahms in *Les amants* [1958]). At its most clichéd, the early Hollywood usage corresponded to a kind of acoustic establishing shot, a musical equivalent of stock footage, designed to illustrate without particular differentiation "universal archetypes or representative epochs."[9] The very notion of cue sheets perpetuated acoustic stereotypes, leveling out national, historical, and ideological overtones that a more discerning deployment of music could retain and evoke as a further narrative vehicle.

In the New German Cinema, "more attention" is "drawn to the music, both because it is often recognized as appropriated and located by the viewer in cultural space, and because the impression it gives of chosenness, on the part of the implied filmmaker, is greater."[10] The way in which such music can open out meanings exemplifies polyphony in a Bakhtinian sense, far beyond the structural dialogue between soundtrack and visuals. It acknowledges a musical auteur behind the film director. Beethoven, Mahler, and Wagner are foregrounded in Fassbinder, Syberberg, and Kluge, and these directors in turn are caught up in the fields of cultural and ideological meanings on which contemporary reception of this music impinges. And in 1970s films of the New German Cinema, numerous examples testify to the ideological associations of music, filtered via Nazi Germany.[11]

Beethoven had been appropriated by the Left as well as the Right up until the Third Reich, and the German Democratic Republic continued to claim him after the war.[12] Nor has Wagner been the preserve of the Right.[13] But, under the Nazis, both composers became the objects of monolithic interpretation, and it was this, alongside other facets of the music's reception, that West German directors drew on in their 1970s films exploring postwar identity. These films then juxtaposed the dual historical levels of the present of the viewing (and listening) public and the recent past of the films' subject matter (including what the music then signified).

Such multilayered music is clearly of a different order to themes specially composed as mood music for a film. Art music used as a cultural marker in film outstrips both parallelism and counterpoint in film music, qualities attributed too sweepingly to Hollywood of the 1940s and the European cinema of the 1930s, respectively. Music thus used approaches the film from a different angle, often a skewed one, because beyond the immediate relationship to images established by originally composed music, preexisting music brings layers of time, relating to the reception of the work. It extends the plane of the film's narrative into a historical dimension, so that sight and sound mesh without the mathematical neatness of either parallelism or counterpoint.[14]

A clear divide between parallelism and counterpoint, and their supposed high watermarks in history, is blurred for a start if we consider the earlier stream of directors emigrating from Europe to Hollywood, among them Billy Wilder. In part 1 of the 1992 series *How Did You Do It, Billy?* (screened on German television), the interviewer, Volker Schlöndorff, tried to get behind the significance of a melody in the Berlin setting of Billy Wilder's *A Foreign Affair* (1948). Schlöndorff's European sensitivities insisted that it must be an instance of counterpoint. But Wilder would not admit to such sophistication, countering that it was a standard Paramount Studio melody, its use primarily attributable to the industrial factor of copyright clearance. Yet the same Billy Wilder, in approaching the "private" life of the amateur violinist Sherlock Holmes, constructed his film around the violin concerto of Miklós Rózsa, an example paralleling the celebrated but exceptional cooperation between Eisenstein and Prokofiev in *Alexander Nevsky* (1938). Availability as a property outside copyright also applies to art music of the nineteenth and early twentieth centuries. But it will be claimed throughout this book that such a reductive approach is not applicable to films of the New German Cinema.

Cultural and National Identity in Germany

Post-unification (post-1990) Germany proclaims the integration of its own national identity into the unknown of an overarching, still crystallizing Europe. What is being submerged—the identity of the expanded nation—has had but a short time to combine its two unequal "halves," adjoining Cold War foes. Common cultural roots are meant to prevail over the interregnum of political polarization. For all the ruptures of twentieth-century German history,[15] this view is really a vestige of nineteenth-century notions of a *Kulturnation,* a nation defining and representing itself through culture, even beyond the belated unification of 1871. This concept compensated for the blighted progress of democracy, while it also maintained the primacy of an apolitical culture. It was one which helped fill the political vacuum of the supposed "Zero Hour" at the end of World War II, and bridge the proclamation of two German states in 1949: "As in the eighteenth and nineteenth centuries, German identity could no longer find support in the unity of the state, and was once again dependent upon a cultural substantiation."[16] Germany, a land of poets and thinkers. Above all, a land of musicians and even, from the outset of the first century of cinema, of filmmakers.

This inherited mind-set still survives. At a post-unification meeting of intellectuals on the question of whether culture can contribute to European unity, the German dramatist Tankred Dorst reminded his audience that one's national identity is largely determined by culture, and that culture is used as a means not of understanding but of exclusion.[17] Within German culture a whole philosophical tradition—Schopenhauer, Nietzsche, Adorno—added weight to the primacy of music by regarding it as the ultimate art form through its supposed nonrepresentational quality, untainted by what Martin Jay calls "too naturalist a mimesis of the given world."[18] The residual effect of this attitude must lend enormous privilege to German music in German film. A soundtrack employing canonized music of the Classical and Romantic eras must then operate at a different level of representation from that obtaining for Hollywood cinema, transcending rather than supporting the mimetic quality of the images.

When preexisting music from an ideologically loaded tradition is cited in contemporary German film, issues of historicity immediately arise. The music evokes not just a different historical stage of German cultural development but an era with a different concept of history, one with a more linear path[19] than in the dislocations of the twentieth century. Inasmuch as music contributes to the cohesion of a society, loss of an uncomplicated concept of *Heimat* for many relocated and dispossessed postwar Germans, and the loss of a musical *Heimat* with the ideological hijacking of key works, would have been two sides of the same coin. Philosopher Kathleen Higgins reminds us, "In the typical case of musical listening, the case in which one hears music of one's own cultural tradition, the environment one feels connected with is the intimately known environment of one's own cultural context."[20]

Nineteenth-century music in twentieth-century film must also evoke the different place in history of culture, a particularly dominant position for German music in the nineteenth century. Norbert Elias explores how the Enlightenment view of culture in Germany was of a dynamic process, not a steady state, with the dynamic operating as a limitless, unchecked progression of humanity.[21] Succeeding this historically, Giesen argues that, "unlike the patriotism of the Enlightenment, the Romantic encoding of the nation insisted upon a radical tension between . . . the identity-securing sphere of culture and the sphere of the quotidian and worldly present." This recoding resulted in the following situation: "While the Enlightenment comprehended the unity and identity of society to be ultimately universal, it is now precisely identity that is taken out of the universalist sphere . . . and reattributed to what is individual and incommunicable."[22] With the last two adjectives we have arrived at those notions which proved so resilient in the reception of classical music, of music as the ineffable, the absolute, and hence the untarnished (not least by the presence of politics). These notions are both evoked and inverted by directors of the New German Cinema, all too aware of music's ideological appropriation just a generation before.

The enhanced status of nineteenth-century culture in general and music in particular is one which the twentieth-century art of film could only dream of in Germany, with local art-house cinema often struggling for acceptance.[23] Alongside the extrahistorical dimensions and ideological overlays that art music made possible in

German film, its function as cultural legitimation cannot be denied. But it also served as a trigger of cultural memory, as a cultural flashback, in line with Walter Benjamin's more general claim that the "shock with which moments enter consciousness as if already lived usually strikes us in the form of a sound."[24]

The most radical break in twentieth-century German history is reflected in the decades of hiatus between Weimar Cinema and the New German Cinema (the latter's heyday extending roughly from 1966 to 1982). Alongside this and other breaks, the art musical heritage has provided a certain cultural continuity,[25] even when its reception has also reflected contemporary history (e.g., the fate of Jewish artists in Nazi Germany). But this continuity must not be overstated: the inflections of reception of this heritage are what interest German directors. Equally applicable to music reception is Marc Silberman's claim for cinema: "The cinema apparatus in Germany has articulated national interests and constructed national tradition. . . . This aspect of national identity is . . . the product of an ongoing struggle between local culture(s) and global pressure(s)."[26] When Fassbinder quotes Beethoven, he is not playing on biographical original instruments, as it were, but is all too conscious of contemporary resonances, both local and more global.

The mix of surviving and discontinuous traditions underpins questions of national identity, one of the main preoccupations of the New German Cinema. But criticism has barely approached this focal point via the use of art music in film. Attention to the latter can then help in reappraising an aspect of German cultural history of almost obsessive interest to Germans themselves.

Historical Context

This overview is designed to set the context for identity issues; in no sense can it give a probing analysis of West Germany in the 1970s. It will emerge that the strong resurgence of identity issues again directed debate to the cultural realm, with a political entity still officially deemed to be provisional (with an eye to reunification at some future time). In the case of classical music used in films, identity issues were channeled into cultural allusions to works with built-in reception histories of their own, exemplifying cultural politics. The bulk of viewers would have been familiar with both the musical examples themselves, at the very least with the Ode to Joy and the "Deutschlandlied," and with the historical baggage these examples brought to films.

Since unification in 1990, the Federal Republic of Germany has largely continued to shore up internally the identity of what at the level of passports, for instance, is primarily a European rather than a national identity. Official opposition to multiculturalism has continued, while moves toward dual citizenship only gained momentum with the advent of the Red/Green coalition in Germany in late September 1998. An ethnically purist [*ius sanguinis*] answer to the question of who is German prevailed up until the introduction of a modified citizenship law, coming into effect on January 1, 2000.[27] A new Immigration Act becomes law on January 1, 2005, finally acknowledging Germany as a country of immigration. But chronologically and geographically remote German ancestry long sufficed for offspring with no command of the language, whereas continuity of domicile and employment did not, for the guest worker of thirty years' residence in Germany. The synchronicity of a postnational view of nationalism with vestiges of an early nineteenth-century Romantic nationalism[28] has been merely the latest paradox in a tradition of national soul-searching and internal (between the two former German states) wrangling.

The question of what is German found a historically unique answer in mid- to late 1990s cinema: comedy. Such box-office successes as Sönke Wortmann's *Der bewegte Mann* [*The Most Desired Man*, 1994], Rainer Kaufmann's *Stadtgespräch* [*Talk of the Town*, 1995], and Thomas Jahn's *Knockin' on Heaven's Door* (1997), alongside the different appeal of Tom Tykwer's *Lola rennt* [*Run, Lola, Run*, 1998], restored to German cinema a commercial viability which Caroline Link's Oscar-winning *Nirgendwo in Afrika* [*Nowhere in Africa*, 2001] and Wolfgang Becker's *Goodbye Lenin!* (2003) have since reinforced.[29] But if not at a thematic level, film as an industry is also reflecting broader historical movements with increasing European coproductions, not least as a unity in numbers approach to the most serious inroads hitherto of Hollywood into the European market. The concept of German cinema was always problematic with regard to national boundaries.[30] But before master narratives of national identity had fallen into some disrepute, and before the fulfillment of Marshall McLuhan's 1960s prophecy of a global village, the New German Cinema, particularly of the late

1970s, thematized national identity as an acutely problematic issue. This was by no means self-evident among German arts.[31]

Paradoxically, the need for a more clearly delineated national identity accompanied a post-'68 shift away from political engagement. This paralleled the receding of earlier phases of the Federal Republic, which had been politically meaningful and contributed to the re-creation of identity.[32] What also receded was the possibility of suspending national identity issues by immersion in a European identity, a combination of new identities which confronted the "new federal states" of the former GDR (East Germany) virtually overnight in the early 1990s.[33] The prominent use of music as cultural marker in films of the 1970s becomes more readily understandable. Its role as accompaniment of a historical stage in identity issues is substantiated by its relative absence from German films of the 1990s and beyond.

The pathological side of a problematic identity was viewed thus by one commentator in 1980: "A people is able to act only when it can tell the story of its own past and identify with it. Germans today cannot do this, or can do it only with great difficulty. Their identity is thereby endangered."[34] In Werner Schroeter's 1980 film *Die Generalprobe* [*General Rehearsal*], the director rephrases the concluding sentence from Ernst Bloch's *Das Prinzip Hoffnung:* "We can construct no positive human system without giving what everyone has always sought and never found, *Heimat.*"[35] The immediately following sound effects are an air-raid siren and a huge detonation. But the double bind is that precisely the "endangered" identity cited above is the kind seeking articulation as a theme, an identity suffering from deficits and disruptions, whose "anchoring in the social world is neither to be taken for granted nor unproblematic."[36]

That a spontaneous self-image was still not easy in West Germany is readily understandable, notwithstanding the beginnings of international reconciliation. Willy Brandt's falling to his knees at the memorial to the victims of the Warsaw ghetto in 1970, and his visits to formerly occupied European neighbors, the first by a West German head of state, came a full quarter of a century after the end of the war. The Federal Republic was still occupied by the Allies, a source of military security and economic investment, but also a seemingly perpetual question mark against national identity (and for the older generation no doubt a reminder of the early days of the

Weimar Republic). The claims by both German states to being sole representative of the German people was succeeded by Willy Brandt's Ostpolitik, an attempt to (keep) open channels of communication, and by their admission to the United Nations in 1973. Within the Western bloc, German identity in the present was fairly and squarely West German identity, an entity without historic roots and with diminished sovereignty (through the presence of the Allies).

Internally West Germany in the 1970s was ravaged by the polarization of society brought about by urban terrorism and the state's ever nervier reaction to it.[37] Alongside the escalating violence of the present, the ongoing process of coming to terms with the past was galvanized among the West German viewing public by the U.S. television series *Holocaust* (first screened in the Federal Republic in 1979). This also provoked the reappropriation of German history by Edgar Reitz in his three monumental *Heimat* series (1984, 1992, and 2004).[38] But in this he was in harmony with one of the clear tendencies of the New German Cinema, in its quest for "a historical memory that runs counter to Hollywood notions of German history."[39]

The identity[40] sought by West German filmmakers of the second half of the 1970s was imperiled "in the wake of political crises during the 1970s which seemed to threaten the self-definition and social consensus of, precisely, West Germany as a nation."[41] Beyond images (e.g., camera shots across the Berlin Wall in Helke Sander's *Redupers*—see chap. 3), the most pregnant formulation of this quest motif is Kluge's quotation from Karl Kraus near the end of *Die Patriotin:* "Je näher man ein Wort ansieht, desto ferner sieht es zurück" [The more closely you look at a word, the more distantly does it look back]. Against the blank background of the screen, the truly arresting inscription is Kluge's addition in capital letters beneath them: "DEUTSCHLAND."

Here Kluge's occasional use of literary quotations functions in the sense of a silent cinema intertitle, as a commentary necessary to more fully appreciate the images. The paradox of a fatherland difficult to approach is not confined to Kluge among 1970s German commentators.[42] In a hefty tome about the history of public language usage in the Federal Republic, the index lists but two instances of the word *Deutschland* outside a brief section entitled *"Deutschland* oder *BRD?* Der 'Kürzelstreit'" [Germany or FRG?

The abbreviation dispute].[43] This controversy, which may now read like a bizarre case of semantic one-upmanship, is a telling reminder of the symbolic function of emotion-laden words and above all of the passionate feelings and convictions connected with this particular debate. In the 1970s two main objections were raised within the Federal Republic to the abbreviation of its official title to the initials BRD (Bundesrepublik Deutschland). First, the disappearance (viewed as "suppression" and "eradication") of the word *Deutschland* was deemed unacceptable by the CDU/CSU opposition.[44] Second, the ostensible devising and propagating of the abbreviation by the GDR, the other German state, was considered a betrayal of the concept of one German nation. That this was historically inaccurate,[45] that the coinage had come into use in the 1950s without exciting the same reactions as two decades later, is of interest for the present focus, the intellectual context of broader debates about nationalism at the time the films under consideration were made.

A seminal film in this sense was the collective enterprise *Deutschland im Herbst* [*Germany in Autumn*, 1978], the autumn being that of the year preceding its release. The film arches the extremes viewed otherwise as irreconcilable, from the state burial of the industrialist Hanns Martin Schleyer, who had been a hostage of the Red Army Fraction (a terrorist organization), through to the very different ceremony for the terrorists who died in the Stuttgart-Stammheim prison. The bulk of the film is taken up with images (and sounds, above all the "Deutschlandlied") produced by a disparate array of filmmakers. All meditated on the question marks raised against national identity and the functioning of the state, by terrorism and the accompanying civil warlike feeling of public life. Syberberg signs off his *Hitler: A Film from Germany* with the time frame of the film's production: "Munich, 25 February–20 October, completed the day after Mogadischu-Stammheim-Mulhouse"— key place-names for the climate created within the Federal Republic by terrorism. Early in the film a monologue by André Heller encapsulates what was perceived to be at stake: "These thirty-two years after the last great European war . . . a major center gone, Berlin, a whole country with no identity. And therefore ominous once again."[46] If the Syberberg and Kluge films analyzed in chapters 4 and 5 largely eschew conventional narrative cinema, they are also to be seen as essays on history in the medium of film, as their directors' highly intellectualized contributions to a "resurrection of history as a popular concern which was so evident . . . in the late 1970s and early 1980s."[47]

Music in This (Film-)Historical Context

> The historical life of classic works is in fact the uninterrupted process of their sociological and ideological reaccentuation.
>
> M. M. Bakhtin, *The Dialogic Imagination*, 421

A number of West German films at this time used either the "Deutschlandlied" or Beethoven's Ninth Symphony. Comparing these films, produced within a span of just a few years, should enable meaningful statements about the significance of these two national icons for probing issues of national (or, in view of the division of Germany, perhaps seminational) identity. With earlier patterns of association, above all of war,[48] still present as one layer of listener/ viewer response, the sites of these two acoustic symbols within late 1970s films lend themselves to a cultural studies approach with "a focus on the elucidation of the specific and historically changing relations between cultural works and practices with social institutions and processes."

That it is not a self-evident paradigm despite ideal subject matter is due to the "fact that, to date, work in cultural studies has been almost exclusively on popular culture."[49] But here the plane is leveled, as "the most German art," music, enters the cinema. Not least through music of such pedigree, this cinema in turn aspires to the art-house variety of film and in some cases even to a nationally representative function. The intersection of national identity and cultural discourse when Fassbinder meets Mahler, or Beethoven encounters Kluge, is clearly a fertile site. The crux of the present project is relocating a canonized musical text in the ideological discourse of a new, filmic text, where this discourse is in dialogue with a stage of the reception history of the music.

It is no accident that Beethoven's Ninth and the "Deutschlandlied" in particular should feature so prominently in these films at a time of acute and anguished self-reappraisal by the Federal Republic. West German film often felt threatened by Hollywood, while being indebted to it, and art cinema served as a form of cultural opposition[50] (particularly, I would claim, the German classical music canon when used within art cinema). Silberman points out how "in Germany the discourse about cinema and nation has developed almost exclusively from 1921 on to the present through competition with American films, technology, and marketing." He rightly qualifies this by drawing attention to the international openness of Hollywood (itself a threat to German cinema with the wave of émigrés like Lubitsch, Murnau, Lang, Wilder), and to the fruitful cross-fertilization of "genres, styles, and themes."[51] Of the directors considered in detail in the present work, this new amalgam defines the very essence of Fassbinder, but (without that invalidating Silberman's point) is less applicable to Kluge, Syberberg, and Herzog. What is truly distinctive in the context of national versus international tendencies is German music within these films.

Nineteenth-century German music in 1970s German cinema: one scale of the balance held an art form, music, which had exerted cultural imperialism in its heyday, and also acquired new trace elements under the Nazis, while the other scale held an art form, film, that was reemerging (above all internationally) from its historical compromise under the Nazis. The convergence of both arts came at a time of considerable national angst.

At the same time the music under discussion here, within a German context, remained immune to "a 'depthless culture,' dominated by the free play of signifiers of culture."[52] The Ride of the Valkyries in Coppola's *Apocalypse Now* (1979), however clever the reworking of the operatic context, is not the same kind of cultural reference as Syberberg's extracts from the *Ring* in *Hitler: A Film from Germany*.[53] In Coppola's film there is no dual-tracked nationality shared by film and preexisting music (though at one level this is clearly music headed toward the global). When Syberberg deploys Siegfried's Funeral March, on the other hand, we have music which drips with connotations of the Third Reich. The music underpins the historical bogey both dramatically in the time frame of Syberberg's film and ideologically in the history portrayed. If reception of Barber's music was modified by its use in *Platoon*, Wagner was never innocent from a German postwar filmmaking perspective. (Syberberg did try to restore our capacity to apprehend his music with a naked ear, free of ideological overtones, as will be seen in chapter 4.)

German cinema of the late 1970s and early 1980s is still close enough to World War II for its ideological accretions to be present as cultural memory. The historical and geographical locations of this film movement resist the leveling of classical music to a "commodity" rather than being an utterance of a "cultural regime."[54] Indeed, German filmmakers consciously factored in the residual effects of a cultural regime for purposes of historical allusiveness. In the 1970s Beethoven, Wagner, or Mahler had yet to become floating signifiers to any significant degree, apart from a couple of chestnuts by the first two.

Both aesthetically and industrially Hollywood could be seen as attempting to colonize German images, stories, and history (and even, as we've seen a Wenders character put it in relation to American popular culture in general, "our subconscious"). But it could never take over German music of the nineteenth century, predating cinema, nor could it take away the stories, however unwanted in retrospect, attaching to this music through its reception within its homeland. The internationalization of a work like Beethoven's Ninth could never totally eclipse its German origins and its changing German ideological reception. The use of art music in German film then came to be a powerful vehicle within the casting about for surviving traditions and valid cultural symbols. It no doubt also accommodated growing expectations of directors, who "between 1974 and 1984 . . . perhaps for the first time ever, were regarded as part of the cultural elite, and by that token, they, too, became involved in what Habermas once called 'the legitimation question.'"[55]

Brechtian distanciation distinguishes German cinema of these years from classical Hollywood, the attempt to address and (politically) activate the mind rather than the emotions. Beyond all finer nuances of "the legitimation question" and the like, Brechtian features operate against conventional Hollywood aesthetics of the soundtrack. For the latter, requiring music to be "invisible" and hence proscribing the familiar are clearly contravened by inclusion of the Ode to Joy or the "Deutschlandlied." In this sense, counterpoint is inherent in the use of nonoriginal music in soundtracks. It is even stronger than the counterpoint, used by Kluge for one, of preexisting images.

The final nuance of art music's German-ness, but also of its frequently compromised reception through the twelve years of the

Nazi millennium, is both a bulwark against Hollywood and a haven for insiders. Its effect on the understanding of a film is akin to the last section of Fassbinder's *Marriage of Maria Braun*, with its virtuosic soundtrack, when that film is screened outside Germany. In accordance with all conventions, and really as the only viable possibility, the banal dialogue of the central figures is what is subtitled. This renders it more comprehensible, given its very low level of audibility, than it is for a German audience. What is missed is where the action really is, namely, in the increasingly loud and hysterical broadcast of the 1954 World Cup soccer final from a radio in the same room. Short of subtitling one track and dubbing the other, the second strand could only be conveyed by the acoustic/subtitling equivalent of a split screen technique. The broadcast brings to a pitch the false solution to the quest for national identity which dooms this construct of a love story.[56]

Musical Quotation

While German films and German music form the core of this book, the issue of quoting music in film exceeds those borders, like other materials assembled here in the attempt to establish the terrain. Is there any parallel at all between preferring known music to commissioning an original score and the use of preexisting images in a film (e.g., photographic and art images with Kluge, or the many directors who cite others' films within their own)? One difference is that visual quotations displace the expectation of new images at that point of the film, with the camera still running. But the same does not hold for music: preexisting music does not replace other music in a continuous soundtrack. Situated between the extremes of a Röhmer film, where dialogue predominates, and the extensive musical soundtrack of many classical Hollywood films, there are only conventions for the entry of music, and they are highly flexible.

What of the citation of music in other art forms? In other music, it exhibits self-reflexivity. But rather than *l'art pour l'art* tendencies, this is likely to point to a historical self-awareness, which in turn anchors the work both in a genre tradition and in a social context (the *William Tell* overture intruding on Shostakovich's Fifteenth Symphony; the reckoning with Mahler, Ravel, and others in Berio's *Sinfonia*, etc.). Music has long been thematized in literature; experimental literature can go beyond descriptions of music in words. Laura Esquivel's 1995 novel *The Law of Love* comes with a CD, so that the reader can, at the cue in the text, hear the music the character is hearing. This is not the same as a CD accompanying a novel (e.g., Vikram Seth's *An Equal Music*) as a sales phenomenon, one which parallels film soundtrack recordings. The Esquivel example has various implications for reader (and listener) response theory, virtual reality, the ineffability of music, etc. The fictional world of the novel inhabits the fantasy of the reader, until the reader supposedly enters that world at the acoustic level and shares an aesthetic experience with an invented character. But the fictional world in turn is validated, and made concrete, by the supposedly shared experience of the historical Puccini. The disregard of chronological constraints matches the story's own hurtling through centuries and across incarnations. But there is a further dimension, too. Accompanying the Puccini arias are illustrations by Miguelanxo Prado, whose projects had included animation in film and television. So the reader is addressed as a listener, and listens to a type of film music, not just because of the music and image combination but also because sounds relating to the images (a baby crying, a helicopter circling) are superimposed on the music. Wagner's notion of the Gesamtkunstwerk envisaged an aesthetic rather than a technological fusion, but this novel points in different directions for multimedia.

In relation to a film soundtrack, matters can be still more complex. A lengthier analysis will establish the dual status of Beethoven's Ninth at the beginning of a Fassbinder film, seemingly both historical broadcast and classically nondiegetic music (i.e., music not emanating from the onscreen space). Quotations of film footage —as opposed to allusions to another film—are generally unambiguously sourced, frequently originating from a TV screen (e.g., documentary footage of a U.S. helicopter during the withdrawal from Vietnam toward the end of Cimino's *The Deer Hunter*), or else a screen within a screen (Chaplin's *The Immigrant* as viewed by the assembled school in Malle's *Au revoir les enfants*). Rare, and highly effective, is a scene in Helma Sanders-Brahms's *Deutschland bleiche Mutter* [*Germany Pale Mother*, 1980] in which mother and daughter in the film's narrative world arrive in Berlin and are cross-cut with documentary footage of a young boy surrounded by ruins. Imaginative splicing sees the mother figure seemingly questioning the boy, but the different film grain leaves us in no doubt that this is also a dialogue of time levels.

The progression from interpolated footage to preexisting music is instructive. The latter is mostly already a "floating" signifier in relation to screen space, rarely emitting from a diegetic source (diegetic music has a visible source [onscreen] or one that is implied, such as a phone ringing in the next room). In that sense it is capable of simultaneously evoking then (and still further back than then) and now. And even that "now" is complex, relating to the music's current reception, not its moment of creation, as with an original soundtrack.

In this sense, music quoted in film is an acoustic simulacrum. Except for reproductions of live broadcasts, the citing of music is a virtual audial reality. But there is a sense in which Beethoven's Ninth at the beginning of *The Marriage of Maria Braun* and certainly Wagner as employed throughout Syberberg's *Our Hitler* are more evocative than a realistic source could be. The already persuasive power of music, when used this way, effects a kind of acoustic suturing[57] of the listening viewer. And the cultural weightings of music ensure a resonance across eras and also across the visual/aural divide.

Historian Robert Rosenstone reminds us of Plato's assertion: "When the mode of the music changes, the walls of the city shake." "If the mode of representation changes," Rosenstone asks, "what may then begin to shake?"[58] The issue of musical quotation in film would seem to combine these two images. My question would then be: if the mode of representation—or its reception—changes through the mode of music changing—e.g., concert music becoming film music which also functions as cultural marker—what then begins to shake?

Theoretical Perspectives

Psychomusicology

The cognitive science aspects of the perception of film music are finally being quantified: an edition of the journal *Psychomusicology* published in May 1996 (although dated 1994) claimed to be "the first collection of articles devoted entirely to the experimental psychology of film music."[59] But here, too, one could expect simpler models of music as a sound source to be complicated by an extra dimension, called here a cultural marker. This involves not just auditory perception but a cognitive act colored by cultural memory. That the latter function is ignored becomes apparent from what the journal takes film music to be, focusing on "background music, music that is not considered part of the drama and is not heard by the actors."[60] It may well be that to take into account the extra factor of the cultural resonance of preexisting music, the number of variables would multiply beyond the viability of the experiment. (Just as I assume the ideal sociological project for the present book was never carried out, namely, investigating the listening habits of late 1970s cinemagoers in the Federal Republic.) Provided the description as background is not understood to exhaust the nature of film music, the findings can still be useful to profile the more complex case of preexisting music, whose reception has frequently been ideologically tinged.

For instance, recent researchers examining the perception of musical sequences conclude: "Strong links will exist between the melodic entry and associative memory for certain tunes. For example, tunes linked with rich environmental information such as films, strong autobiographical or emotional events in specific limited contexts, or subjected to extensive reflection, study, or analysis are likely to elicit elaborate and specific cognitive and emotional associations."[61] When preexisting music is used in films, these "strong" levels of association often multiply. In the case of music used for propagandistic purposes and subsequently subjected to a more sober gaze, the sequence of "strong . . . emotional events" leading to "elaborate and specific emotional associations," and in turn leading back to "tunes linked with . . . films," reflects the use of the "Deutschlandlied" in New German Cinema. Such melodies are then connected with "rich environmental information" at all levels listed, leading presumably to visual associations at each level. If this is so, superimposed layers of visuals are involved as multifaceted "auditory imagery," creating a cognitive hypertext that embodies and releases cultural associations. This is over and above the act of hearing a tune, often construed all too passively as a physiological process of registering. Carroll-Phelan and Hampson plead for a perception of auditory imagery "as the playing or performing of tunes in one's head, rather than merely hearing the tunes play."[62] Certainly such an activation of the audience is inherent in the approach of Kluge, as also in the more generally Brechtian thrust of auteurs like Fassbinder.

Still needing vigorous defense is the notion that film music is part of the film, and that once the film has been seen, the auditory and visual tracks cannot be totally divorced. Art music used as cultural marker in cinema modifies more standard views of film music, involving a fresh contextualization of the music, and acoustic events that contrast with the foregrounded narrative of films. Similarly, psychomusicological approaches to film music need to take into account this culturally more complex possibility.

Film Music, Narrative, Semiotics

Music can dominate the narrative drive of a film, as with the "Euromelody" of Kieslowski's *Three Colours: Blue* (1993), whose musical stakes parallel the Prize Song in Wagner's *Die Meistersinger.* Music can even replace conventional narrative, as in the Philip Glass scores for Godfrey Reggio's *Koyaanisqatsi* (1983) and *Powaqqatsi* (1988). Herzog's *Lessons of Darkness* (more fully analyzed in chapter 7) might be seen as a high art equivalent of *Powaqqatsi*'s narrative structure (with Mahler and Wagner standing in for minimalism). Both Reggio films share the problem of images that cry out for political commentary or at least reflection, as well as a soundtrack that has become rarefied through drastic reduction of speech and sound effects. One level of narrative demands speech, the other removes it. This, more than anything else, is what seems to seal these films off hermetically from their respective profilmic events. But these examples are the exception: in most films the musical score is subordinate to the other components of the film to a far greater degree, and the "meaning" of the whole score differs from the sum of its parts. This is a result of its interaction with the visuals, with other elements of the soundtrack, and with dramatic contingencies of the narrative such as the spacing of silences or the adornment of sequences conventionally accompanied by music.

When preexisting, historically charged music is used in a different medium, the resulting discourses are all the livelier. The present project involves examples where music, film, narrative, ideology, and history intersect, through the overlay of the music's reception history on a new artwork and a cultural context outside the normal ambit of the music. The resulting site of film and music combines signs from each without dissolving them totally into a new blend. This music has an extramusical historical past, whereas original compositions only have a historical present (beyond references to the past: Dixie in the overture to *Gone with the Wind*, etc.). Not just conservative musicological methodology (challenged by all film music studies) but even an iconoclastic cultural critic like Roland Barthes, in *Le grain de la voix* (1972), "regard[s] a musical work as a single sign (of its times, its culture, its author's personality, etc.) rather than as a discourse or text that unites distinct signs into a meaning which is not be [*sic*] predetermined by context."[63]

The present study consciously foregrounds questions of reception over the internal semantics of a work's musical language. The latter are also crucial: the musical excerpt employed in a film sequence will always reflect decisions about aligning dynamics, melodic line, tempi, and the like to the dramatic structure of the film's visual narrative. Nonetheless, a semiotic approach to music used as cultural marker must further expand a more monolithic view which prevailed up until a range of approaches ushered in by the New Musicology. For an overview of what semiotics can mean in relation to music, and what it can offer the discipline, the reader is referred to Kofi Agawu's chapter "The Challenge of Semiotics."[64] Its tools are regarded by another writer as applicable to "a model which considers music as a composite of significant units, the whole having a meaning of a different order than that of the parts."[65] Such a model applies doubly to originally composed film music, where the whole of the sum of the musical parts is itself but a part of the whole film. This alone suffices to explain why in earlier days a musical establishment preoccupied with notions of organic unity might have regarded film music as primarily a commercial compromise, a tonal scarlet lady.

A "soft" semiotics approach[66] considers the music as text without claiming—how could it?—that this exhausts its meaning. The "Deutschlandlied" and Beethoven's Ninth become cultural "topics,"[67] in the sense in which Agawu uses the term, when New German Cinema directors play with musical and historical signs. At one level the orchestral variations of what has become synonymous with the Ode to Joy imply that text; in a particular context the Haydn melody implies the text of the "Deutschlandlied"; and orchestral statements of Wagnerian leitmotifs imply, or at the very least evoke, the written text of their vocalized version. Anything less would sunder the parts of the Gesamtkunstwerk.

In one sense (profiling it against original film music), preexisting music is extrafilmic. But films (like West German films of the 1970s) not overdetermined by genre formulas are such an open entity that a term like *extrafilmic* does not have the same validity as *extramusical*. Music thus used also largely eliminates distinctions between the "nonconceptual" hearing of "an ordinary listener, untrained in musical theory" and "the trained musical analyst, whose hearing is typically conceptual and theory-laden."[68] If the addressee of a film has a sufficiently musical ear to recognize the melody in the first place, the ensuing act of musical reception owes more to general cultural awareness than to musical literacy. With the use of art music in film, especially in film originating in the same country as the music, a cultural code comes into extended play. While often relying on a prevailing connotation, musical examples are not confined to a single resonance in each context.

While music is conventionally regarded as having no code and being without semantic structure,[69] many of its structural devices bear strong resemblances to features of film language that are susceptible to such analysis. Thus continuity editing finds a counterpart in smooth modulations and bridge passages, while a concrete instance of such editing, match-on-action shot, can be meaningfully compared with linking chords, a convergence of unrelated keys to a single harmonic, vertical hinge. The work of Metz, celebrated for submitting the visual aspect of cinema to a semiotic gaze, locates vision on a psychoanalytic plane without pursuing the implications for hearing: "Cinema practice is only possible through the perceptual passions: the desire to see (= scopic drive, scopophilia, voyeurism) [and] the desire to hear (this is the '*pulsion invocante,*' the invocatory drive)."[70] Music as cultural marker in film might be regarded as a culturally specific instance of this invocatory drive, its acquired cultural referentiality answering a need for a more multifaceted historical perception. For beyond all semantic nuances this remains its ultimate determinant: "Musical meaning, inherent and delineated together, is a social construct, collectively defined through history."[71]

Art viewed as "a mediated version of an already textualized socio-ideological world"[72] describes accurately the role of nineteenth-century German music in late 1970s German cinema. The music frequently embodies cultural and historical discourses, in particular of the Nazi era, within films addressing contemporary issues of national identity. Viewed this way, music, once the greatest glory of the German *Geist,* and a vindication of the apolitical, becomes an intensely social sign within the overtly cultural and political concerns of these films—just as it had been in the Nazi era, which still preoccupies these films. Approaches via psychomusicology and semiotics are tacit in the analyses that follow, the foregrounded social context of the subject matter making them immediately relevant. These interdisciplinary areas are also potentially among the most fertile for future work expanding the frontiers of film music studies.

3

History on the Soundtrack
The Example of Beethoven's Ninth

Germanic Songlines or Global Music?
The Symphony as Cultural Document

In the introduction to his monograph on Beethoven's Ninth Symphony, Nicholas Cook writes: "And so, in a way that has perhaps never been the case of any other musical work, the Ninth Symphony became a trope, a focus of cultural discourse." He sees convergence within a range of interpretations of the work, inasmuch as "they treat the Ninth Symphony as a cultural symbol of enormous importance."[1] Yet in the sections titled "The Ninth as Ideology" and "Consuming the Ninth," his wide-ranging work foregrounds reception in China and Japan at the expense of some of the symphony's significance for an audience of compatriots. Films featured in the next three chapters of the present study incorporate this significance within a German context. The Ninth is an international work, too, but its own cultural roots, and the resonance of these for other German art forms, are a rich terrain for German filmmakers. However, this further cultural site has barely been acknowledged. And while Cook's choice of scope is perfectly defensible in a relatively short monograph by a non-German musicologist, it is puzzling to note the absence of Nazi reception in a German monograph profiling itself not only as a performance history of the work but also as a history of its reception, ideological as well as aesthetic.[2]

47

Cultural symbols are not static, historical givens, but in turn have their own reception history. Alongside a common reservoir of connotations, mostly relating to the message of universal brotherhood in the last movement's setting of a Schiller ode, Beethoven's Ninth has meant different things to different generations.[3] Beethoven was the first composer whose compositions Jewish musicians were no longer allowed to play under the Nazi regime. In the concert season of 1941–42, Beethoven's Ninth was performed more frequently than any other symphony.[4] Furtwängler, already associated with the work beyond the concert platform via a filmed prewar concert screened in cinemas,[5] conducted it for the Führer's birthday in 1937 and 1942, on the first occasion at Goebbels's behest, on the second at Hitler's. Yet when the Bayreuth Festival was reopened for the first postwar season in July 1951, it was again Furtwängler who, echoing the original 1872 program, conducted Beethoven's Ninth in "what amounted to a re-consecration of the house that Richard Wagner built."[6] The choice of music was unchanged, but the successive names of (a) conductor, (b) composer performed, and (c) composer enshrined encapsulates the whole point being made here. In 1872 the triad was Wagner–Beethoven–Wagner. In 1951 the only change on the surface was Furtwängler for Wagner in the first capacity.[7] The conductor's contentious relationship with the Nazis has recently been reexamined in Szabó's film *Taking Sides* (2001). This relationship plus the Third Reich's ideological coloring of music, not least the two composers mentioned here, made for a transformed constellation.

Worldwide attention focused on the phoenix of Bayreuth. Beethoven's work had caused the Nazis problems with the "internationalist" tendencies of its final movement's text. But here it served as a bridge, no doubt a combined German and international bridge, to the works of a composer identified with the Nazi state, Israel refusing to allow performances of Wagner (and Richard Strauss) in the wake of World War II. The tension between nationalistic German and international symbolic value was no more glaringly apparent than in the performance of the final choral entry of the Ninth Symphony at the opening of the 1936 Berlin Olympics.[8] At the 1960 Games in Rome and those of 1964 in Tokyo, it featured as the anthem of the combined team from West and East Germany, a utopian

Enlightenment vestige recalling the cultural/historical links of Cold War foes.[9]

Preceding the new Germany's evolution within a new Europe, the Ode to Joy had become the supranational anthem of the European Community.[10] Just fifty years on from Hitler's birthday of 1942, the closing ceremony of the Barcelona Olympics included a Reader's Digest (or Listener's Digest) version of the Ode to Joy. It was reduced to a reinstrumented variation on a melody, effecting all the more readily the merging of German with European identity. To oversimplify, the reception of Beethoven (and particularly the Ninth) has completed the cycle of being deemed internationalist, nationalist, and then again internationalist—paralleled in its reception history by the following stages of the Olympic Games: (a) Baron Coubertin's original suggestion that the Ode to Joy accompany the opening ceremony,[11] (b) Berlin 1936, (c) Barcelona 1992 and Atlanta 1996. The internationalist dimension has officially exceeded a European frame with the score of this symphony becoming the first composition added to the UNESCO Memory of the World program (an archive of international cultural treasures) in January 2003.

In the late seventies, German film directors drew on the ambiguities of the work's earlier status and especially any residue of Nazi associations. The tension between national and international resonances makes this cultural icon an ideal vehicle for exploring questions of German identity, since its blend mirrored the whole *Deutschlandfrage*—the question up until 1989 of the desirability/feasibility of a (re)unified Germany. The multiple and opposed meanings residing in the Ninth in a German context are what generate its power in the hands of a filmmaker sensitive to the soundtrack, where its actual quotation in an estranged context makes it so much more plastic than in literature—for example, its significant but abstract role in Thomas Mann's *Doktor Faustus*, when revoked by the composer Leverkühn. The same estranged context furthermore creates ambiguities. Caryl Clark asks, "Is Beethoven's Ninth inviolable? As an artwork, yes, but not as a political symbol."[12] When this symphony is used in German cinema, it functions both as cited artwork and political symbol, and hence the boundaries of its inviolability are far less assured. It simultaneously functions (a) as a dramatically secondary artwork within the primary artwork that is the particular film; (b) within a culture ranking music aesthetically higher than film; and (c) as a symbol of different historical stages of German politics.

While Adorno branded poetry after Auschwitz an obscenity, Marcuse found this symphony's illusionary—utopian—quality untenable in the same historical context.[13] Nonetheless, the staging of music deemed still more compromised by this criterion could find an injection of new symbolic energy from film. A telling example was the centenary Bayreuth production of the *Ring* by Pierre Boulez and Patrice Chéreau, with the opening sets of *Das Rheingold* (the hydroelectric dam on the Rhine) evocative (via the stage prop of Moloch) of a comparable vertical configuration of power in Fritz Lang's *Metropolis*. Film has at the very least found inspiration in the formal qualities of Beethoven's Ninth, before adding nuances to Marcuse's verdict. The cyclic principle of its last movement, utilized by Syberberg in *Hitler: A Film from Germany*, informs the director's view of the progression of German history. In this it is in tension with the Enlightenment view in Schiller's text that the perfectibility of humanity could pursue a smooth path like the course of the stars—that is, a linear (ever ascendant) view of history embedded in an eighteenth-century literary and philosophical topos for the sublime.[14] To anticipate arguments to be developed in chapters 4 and 5: the point at which Syberberg leaves the Ninth suspended (the concluding bars of the section "Adagio ma non troppo, ma divoto" of the fourth movement) could also be seen as an equivalent to Leverkühn's retraction of the work. Kluge's *Die Patriotin*, on the other hand, doesn't just take back the work in a negating sense. It repositions it, relocating the utopian impulses of the last movement in the political Left, where its text would seem more at home. This was expressed most emphatically by Hanns Eisler in 1938: "This Beethoven is not a witness for the fascist dictatorship, but he is the model for the anti-fascist, and the great witness for truth and the justice of our struggle. In him are embodied the best ideas and thoughts of the progressive bourgeoisie of the French Revolution."[15] Ideological accretions it has, or had, but these never sufficed to make it irredeemable.

The virtuosic way in which film can suggest these associations is illustrated by a brief example from Godard's *Allemagne 90 neuf zéro* [*Germany Year 90 Nine Zero*, 1991]. This film features a wide-ranging dissection of German philosophy, literature, cinema, and music alongside its distinctive slant on political reunification. Behind visuals featuring a kind of intellectual guided tour of Weimar, the soundtrack briefly features a snatch of Beethoven's Ninth Symphony, not the usual fourth movement, but the second, not with full orchestra, but in Liszt's piano transcription. At the level of cultural history this recalls how Liszt's settling there as musical director to the Prince revived the fame of the city of Weimar classicism. Dramatically it brings out the non-iconic in an iconic work, in a version that is still avowedly artistic. In short, the reference is (also) a cipher for the signature of Godard himself, also (like Liszt) not German-born, but steeped in German culture, reworking classically German material in often iconoclastic fashion. Behind this establishing of his own position as filmmaker/commentator lies the archaeology of an artistic tradition, palimpsest layers superimposed on the German original, which paradoxically can reveal more through their combined insider/outsider perspective. The historical moment for making a comparably probing German film about the fall of the Wall is past.[16] This cultural layer inevitably intersects with political and historical strands. Without further narrative pointing by Godard, Weimar also evokes the failed Republic, the precursor to the Hitler era, while in the later time frame a Liszt fanfare served as a signature prelude to radio announcements from the Eastern front.

Film's built-in dialogue as a technological and narrative medium —above all in the hands of a director like Kluge—can unmask the unilinearity and absolute claims of ideological overtones. This holds not just for a state apparatus, as in liberating an artwork like Beethoven's Ninth from the aesthetic cast lent it by Wagner. The interplay of visual and acoustic tracks is further complemented by the possibility of simultaneously overlapping historical layers. In Kluge's *Die Patriotin* this occurs with the central figure, forever interrogating German history, listening to a live broadcast of the Ninth on New Year's Eve. This timing evokes a tradition of the Left going back to the turn of the year 1918/19 and a concert staged by the Leipzig Workers' Educational Institute. It thereby honors an alternative strand submerged by actual history, which had lent this work very different associations. Historical layers are perhaps best

Unsettling Scores

52

exemplified by the program for the 1937 "Celebration of Germanism" in Paris, itself an adjunct to the feting of Leni Riefenstahl's *Triumph of the Will*. As preludes to Beethoven's Ninth, the Berlin Philharmonic under Furtwängler played the "Deutschlandlied" and the "Horst Wessel-Lied," the latter becoming a compulsory tandem accompaniment to the national hymn from 1940, until both were banned by the Allies after victory in 1945.[17] The fluctuating historical fortunes and resonances of the "Deutschlandlied" will be detailed in chapter 5: its original form and purpose were quite different from its reinstrumentation as a march. The "Horst Wessel-Lied" seems to have plagiarized a pre–World War I workers' song, "Die Fahne hoch."[18] It is easy to forget that in terms of voter patterns, German history around 1930 faced alternatives of the Far Left or the Far Right; their rhetoric, as this example indicates, was to a degree interchangeable. The grouping of Beethoven's Ninth with these two martial pieces showcased its baneful appropriation by the Nazis to represent a supposedly superior national(istic) culture. The performers in 1937 Paris only furthered this ambiguity. Strengthening this strand of associations attaching to Beethoven's Ninth was its performance by the Berlin Philharmonic at the first Reichsmusiktage in Düsseldorf in 1938.[19]

When art music is cited in a film, conventions of instrumentation, rhythm, etc., are predetermined, unless an adaptation is involved. Certainly musical arrangements can achieve a strongly Brechtian effect, as in the harmonica-type reductions of Beethoven's Ninth in Tarkovsky's *Nostalghia* (1983). But faithful quotation of a musical text—in a particular interpretive performance—raises the question: to what degree is an earlier musical context carried across when an excerpt is used? Or is it precisely the triumphant chorus(es) of Ode to Joy that is/are relevant, as a popular icon, and not the whole symphonic setting of the movement, let alone its place within the structure of the symphony? The following examples explore the use of Beethoven's Ninth in a wide range of European films, to approach an answer to this question.[20]

Helke Sander's *Redupers*
[*The All-Round Reduced Personality*, 1977]

"I ask the viewer to consider a given situation from an alternative perspective, namely, a divided Berlin from a woman's perspective.

It's a subversive procedure, perhaps even a form of utopia."[21] How to express musically such a utopia from a woman's perspective? What Helke Sander employs is that long-serving utopia from the German idealist tradition, the "Alle Menschen werden Brüder" section of Beethoven's setting of Schiller's *Ode to Joy*. This strongly gendered film makes relatively sparse use of music, and with one exception the other examples are popular forms. But at a crucial stage of Sander's film, the turn to German music with international overtones in the text is itself utopian.

Earlier sequences establish the absurdity of Berlin as a linguistic and ideological Babel, illustrated by a medley of radio voices, a device taken up by Wenders's *Der Himmel über Berlin* [*Wings of Desire*, 1987]. A utopian perspective is also present early with a body keeping alive the hope of returning to an undivided Germany, the Kuratorium unteilbares Deutschland (Office for an Indivisible Germany). In this narrative about the processes of photography, both aesthetic and industrial, the capacity of telephoto lenses to traverse the no man's land surrounding the Wall becomes a further utopian element. It seems to be one of the assumptions of the film that the project for which the women's collective gains financing, "women photographers see our city," entails an ability to see through the political fences created by the patriarchy in the name of ideological coexistence. Not discrepancies but similarities between the two cities, or parts of the one city, interest the group, and likewise public graffiti rather than the slogans of ideologues.

Roughly halfway through the film comes a sequence that generates musical intensity until there is a direct transition from the triumphal final chorus of the *Choral* Symphony to a pop song, as the main figure looks at photos in her car. The Schiller text of "Alle Menschen werden Brüder" (written well before the first unification of Germany) is both ironic commentary on, but also utopian transfiguration of, the palpable division of the German nation, which in turn signaled the division of Europe into Western and Eastern power blocs. Later a gallery browser states categorically that culture in Berlin is a political matter, not just culture. In this he consciously differentiates Berlin from Stuttgart or Hamburg: without further internal nuancing, this politicization of German art in the late 1960s and the 1970s is one of the main springboards of the present study. The ironic side of the Beethoven/Schiller quotation has been compounded by the immediately preceding news of UN Secretary-

The Berlin Wall as Russian doll effect, visually and musically gendered:
The Allround Reduced Personality.

Courtesy Basis-Film / The Kobal Collection.

General Kurt Waldheim sending greetings to other intelligent be-
ings with the Voyager space capsule, on behalf of humanity, as it
were. The cosmic unity projected there, contradicted most tellingly
by the division of Berlin, is itself a kind of macrocosm of Schiller's
text vis-à-vis the reality of German politics, then and now (in the
film's present). Sander's Berlin has become the point of geographic
convergence of Eastern and Western power blocs, a division which
has sundered former "Brüder" within the one land. With the underscore of universally revered German art, the visuals testify to the
inversion of universal brotherhood.

But there is a further link to this chain of associations. Earlier in
the film the women erected a curtain over their exhibition, but it
was still not impressive enough. This simply reflects the paradoxes
within the photographic material itself, as the voice-over ruminates
on the view into the East: "Is not the glance into the workers'
fatherland enhanced by the curtain? Is this also the motherland for

the hopes of women?" There follows a sad sigh for the mind's con-
structs so outstripping the tangible evidence that utopias can seem
escapist rather than visionary.[22] Directly adjacent to the subject
matter it depicts, the photograph of a section of the Wall creates a
mise-en-abîme effect that is in turn a metaphor for the representations through female eyes that are dwarfed by the monumental political realities of what they seek to show.

All this is accompanied by music that gradually builds up from
instruments in dialogue with a piano to an orchestral tutti. The accompanying visuals show a cross-section of Berlin's multicultural
masses going up to an observation point affording a view across
the Wall. The music crystallizes as Beethoven's Fantasy for Piano,
Chorus and Orchestra, op. 80. Using this precursor of the Ninth
Symphony exemplifies the director's concern with the processes of
evolution rather than with their concealment in the final product,
and is a highly ingenious example of music supporting both process
and theme of the visuals.

The use of the *Choral Fantasy* is to my knowledge unique in the
New German Cinema. It gives a refreshing new slant to the effective integration of a set piece such as the conclusion to the Ninth.
Formally the conjunction of the Fantasy with the Ninth provides
an acoustic mise-en-abîme that parallels the visual one discussed
above. It also reflects a mise-en-abîme of gender politics. The work-
in-progress Beethoven accompanying the women's photographic depiction of the Wall at least sheds new light on the objects scrutinized and stresses their provisional nature. As used here, the Ode
to Joy itself and the real Wall are bastions of male monumentality.
But nothing seems capable of bridging the political and gendered
discrepancies.

Sander's bookending of her sequence with the *Choral Fantasy* and
the Ode to Joy is far from just the primitive prototype that the final model perfects. In *A Thousand Plateaus*, Deleuze and Guattari
claim that "when development subordinates form and spans the
whole, as in Beethoven, variation begins to free itself and becomes
identified with creation."[23] This is one of the many senses emerging
from the juxtaposition of the two Beethoven works here and what
they accompany. The *Choral Fantasy* embodies a jaunty multivocality
—a whole range of instruments having riffs with the piano; a sense
of a new perspective on familiar territory, both with the women's

artwork itself and the way it frames the gray reality of the Wall and the other side. Indeed, there is a sense of variation freeing itself and becoming creation: Sander's use of this Beethoven work is highly creative. But it is still Beethoven, not some German Laurie Anderson.

The male giant prevails, just as the Berlin Wall prevails, the monument to politics at its most economically rational extreme: if the workers you have educated persist in crossing the border to power the enemy economy, you deny them freedom of movement to protect your own economy. On the other side of the film's own Wall, a Wall in the head that is gender division, we have far less fluid camera movement to accompany the immovable Wall and the unshakable musical icon, grand, monumental, but ultimately sterile, defying the high-sounding rhetoric of male words, "Embrace, ye brothers in your millions." The clash between the Wall and Beethoven's Ninth in this film is not unlike that between the same work and the Nuremberg Rallies in Kubrick's *Clockwork Orange*.

But there are also bigger issues implicit in the use of Beethoven on a film soundtrack, especially a film with a female director. Cultural theorist Martin Jay raises the issue of a hierarchy of the senses, claiming the German hermeneutic tradition favors hearing, where the French is captive to vision.[24] Coming from a different angle, John Shepherd claims that "male hegemony . . . is essentially a *visual hegemony*."[25] And in the foreword to Michel Chion's *Audio-Vision*, none less than Walter Murch speaks of film as a marriage between King Sight and Queen Sound.[26] Are the senses gendered, and what do we make of complex interplays between sight and sound such as we find in film, not least in German film using the canon rather than originally commissioned scores, and in the present case, directed by a woman?

And where might Beethoven fit in all this? In an article provocatively titled "Model: Beethoven as a Chauvinist," Albrecht Riethmüller sets about addressing claims that Beethoven might have been a chauvinist either in a nationalistic sense or in a gender sense. But on the first score, at least, it is impossible to dispose totally of the Beethoven reception, a paler but still significant reflection of the Wagner phenomenon. Indeed, Beethoven was almost certainly an instance of chauvinism in both senses at one historical stage of German musicology: Beethoven, as Riethmüller puts it in relation to

Nazi reception, "as the essence of German music, and this taken to be music full stop."[27] *Redupers* and *Felix* show that this might also apply to Beethoven reception in a gender sense.

A less reflective, more outright parodic use of Beethoven's Ninth is found in a scene of the 1987 film *Felix*. This was directed by four women, including Helke Sander. In this respect, it functioned as something of a transfer of the women's photography cooperative of the earlier film into cinematography. Toward the end, the main figure returns to his hotel after a lonely night out on the town, to be told there is someone waiting in his room. The someone turns out to be a strange woman in his bed, and the potential change in his fortunes is signaled by a section of Bizet's youthful Symphony in C (not acknowledged in the end credits). But she has no chance against the tirade of existential angst and male self-doubt that he unleashes. She fails to get in a word, as his harangue is underpinned by the Ode to Joy, almost as a marker of the patriarchy. His rantings vary the Schiller text, with *sturzbetrunken* [hopelessly drunk] replacing *feuertrunken*, and this in turn follows his almost expressionless rendition of the Heine lines: "When I think of Germany at night, I am robbed of sleep." The classical legacy, literary and musical, is dumped on this pathetic male in a whimsical sideswipe.

Tarkovsky's *Nostalghia* (1983)

To better profile the cluster of German examples, a number of films by other European directors will be drawn on to examine their use of Beethoven's Ninth (always the Ode to Joy section). An ideal counterexample to music weighted as cultural marker is the Russian director Tarkovsky, with whom "any possible political interpretation quickly becomes secondary to his moral and philosophical concerns."[28] Here, if anywhere, we would expect to find music chosen with a view to its super-humanism or at least its internationalism, the very attribute that made the last movement of the Ninth suspect in the eyes of the Nazis.

Over the opening sepia shots of a Russian landscape into which figures spill to form a statuesque tableau, an unaccompanied woman's voice intones "the keening death-chant of Russian peasant women."[29] This then intertwines with, before yielding to, the Requiem aeternam section of the Verdi *Requiem*. The counterpointed styles and melodies anticipate the twin pulls on the main character of his Russian homeland and present Italian domicile. They also, in the seamless acoustic progression from one to the other, anticipate the prominent theme of linguistic and cultural translation and its limits. This is taken up by the main figure, the poet/musicologist Gorchakov, and his Italian guide/translator, Eugenia. Like all art, he claims, poetry is untranslatable. To her objection, "But music . . . ," he replies by singing a Russian song, which she fails to recognize and which combines the two art forms mentioned so far. The cultural divides are taken much further when he suggests the frontiers between states must be broken down, but unlike the invocation of great names from both Italian and Russian art, this suggestion seems to remain totally abstract. And at a political level it does. But further into the film Gorchakov enters the abode of Domenico, himself a case of cultural translation in being an Italian version of that Russian topos, the holy fool (and aptly portrayed as something of a Doppelgänger to Gorchakov). His summons across the threshold is accompanied by the passage of the last movement of Beethoven's Ninth that immediately precedes the breaking of the double fugue, where the text speaks with confidence of a Father enthroned above the stars. The final headlong rush of the music is cut off, the joyous embrace of the millions in the text, which nonetheless seems to be the foreshadowed removal of national barriers at a still higher level, the one that ultimately interests Tarkovsky. The divine is contemplated but not attained, a state consistently anticipated in the director's œuvre and only realized in the largely frame-breaking epiphanies at the end of various films. Beyond the nostalgia for one's homeland signaled by the film's title, there is a more diffuse nostalgia for a European humanism, embodied here by its most famous musical/textual statement.

But the music is reprised, at a slightly more advanced stage of the symphony, when Domenico takes up cudgels against the evils of the time, an Old Testament figure atop a statue of Marcus Aurelius in Rome. His onlookers form a frozen tableau, with only the dog seeming to sense what is imminent, the madhouse mise-en-scène resonating with Wiene's *Cabinet of Dr. Caligari* and Bertolucci's *Conformist*. As Domenico incinerates himself, the invoked musical accompaniment finally materializes, but with mocking distortion at both beginning and end, a fairground reduction of some of the lofti-

est music written. But between these points of conscious ludicrous-
ness the final chorus is unleashed with full clarity, the text coming
to an ignominious end on the word *Brüder* in the key phrase "Alle
Menschen werden Brüder." The scene undercuts any notion of
brotherhood at a broad level. But the next sequence realizes it in
(and confines it to) a more intimate sphere, as Gorchakov manages
at his third attempt to fulfill the task assigned him by Domenico of
carrying a candle across the thermal springs. In the hands of a
Buñuel the self-immolation scene would totally negate idealism,
and yet Tarkovsky only seems to demolish the realization and not
the substance of visions. In a similar sense Beethoven here survives
the caricatured rendition of his music, and the Ninth remains a humanistic icon, though nothing more focused than that.

The successful sheltering of the candle flame across the waters
seems to snuff Gorchakov's own life's candle. As he reaches the
opposite bank, Verdi's *Requiem* returns, and the musical arc is completed when, with the Russian farmhouse now framed majesti-
cally by Romanesque architecture, the female singer of the opening
frames returns with her timeless song.

Makavejev, *Covek nije tika*
[*Man Is Not a Bird*, 1965]

This film employs Beethoven's Ninth both diegetically and, at the
end, nondiegetically in highly innovative fashion. At the beginning
a factory manager reports to Belgrade in anticipation of the concert we witness toward the end of the film, evoking the "passionate
words of Schiller's ode . . . reflected on the gleaming faces of the
workers." Instead of the latter prospect, however, there is an immediate cut to the yokel-type faces of those present at the performance of a nightclub singer, just as at the later workplace performance of the symphony the idealized worker Barbulovic is restless,
not rapt. The universal brotherhood of Schiller's text is similarly
demystified, as a brawl erupts after the singer's provocative performance.

With this anti-idealistic tone the viewer might expect a parodic
depiction of the Beethoven/Schiller work, but instead it serves as a
multifaceted site for a socialist Vanity Fair. When the engineer
Rudinski completes his project ahead of time, an orchestra and cho-

rus are sent to the factory to perform the Ninth for the edification of the workers (and in this context Schiller's text about brotherhood is undoubtedly viewed as a paean to the ideals of socialism). Seating at the workers' concert is hierarchical, contravening the Beethoven/ Schiller message. Rudinski, the feted hero of socialism, acknowledges that "it is a man's duty to build his future," but this message is more than a little modified by the succeeding excerpt from the Ninth, the orchestral dissonance preceding the entry of Schiller's text with the words "O Freunde, nicht diese Töne" [O friends, not these tones]. Further into the performance a parallel spectacle is staged, involving Rudinski's neglected lover and her new man. The continuing Beethoven concert is crosscut with the ode to more sensuous joys in the cabin of a truck out in the countryside, and the music climaxes feverishly as she does with calmer delight.

At the end of the film a circus barker says that under hypnosis a man carries out any order, even to kill. This cuts to an extreme long shot of a figure in a landscape, Rudinski, now bereft of all exaltation through the "'collective' joy expressed in Beethoven's music," which "is associated with his devotion to the 'collective' interests of the factory and the sacrifice this has entailed."[30] Nonetheless, it is the conclusion of this very music which accompanies his final appearance and sees out the film. Prior to this the camera pans across the industrial wasteland setting of the city behind the fairground, where the circus performance has briefly diverted the audience. It is as if the whole ethos of industrial work is seen in its soul-destroying capacity, if not as an act of literally killing, then as an act carried out under the hypnosis of the state. This in turn is an extension of male authoritarianism: once Barbulovic's wife sees through the hypnotist, she is able to take wing.

That the soundtrack should end with Beethoven is apt because of the work's double-pronged signification in this film. The bombast of its staging and the pathos of its Schiller text, both filtered through social realism, unmask the ultimately bourgeois pretensions of those parading its performance. But this fails to undercut the genuine exaltation of Rudinski as he surrenders his resistance to soaring, and it does not diminish the offstage joy of the collective of two in the truck cabin. In relation to the figure in the empty landscape at the end, the music is elegiac, reinforcing his isolation. But it also celebrates his capacity to rise spiritually, in synch with the different delights of the couple away from the concert. The realization of the socialist state, whose foundation myth creates a continuity with the Enlightenment and the French Revolution, betrays the Beethoven/Schiller challenge to humanity, but the challenge and the potential to meet it remain.

Still, the Ninth emerges as a far from unqualified icon of European idealism. The identification of its staging with the "authorities," imposing a culturally higher level of bread and circuses on the masses who are shown to prefer their circuses unadorned, aligns it with the very processes of hierarchy underlying hypnosis that Barbulovic's wife alone sees through. The quirky Makavejev is not to be reduced to a debunking role, but the more ritualistic side of the whole Beethoven event—venue, style, provenance, and the chasm, but for Rudinski's raptness, between performers and audience—winks at the text, while filtering the institutionalization of the music. In this sense Beethoven's music is dramatically mounted within Makavejev's film as akin to the original impulses of socialism.

Tarkovsky, *Stalker* (1979)

In a key scene halfway through this film, the stalker—the physical and metaphysical guide for his companions—is declaiming from Luke's account of the appearance of Jesus to two disciples on the road to Emmaus. The rendition trails off at the point where one disciple is identified as Cleopas, as the camera pans to the professor, now awake. The biblical story continues, beyond the excerpt chosen by Tarkovsky, with Jesus berating his listeners for not realizing that Christ's suffering was a necessary prelude to His glory, and then retracing the preparing of His path in scriptures from Moses on. The apparent paradox of suffering leading to hope is repeated at the end of the film by the stalker's wife. Transfigured from her earlier resistance to his return to the dreamlike landscape of the Zone, she has become the moral prophet of the film. Delivering the stalker from momentary despair, she utters the film's final wisdom and benediction before the coda of their miraculous daughter, whose telekinetic faith is capable of moving mountains at the level of the microcosm. So this elided section of Luke is nonetheless implied as part of the narrative arc of the film. More self-evident is the eliding, as in Luke's gospel, of the distant prehistory of the Resurrection.

But it is possible to view the following "sermon" by the stalker as its equivalent.

He addresses the professor and writer thus: "You were talking about the meaning of our life, the unselfishness of art. Now take music. It's connected least of all with reality. Or, if connected, then it's without ideas, it's merely empty sound, without associations. Nevertheless, music miraculously penetrates your very soul. What chord responds in us to its harmonies, transforming it into a source of supreme delight and uniting us . . . and shattering us?" In a film with less music this would sound like a programmatic utterance. But beyond the function of the "hidden" music we are coming to, the camera work during the expounding of the program should alert us to its limits. During the above speech the camera, in a slow dolly shot, traverses the expanse of water between (we assume) the bank where the stalker is standing and the far bank. The surface of the water is glasslike, so that as the camera skims it at the section "It's connected . . . without associations," the screen seems to be correspondingly blank. But what the text also proclaimed, the miraculous penetration of the soul by music, is matched by the breathtaking beauty on which the camera comes to rest, the opposite bank, and above all its reflection in the water. An unmediated shot of this natural tableau would have been far less arresting, so that the apparent intervening blankness is necessary for the final effect.[31] Tarkovsky's visuals qualify the logic of the stalker's exposition of an artistic credo; his handling of music within the film works similarly.

Critics draw attention to the paring down of music in Tarkovsky's later films. There is some originally composed music here, from the pen of Eduard Artemiev, as an accompaniment to the setting of mood and atmosphere, which is largely left to mise-en-scène and lighting. But beyond that, critical attention virtually stops at the muffled tones of the Ode to Joy at the film's conclusion,[32] whose significance is misjudged if it is viewed in isolation. It is but one of four musical stations of the Cross in the spiritual odyssey of the film, the last of a sequence of references to the musical canon which functions as the cultural memory of Western civilization. We have seen this function in a nightmarish sense in *Clockwork Orange;* here the canon, culminating in the Ode to Joy, is used as an antidote to the arid technological landscape of the film.

Like three of the four musical entries, the first is obscured by the rhythmic propulsion of trainwheels, their purposefulness feigning a sense of direction we never witness. It comes after the stalker's announcement that he is returning to the Zone, whereupon his wife curses him and writhes on the floor. Like the other extracts it is no more than a snatch of music, because that is all that is necessary—contrary to the stalker's credo above, it conveys immediate associations. The music is the Pilgrims' Chorus section of Wagner's *Tannhäuser* Overture, and it lends this latest stage of the stalker's quest a sanctity which at this stage eludes his wife but to which the narrator thus gives his blessing.

The second comes when the stalker's familiarity with the terrain of the Zone frustrates his companions, who see no reason for his caution and are inclined to take more direct paths to the Room. As the writer figure, back to camera, follows the professor, a snatch of music is whistled. Its source, we surmise when the writer ultimately turns but still betrays no facial movement, seems to be the stalker.[33] What he whistles was to frame Tarkovsky's later film, *The Sacrifice*, namely, "Erbarme dich, mein Gott" from Bach's *St. Matthew Passion*. There it follows Peter's threefold denial of Christ. The aptness of this music with its text's dramatic content is clear, as the stalker exhorts his companions to humility. Its original setting reinforces the religious aura of the expedition, which in itself represented a major provocation to East bloc aesthetics.[34] In the context of the film, the inevitability of human weakness even after direct contact with Christ must be of some comfort to historically remote pilgrims.

The transition from the Zone back to normality, from the magic golden pond before the Room to the sepia hues of domesticity, is eased by a soundbridge of the recurring trainwheels. Beneath these, with similarly relentless rhythm, a snippet of Ravel's *Bolero* can be discerned. Again the mere suggestion of this piece suffices, precisely because it does have associations: after the rigors of the inner journey it signals the return to the garish world of fleshpots. But this music is least connected with the narrative reality. The austere return to sepia before the celebratory use of color in the final sequence belies all gaudiness, while the tortured writhings of the stalker's wife before his departure have yielded to a serene spirituality that sustains her. (A degree of irony is cast on the whole enterprise of the quest by the spiritual development of the wife and the exceptional gifts of the daughter, both outside the Zone.)

The final example crowns the panorama of the Western musical tradition, completing the film's miniature, four-movement symphony with *the* fourth movement, that of Beethoven's Ninth. As the table reverberates to yet another passing train, the glass and jar which the stalker's daughter had set in motion shake on the spot but do not otherwise move. Just as the magic of her telekinetic capacity prevails over the more prosaic phenomenon, the musical examples, while they do not prevail acoustically, do so spiritually. Three of the four are distorted by the sound of the trainwheels, and the fourth through being whistled. But they all assert cultural memory and enact a minimusical drama of their own in four allusive movements. They culminate in the ultimate expression of "uniting us," as the stalker's musings had formulated it, the "Alle Menschen werden Brüder" section of the Ninth. The new universal harmony[35] that preoccupied Tarkovsky in his later years here finds its expression in the pinnacle of musical humanism. The Ninth may be barely heeded acoustically, but it is a voice in the (industrial, ecological, above all spiritual) wilderness that is not to be silenced. The nature of the quest in *Stalker* seems to combine a latter-day Holy Grail with Kafka's *Vor dem Gesetz* [*Before the Law*], with the gatekeeper personifying one's own heeding of inner voices. The object of the quest, too dazzling to contemplate directly, can still be intimated (the unquenchable glow through the door of the Law in Kafka) via a spirituality mediated here by music and elsewhere in Tarkovsky by literature or painting.

That music culminates in the Ode to Joy section of the Ninth, which since has indeed been elevated to the position of European anthem in the new, post–East bloc Europe. (*Stalker* as anticipation not just of Chernobyl?) This more generalized sense profiles Tarkovsky's two films treated here against contemporary filmmakers of the New German Cinema. In a purely German context the progression Wagner–Bach–Beethoven, with a diversion to Ravel, would have quite different associations, the very element which the stalker's programmatic utterance denies but which the above analysis strives to affirm. That Fassbinder, Kluge, Syberberg, and Sander reexamine the Ninth as part of their broader reassessment of iden-

tity points to a pathology of national psyche from which Bergman's
Till glädje [*To Joy*, 1950], Makavejev, and Tarkovsky remain exempt. Each axis yields archaeologies of reception, the first via the
overpowering intervention of Nazism, the second via more pan-
European resonances to which German cinema, and German society, would as a utopian wish like to return. But then with many
different gradations of detail, the Ode to Joy has always incarnated
utopian aspirations, the holy madness of this being exemplified by
its signature theme status for Domenico in *Nostalghia*. In these two
films of Tarkovsky, Russian culture achieves what was denied the
German equivalent of both Westernizers and Slavophiles, namely,
the transvaluation of the pinnacle of German humanism, Beethoven's Ninth, into European idealism.

4

A Wagnerian German Requiem
Syberberg's Hitler *(1977)*

In a book linking music and film, the name of Hans-Jürgen Syberberg most likely evokes his *Parsifal* (1982), a landmark approach to the genre of the opera film. In this genre, preexisting music is a given, and innovations relate to the production within the new medium. But the director was no stranger to a radical staging of the familiar or the music of Richard Wagner. On that score alone, the film examined here has a central place in an investigation of music as cultural marker within the New German Cinema.

A plot summary of *Hitler: A Film from Germany* is impossible, which immediately reflects the fragmented view of German history that emerges. Far from norms of the historical documentary, the film functions like a succession of outtakes. Its importance is not confined to the controversies it has aroused; however idiosyncratically, it attempts to approach twentieth-century German history and German cultural history via their common link in nineteenth-century Romantic nationalism. The following selection of details can be a mere taster, but it should amply locate those aspects of music which remain the focus.

The remoteness from documentary does not locate this as a narrative feature film. Lasting over seven hours, it avoids newsreel footage and comparable "authentication," instead lending Hitler's features to a ventriloquist's puppet or even, drastically, a dog-shaped puppet. The provocative alternate title in English, *Our Hitler,* foregrounds the uncomfortable link, the continuous spectrum between him and us. He is stylized as the fulfillment of our desires, and the device of ventriloquism is the perfect dramatic means of suggesting this. Against our wishes, we are plunged into audience identification with this Hitler styled as a film from Germany.

In a balanced, often critical appraisal of the film's qualities, Anton Kaes acknowledges that it "represents one of the few attempts to come to terms with the Nazi phenomenon in a way that challenges Hollywood storytelling and, above all, utilizes the specific potential of film in the representation of the past."[1] If documented visual images of Hitler are absent, his speeches continually stud its rich soundtrack. It is a soundtrack that utilizes music to represent and interrogate the past. Rarely treated in any detail in the considerable literature on this film,[2] music is a crucial presence in its dramatic and narrative structure. Above all, Syberberg confronts the baleful link between Hitler and the historical reception of the music of Wagner.

A Wagnerian German Requiem

Syberberg's film is epic in length but of chamber-opera dimensions in its dramaturgy (in this, too, not unlike postwar reappraisal of more bombastic elements supposedly inherent in Wagner). The dominating composer on a prominent soundtrack is Wagner. This tallies with expectations aroused by the film's title alone, a clichéd parallel[3] both foregrounded and challenged by Syberberg. His project quickly dispels this triggered association and signals its intention to seek the roots of Wagner's music beneath the patina of Nazi reception. Through the saturation of its soundtrack and its own length, his film acquires a dramatic kinship with the composer. Yet the film's own balance diverges from that of opera, not just Wagnerian opera. It heavily favors orchestral excerpts, which is of particular interest for Carolyn Abbate's view of Adorno, a key influence on German intellectual life of the 1960s and beyond: "Yet Adorno, by fixing obsessively on Wagner's orchestra, ignores the *singers*—but perhaps with reason, for the singers undo the Marxist shades of his interpretations. Wagner never swerved from operatic composition; he never 'hid' the singers."[4]

But he did hide the orchestra, with the Bayreuth pit unique

among contemporary theaters in removing conductor and musicians from complete visibility. The lack of visual distraction for Wagner's audience compounds in Syberberg's film the standard effect of non-diegetic music, offscreen but directing our emotions, at the very least subliminally. This yields the situation of watching a film from the same viewing/listening situation as for a Wagner opera, with a significant portion of the visuals accompanied by Wagner's music. Still more ambitious than Syberberg's assault on Hollywood as cultural agency is his attempt at the acoustic transformation of Hollywood into Bayreuth, the reclaiming of classical Hollywood's ideal of music being "invisible" to the "spectator." Because Syberberg's Wagner is a nonvocal Wagner, it is as if we were watching his stagecraft enact the hidden orchestra—either sunk in the pit or offscreen—with its wash of Wagnerian sound. Syberberg's shades are Wagnerian, not Marxist, and he interprets and stages Hitler as a shade.

With Syberberg, music as cultural marker becomes marked, even scarred, music. Like references to Romantic painting and cinema history, it is part of the cultural bric-à-brac of this film, but it is also tainted through its identification with artistically brilliant but politically compromised conductors like Knappertsbusch, Furtwängler, or von Karajan. With Syberberg, however, the thrust is frequently reversed, and the reduction of Wagner's Romantic aura by the tawdry attributes of Nazism becomes the real object of lament. Wagner is simply the most focused object of the director's sense of affront at the destruction of German art in the twentieth century.[5]

While certainly not an apologist for Hitler, Syberberg thereby aligns himself with a politically blighted nineteenth-century tradition. In the wake of German history of the twentieth century, this stance seems willful. At one level, in his introduction to the script, he even links Wagner with Mozart as a common site of resistance to Hitler: "Hitler is to be fought, not with the statistics of Auschwitz or with sociological analyses of the Nazi economy, but with Richard Wagner and Mozart."[6] Music per se is viewed here as legitimate irrationalism, the converse to Hitler's. But elsewhere his Hitler figure, having emerged from the grave of Wagner (see cover illustration), acknowledges the alien mold of the cosmic laughter of Mozart. This is a more realistic acknowledgment of the ideological component of musical reception. Like Kluge, Syberberg presents a panorama of German musical history. But where Kluge opts frequently for an alternative lineage or at least a redirection of the familiar, Syberberg draws on the mainstream of art music, with many of the inflections of its historical reception.

The soundtrack of this film frequently bombards the viewer with acoustic information, as a re-creation of the Nazis' exploitation of the media for propaganda purposes. But the normal dramatic dictates of film music do not constrain Syberberg. A particularly long monologue (by André Heller) near the beginning of part 4 (*Hitler,* 211) has no "background" music, at a point where more conventional film aesthetics would demand it, to work against the static quality. The images behind Heller are admittedly the most animated of the film, drawn from private footage shot on 8mm film or from "home movies taken by a member of Hitler's entourage at Obersalzberg" (*Hitler,* 216). But precisely because these lack the sound effects that have been such a crucial component of the film, they seem totally disembodied, and Hitler has indeed become a home movie at a comfortable (because soundless) aesthetic distance, while the Cassandra-like commentary of Heller is diluted. Just as the visual and script levels of the film text are multifaceted, with overlapping references in various historical directions, the examples of art music are frequently but one acoustic element on a multistrand soundtrack. For all its grappling with the era, and with Kracauer's thesis of a continuity of collective fears in *From Caligari to Hitler* (1947), *Hitler* is far from being a silent film from Germany.

Syberberg goes back one step further from the late 1970s identity crisis besetting (West) Germany and its filmmakers. Before the questions "What is Germany after Hitler?" and "How is post-Hitler Germany to be represented?" Syberberg asks, "How is Hitler to be represented?" In the view he adopts, his chosen medium of film is closely allied to music. At the end of the opening credits, special thanks are given to Henri Langlois and the Cinémathèque Française, acknowledged as the spiritual progenitors of the film with the publication *Film—The Music of the Future.* The title evokes *Zukunftsmusik,* in Germany associated with Wagner and Liszt; film as latter-day *Gesamtkunstwerk,* a commonplace that for Syberberg functions as palimpsest, not effacement.

Early in his film, the circus barker sets out what is not to be found here, listing representative "highlights" that are absent because they belong to an "unrepeatable reality": "Stalingrad . . . the Twentieth of July plot . . . Riefenstahl's Nuremberg" (*Hitler*, 43). By implication we are instead to be offered repeatable reality, history primarily as myth, Wagner's Nuremberg, the leitmotifs of history. And yet this summary begs questions of representation. Wagner's Nuremberg is artistically framed, but then so is Riefenstahl's. Any historical unrepeatability of Riefenstahl's Nuremberg implies the uniqueness of her take on the city, both as art and as quasi-documentary. Nazi film had in turn left Hitler as a mythical, and hence limitlessly allusive, gap in the text, a feature present in *Die Patriotin*, and satirized by Fassbinder in *Lili Marleen* (see chap. 6). Here the unrepresentable figure is reduced in stature, but not in chameleon quality, to Hitler puppets.

Syberberg's convergence of film and music relates the two art forms as quarries of cultural history and as dramatic hinges in the film narrative. His use of nineteenth-century music links with a view of music as an expression of the ineffable, while his film features the visual absence of the historical icon Hitler, a twentieth-century expression of the ineffable. Well beyond this film, the cultural embedding of the soundtrack is an as yet neglected aspect of "re-visioning history." When Rudy Koshar sees the prime achievement of "*Hitler*, and perhaps filmic history in general" as giving "a rather distant visual representation to such things as the 'structure of feeling' in which Nazism developed and to which it gave political shape,"[7] then a more differentiated approach calls also for an acoustic equivalent of re-visioning, a renewed listening to history.

Syberberg's own approach to his subject matter is encapsulated by the snow-filled glass sphere holding an image of Edison's Black Maria, at the beginning of part 2. As well as evoking the historical development of film technology, the sphere naturally conjures up *Citizen Kane*,[8] especially in conjunction with Kane's dying word. The demystification of Rosebud, which for all the sleuth work of Kane's fellow actors is confined to the viewer, is an effective cipher for the view of Hitler that emerges from Syberberg's film (and its hope of exorcising the Hitler in us).[9] Plausible leads proliferate but do not bring the investigator closer to Rosebud/Hitler as profilmic event. Where rationalism is exposed as inadequate in *Kane*, irrationalism is celebrated in *Hitler* with music.

The progress of the war is acoustically documented by broadcasts ranging across Stalingrad (from both sides) to many other spheres of combat. It culminates in a famous broadcast of "Stille Nacht" on Christmas Eve 1942.[10] Its rendition by German fighters from the uttermost reaches of the expanded Reich feigns a sovereignty that the imminent collapse of Stalingrad was to negate totally. By the end of Syberberg's film, the sentimental words "Sleep in heavenly peace" have been replaced by the death wish of the "Liebestod" from *Tristan und Isolde* (*Hitler*, 247).

In a film permeated by music, there is so little outside the Germanic tradition that the odd example stands out prominently. The course of the war is dramatically reinforced when, while Himmler is undergoing a massage, we suddenly hear the liberation of Chartres sealed by "La Marseillaise" filling the airwaves. Just as the masseur's elaborate gestures after body contact are meant to expel the poison from the body, the note of hope sounded by this turning point in the soundtrack of history expels the poison from the body politic, embodied in Himmler.

A little later in the film we hear a further example of non-Germanic music, in fact the only one mentioned by Ellerkamp in a list of his leader's favorites. A Hitler acolyte imagining himself to be the synonymous film projectionist for the real Hitler, Ellerkamp walks through the ruins of Obersalzberg, a transistor under his arm. "The Stone Has Closed above Us" is clearly audible, continuing throughout a speech by Hitler in Munich, 1943, broadcast on the soundtrack. The *Aïda* excerpt functions as a kind of ghostly aria from the tomb of the Obersalzberg, as well as alluding to the far from grand opera ending met by Hitler and Eva Braun in the Berlin bunker. It also links up with a solitary earlier example from the opera, whose finale (*Hitler*, 102) prefaces the return to the Eastern front of soldiers on leave. Strangely juxtaposed with the trivializing of Romantic art, these soldiers are the human object of lament in this film.

Photosonics

Syberberg's film is a virtuosic blend of cultural overtones with formal conventions. The prominence of its soundtrack can be gauged from the beginning of its script:

Stars flying toward us. A voyage into the darkness of outer space. The noise of static familiar to us from the radio of the 1930s and the opening of Mozart's Piano Concerto in D Minor softly fade in and out. More static as the following text appears in the form of subtitles:

> We all dream of traveling
> through space—into our
> inner self.
> The mysterious path
> goes inward,
> inward into night.

The figure 1 for part 1 of the film flies toward us and vanishes. Suddenly we see a landscape with Himalayas, palms, and a lake—a painting of the Winter Garden that Ludwig II had built on the roof of his Munich palace. We hear the prelude to *Parsifal*. (*Hitler*, 26)

For a start, Syberberg signals his technique of recycling images—the exoticism of Ludwig's Winter Garden—used in earlier films, a further linking device within the trilogy constituted by his *Ludwig, Karl May*, and *Hitler*. The process extends beyond the visuals to the music of Liszt, Mahler, and above all Wagner. And with the counterpoint between Mozart and 1930s radio static (even though in this context it doubles as a science fiction–type sound effect for outer space), we have the recycling of sound technology, producing a very particular effect within the film's larger project of cultural memory.[11] I have tried to capture some of this effect in coining the title for this section.

The subliminal impact of the music is enhanced at the same time that it tugs at coordinates of time and space. For the viewer/ listener, the music is both there in acoustic space and not there in visual space. Temporally it is both present (its acoustic reproduction) and absent (its historically distant origins), the latter feature distinguishing it from originally composed film scores. To this absence can be added a technological pastness, obligatory for the authenticity of early jazz recordings and drawn on by Syberberg in the juxtaposing of Mozart with static. But music is not past (nor yet present) once the ink dries on the score. Perception of the original notes is modified not just by the acoustic trace patterns of technological progress but also by the intervening reception, changes in aesthetic taste and in performance practice, the layering of cultural markers, and in many cases the whole original instruments debate. Nonetheless, a soundtrack feigning the datedness of a Mozart recording is a kind of acoustic freeze-frame, confining not the music but its (re)presentation.

This line of thought leads back to Barthes's approach to photography in his "Rhetoric of the Image." Relevant to the Syberberg example is the awareness in Barthes's viewer of a photograph's *"having-been-there.* What we have is a new space-time category: spatial immediacy and temporal anteriority, the photograph being an illogical conjunction between the *here-now* and the *there-then.*"[12] A third dimension is added in examples like static superimposed on Mozart, inasmuch as the *there-then* in turn bifurcates into the then of the static and the then of Mozart, the tuning fork of history that emits two tones.

Inexact though the match may be, it can be asserted that the acoustic equivalent of Barthes's photograph involves a conjunction that is still more defiant of logic. This is precisely the kind of creative irrationalism that Syberberg is at pains to defend, one which he finds primarily in music (see Susan Sontag's preface in *Hitler*, 6, 19). A more direct equivalent, and one undoubtedly factored into his film by the director, is the following: "The inevitable aura of a lost past attached to *all* photographs suggested an implicit trauma as well: the pain associated with mourning that loss."[13] One of the catchcries of approaches to *Hitler*, following Syberberg's lead (*Hitler*, 4), is grieving, "Trauerarbeit," the very process foregrounded by Jay's reading of Barthes. Art music in German film can in itself have this narrative function—see in particular the opening of *The Marriage of Maria Braun* (see chap. 6). In the opening of Syberberg's film, the archival aura of the historical soundscape reinforces that quality. It is as if the Mozart excerpt were the last bastion of aesthetically and ideologically absolute music before the Nazi takeover, before the static yields to the different subliminal effect of propaganda-drenched airwaves. And indeed, when the first (1932) Hitler speech intrudes on the welter of Wagner, the presence of static is prominent. An acoustic suturing[14] of the listening viewer parallels the effect of the historical hypnotist/ventriloquist Hitler.

Syberberg's Wagner:
Film Music from Germany

As a prime example of music as cultural marker, the Wagner Syberberg is trying to rehabilitate is inevitably permeated with overtones
of Nazi-directed reception. No postwar German film could avoid
these overtones. Among a host of Wagner quotations, *Hitler* avoids
the more hackneyed "Hollywood" Wagner (of, say, The Ride of the
Valkyries or the *Lohengrin* Wedding March—compare the current
Classics from the Silver Screen Web site).[15] Instead, it opts for excerpts that have dramatic and textual significance (via the libretto
they imply) for the whole opera or cycle. This seems to be a built-in
defense against popular culture. Commenting on TV advertisements featuring melodies by Grieg, Dvořák, or Delibes, David Huckvale points out how "Wagner's *parlando* is too specifically rooted in
the drama to be so easily extracted. Popular culture decontextual-
ises operatic music and Wagner's highly integrative system of *Leit-
motiven* with poetic text makes this harder to achieve than with a
conventional number opera. Consequently, whenever Wagner's music (as opposed to his techniques) is exploited in popular culture, it
is rarely without some ideological connotation or reference."[16] While
not making a quixotic attempt to sidestep the ideological connotations, Syberberg does celebrate the music's "integrative system,"
and he tries to reinvest Wagner with musical value.

Syberberg's editing of the soundtrack enabled a length of musical excerpts that is rare in film. His handling of Wagner, in particular, is an acoustic equivalent of Wim Wenders's attempts to salvage
images from the pace of Hollywood editing. This greater fidelity to
the original score in turn makes music less of a collage component
and more of a primary source, a profilmic acoustic event.

At the same time, Wagner is an iridescent weapon in Syberberg's
attack on Hollywood as cultural agency, a crucial subtext of this
film. He confronts stereotypes of Wagner's kinship with Nazi excess, mythological obscurity, and irrationality. Except for Werner
Herzog, whose penchant for Romanticism resembles Syberberg's,
directors of the New German Cinema largely avoided Wagner. But
Syberberg tacitly addresses the historical irony of Hollywood film
music of the 1930s and 1940s emanating largely from European

émigrés (e.g., Max Steiner, Franz Waxman, Miklós Rózsa), in a style based strongly on late Romanticism, not least on Wagner.[17] In other words, the latter-day exponents of Wagner's musical lineage were in the United States, at the forefront of the dream industry. Syberberg's musical rehabilitation of Wagner from the trivialization of Hollywood then anticipates the attempted reclamation of German history at visual and dramatic levels by Edgar Reitz in his monumental *Heimat* cycles.

These are the larger parameters. But how, concretely, does Wagner look/sound with Syberberg? After an opening sequence in which Wagner permeates the soundtrack, potentially as highbrow mood music or operatic film narrative, there follows a section (*Hitler*, 44ff.) where his music is intercut with Nazi or at least Nazified songs, so that the effect is of longer- and shorter-term cultural memory. The counterpoint is most striking when one of the narrators, Harry Baer, proclaims that "music . . . overcomes everything" while holding the Ludwig puppet. This is underpinned by the *Parsifal* Prelude, which yields to an archival record of the song "Today Our Germany Hears Us." The hinge between the two worlds, as it must have been for the febrile imagination of the young Hitler, is the Wagnerian martial music of *Rienzi*. And a still more striking amalgam, less direct, is created by the repeated funereal drumbeat of the roll call of the 1923 Nazi martyrs and the recurring evocation of the archetypal Germanic hero Siegfried with the Funeral Music from *Götterdämmerung*. When the Hitler puppet says, "So long as Wagner's music is played, I will not be forgotten" (*Hitler*, 207), this is the musical example chosen. The Funeral Music ruminates on the life of the dead hero (as a cluster of leitmotifs), and at the point where the exultant theme from Siegfried's Rhine Journey enters, Harry Baer takes up the narration with the words "Thus spake the devil" (*Hitler*, 207). Hitler, the authentic historical figure, is demonized, shrouded in mythological mist, while the Wagnerian hero Siegfried is projected via Third Reich reception into the realm of the historical.[18] With this degree of precision are the musical entrances planned in this film.

Syberberg quotes *Parsifal* extensively, with the quest for the Grail becoming synonymous with German Romantic striving for the transcendental. The first Wagner excerpt among many throughout the film is the Prelude, and this clearly stakes out Syberberg's Wagner, to be reclaimed from Hitler's. Performances of this work were banned by the Reichskulturkammer after the Bayreuth Festival of 1939. While reasons were never stated, the more passive mold of the central figure ("durch Mitleid wissend" [coming to knowledge through sympathy]) was clearly far from Siegfried-type heroism.

Syberberg's critique of the way Hitler had trivialized Romanticism still draws on the connotations of Wagner under the Nazis. The Hitler puppet's speech quoted in the last paragraph but one goes on: "I will not be forgotten. I've made sure of that. Branded forever in the history of Wagnerian music. The source of our, the source of my strength" (*Hitler*, 207). But whereas Kluge in *Die Patriotin* realigns Beethoven's Ninth with traditions of the Left (see chap. 5), which had been totally submerged by Nazi reception, Syberberg would ideally remove Wagner from the embrace of both the Right and the Left, although the weight he lends the nineteenth century might have led him back to the historically arresting phenomenon of the latter.[19]

The preponderance of Wagner from the outset stakes out an expansive and allusively rich acoustic terrain for this film. The Prelude to *Parsifal* is followed by excerpts from the scene from *Das Rheingold* in which the Ring is forged, the orchestral flourish and Donner's hammer blow before the entry of the Gods into Valhalla, the final scene from *Götterdämmerung*, and a return to the *Parsifal* Prelude, all within the opening fifteen minutes. The Wagnerian plot, the forging of the Ring that is to unleash such greed and ultimately destruction, is perfectly positioned, as André Heller speaks of the legal claims advanced by thirty Hitler heirs (*Hitler*, 31–32).

The film's frames of reference extend still further. Musically the most dramatic of the above examples, a furious drumroll prefacing the Gods' entry is qualified by a yodeling voice, and the sequence of this intruder surrounded by the two Wagner excerpts is the same as at the end of *Ludwig*. The yodeler deflates the high pathos of Wagner's music as well as asserting Syberberg's German trilogy alongside Wagner's tetralogy. The musical combination also signals the director's use of his own leitmotif cluster to combine film narratives. The title to part 1, "From the World Ash-Tree to the Goethe-Oak of Buchenwald," links *Die Walküre* to the Weimar of Goethe and beyond. The name *Buchenwald* summarizes Syberberg's own lament, incarnating the reduction of a once highly poetic word to a single connotation, a linguistic barbarism matched by the preservation of the link with classical Weimar (the Goethe-Oak) in a concentration camp compound. The span of Syberberg's title for part 1 then reflects the enterprise of the whole film, the attempt to resuscitate archetypal myths which once fed into a great Romantic tradition and have since been hopelessly compromised. Wagner is a major player in advancing this thesis.

But the salvage operation is reversed with the appearance of *Rienzi*. The composer came to distance himself from this early opera, but the latter-day orator Hitler embraced it. Its more martial instrumentation (e.g., *Hitler*, 57) blends effectively with the marching songs of the Hitler era that feature in this section of the film. The Funeral Music from *Götterdämmerung* undergoes similar recontextualization alongside jaunty renditions of military marches and songs (*Hitler*, 108–109).

Still more arresting are the occasional minidramas that Syberberg creates, both parallel to, and dramatically deriving from, the Wagner he is citing. During ravings from the Man of Destiny about the Eros of ruling and of violence, culminating in an invocation of the charismatic leader (*Hitler*, 126), Donner's "He da! He da! He do!" rings out, leading into the orchestral flourish quoted briefly near the beginning of *Hitler*. The fanatical voice of invocation is joined by a crowd intoning, "Sieg Heil, Sieg Heil," Goebbels's pledge of total submission to the Führer's will, and a snatch of the "Deutschlandlied." At a dramatic level the intoxication of the voices is matched by the upward surge of the music, resolving in Donner's hammer blow and the thunderclap of the kettledrums. The effect is a flashforward on the soundtrack to the foundations of the Nuremberg Rallies. And the Wagnerian viewer whom Syberberg ideally is addressing will make the further (dramatic/historical) connection that this music immediately precedes the entry of the Gods into Valhalla, the mirage of grandeur penetrated only by Loge's prediction:

Ihrem Ende eilen sie zu,
die so stark im Bestehen sich wähnen.
[They who delude themselves that they will endure are in fact
hurtling toward their end.]

Occupied Territories:
Liszt, Mozart, and Haydn

Syberberg introduces *Les Préludes* a number of times during the carnival booth scene early in part 2. The Liszt functions as a fanfare for mountebanks and a succession of the Magician's rabbits (*Hitler*, 106), climaxing with "das germanische Urpferd Himmlers" [Himmler's Germanic horse]. Underlining the showmanship of the music, the Magician's drumbeats are in synch with those of Liszt's score. In a short film called *Brutalität in Stein* [*Brutality in Stone*, 1961], Kluge had blended the theatricality of this piece with its Nazi associations. His film treated the grandiose plans of the frustrated architect Hitler for Berlin, with the towering edifices on paper accompanied by *Les Préludes*. At the end the buildings collapse as the music reaches an upbeat leading nowhere, disintegrating in parallel with the visual images beneath musical bombast and the hollowness of its ideological associations.

This music returns in less fragmentary vein toward the end of part 2 of Syberberg's film, which also concludes a long catalog of banal sartorial details about Hitler given by his valet. At first the fact that the Führer wore "only short underpants, even in winter, during the greatest cold" (*Hitler*, 154) seems a bizarre "text," debunking the grandiose gestural quality of both music and its appropriator. But in context, even a detail like this has its place. The music was indelibly associated with special announcements from the Eastern front,[20] and via a broadcast which suggests the Stalingrad station is intact, we are shortly to reach the turning point of the war for Germany and appropriately the end of "A German Dream" within both film and outer history, the capitulation of the Sixth Army. So Hitler's heroically spartan attire is in a sense matched with that of many of his forces, defeated by the Russian winter and without Hitler's compensating comforts. The servile valet, last viewed in what is literally a freeze-frame (he is weighed down by snow), provides the human link. But the Liszt, via its deployment by the Nazis in a specific context, is a strongly suggestive symbolic link.[21]

A further rich example of this technique is Syberberg's use of the station identification signal for the Deutschland Radio Network,

"Üb immer Treu und Redlichkeit." Syberberg sketches in the background to this reference: "It was the glockenspiel tune in Potsdam until its destruction, the melody by Mozart and verses from Germany's pietistic eighteenth century. Then it was taken over by the Freemasons and engraved on Frederick II's church as the hallmark of Prussia. And thus it must be understood here too as a signal and the dismal, macabre, tragic ending of a Hitler-history of Germany: 'Be ever loyal and honest until the cool grave'" (*Hitler*, 18). The station signal is reduced to the first part of the motto; the whole trajectory of the film is toward the second. Even without awareness of all the multiple layers of allusion opened up by Syberberg's filmscript sketch, the viewer/listener registers the displaced artlessness of the little snippet of melody, its illusory still point ushering in ever more disastrous news of the collapse of the German nation with its Prussian inheritance. But the director's commentary above, as elsewhere, also highlights the dramatic problem of realizing this level of detail in the film, rather than in footnotes to the script; some ironies remain embedded there for all but the most historically versed viewer/listener. Nor does Syberberg expect a totally versed viewer, just as for Kluge the most important text is the film within the viewer's head, a range of possible associations triggered by his film.

The appearances of the Mozart melody in the film constitute a minidrama. First it ushers in a Berlin crowd of 1933 shouting, "Sieg Heil!" and a blind veteran of World War I, his faith unshaken, exhorting his compatriots to the virtues of the motto (*Hitler*, 59). His appeal is punctuated by the singing of "Deutschland, Deutschland über alles," both perversion and logical end point of the motto's message. Then the signal accompanies the beginning of transmission on a Sunday in October 1941, but the actual news broadcast, in a kind of acoustic jump cut, is the Japanese announcement of Pearl Harbor, one of the supreme examples of perfidy and hence a drastic counterexample to the motto. The signal ultimately introduces "the final Wehrmacht report of the war" (*Hitler*, 234), with news of last-ditch stands by German troops as the *reductio ad absurdum* of the spirit of the motto.

The "Deutschlandlied," with its Haydn origins, undergoes transformation. After earlier underpinning the confidence of a conquering people, it is virtually deflated in a scene whose soundtrack

marks the stations of the cross of Nazism (*Hitler,* 127ff.). Goebbels's New Year's Eve address of 1942 (just weeks before the fall of
Stalingrad), punctuated by the crowd's chants of "Sieg Heil," is
succeeded by a rerun of the roll call of the 1923 martyrs. Hitler
emerges from the grave of Wagner wearing a Roman toga, appropriately instrumented by *Rienzi;* Goebbels celebrates the tenth
anniversary of Hitler's takeover on what proves to be the eve of the
fall of Stalingrad; the crowd still chants, "Sieg Heil"; and the
"Deutschlandlied" rings out one last time before the façades of
German historical consciousness fall along with the Sixth Army.
The total confounding of national pride and racially purified preju-
dice is encapsulated with the next images, showing African American GIs dancing with Aryan partners round the grave from which
Syberberg's spectral Hitler had appeared, a bombed out Wahnfried
in 1945 forming the backdrop. The tombstone scenes form a most
provocative historical arc, matched by the musical progression from
Rienzi via a compromised "Deutschlandlied" to the ghostly symbolic dance on the grave.

The anthem's words are often obscured by other elements of the
soundtrack. The sole clear rendition comes when the 1970s Hitler
fan Ellerkamp sings the first stanza, no longer part of official versions of the national anthem by then, and breaks down in tears of
frustration at the end of the scene. By this stage the recurring musical motifs of the film have gathered a momentum of their own,
combining like a Wagnerian leitmotif their earlier associations in
the new context. This accumulation of meanings is the very nature
of music as cultural marker, facilitated by the allusive layers of
visual markers in film, especially film as realized by a Syberberg. In
this case the musical constellation captures all the complexity of the
acquired ideological overtones. The German boundaries fantasized
in the first stanza of the "Deutschlandlied" match as a phantom, if
not in geography, those proclaimed by the equally misleading linkup
of German outposts on Christmas Eve 1942 (especially since the
day before, the Sixth Army had found itself hemmed in between the
Volga and the Don). And indeed the shattered nostalgia of the first
stanza of the "Deutschlandlied" is preluded by the song at the center of this linkup, "Stille Nacht," plus a repeat of the Deutschland
Radio Network signal. Again it is worth quoting Syberberg in full
on the significance of the "Deutschlandlied":

Nor is it necessary to know anything else, for instance the history of that unhappy anthem, which was carried by Hitler to all European countries, but which was written as a poem of freedom in the revolutionary days of the nineteenth century. By a poet who dreamed of national unity and freedom and was therefore persecuted. Nor does one necessarily have to know that the melody comes from Haydn and was originally that of the anthem of the Hapsburg monarchy and then, combined with the verses of the revolutionary period, it became the national anthem of the Weimar Republic, that first German republic, from which Hitler took the song. One does not have to know all these things; nevertheless, this neo-Nazi [Ellerkamp], unappealing to both our emotions and our political convictions, is a dismal figure. (*Hitler,* 17)

The subsequent fortunes of this melody give some idea of the dense texture of this film. At the end of a late 1944 broadcast, we hear the same tune with very different instrumentation in Haydn's *Emperor* Quartet. It is as if the chauvinistic veneer will no longer hold, raising hopes of reclaiming the melody for its intended context. But a little further on, at the end of a long monologue at the beginning of part 4, the patriotic song version returns, followed by the melody without voices but still in military arrangement. A snatch of the song is heard after a Hitler speech broadcast at the new theme park in his honor. Then the Haydn version is heard behind one of the key speeches in this highly verbal film, the monologue in which André Heller laments the travesty of the true Romantic legacy, its reduction to kitsch, by "the executor of Western civilization" (*Hitler,* 242). The music illustrates the object of lament, for despite its extended performance in its original version, this particular Haydn, as projected in Syberberg's film, can no longer be just Haydn. Its identification with an alien sign system is too strong, the politicization of its aesthetic too complete. In short, its fate is symptomatic of the cultural victims of German political culture, whose rehabilitation was essential but still historically impossible at the time of Syberberg's film.

Syberberg's Beethoven

Toward the end of the second of the film's four sections, entitled "A German Dream," the third movement of Beethoven's Ninth is blended in. At the same time, famous examples of German Romantic painting are superimposed on a text about astronomy, as Syberberg's film, like Kluge's *Die Patriotin*, prods the viewer to make private connections. Susan McClary has described the movement as a "dream of utopia" that "can never be reality,"[22] and as in the opening scene of Fassbinder's *Marriage of Maria Braun*, it seems to have a primarily elegiac function. Within Syberberg's narrative it is positioned directly after the fall of Stalingrad, which in turn undercuts German dreams of expansion to the uttermost parts of the world. The substance of those dreams seemed intact with the historical Christmas Eve broadcast (a month before the fall of Stalingrad) from the furthest reaches of the German-occupied world.

More elaborate is the accompaniment of the final scene of the film by the chorus from the last movement, the setting of the Schiller text from "Praise to Joy, the God-descended" to "O'er the stars enthroned, adore Him."

> The child goes back to the huge eye. In the eye: the crystal sphere and the Black Maria, the black mother of our film imagination, and then (a projection from the Ludwig film) the small weeping Ludwig. To Beethoven's Ninth Symphony, the sphere turns into the landscape of Ludwig's Winter Garden from the start of the film, torn now, with a deep crack through the world, a huge tear hanging down. Camera moves toward the tear, in which the girl sits, folding her hands in prayer, closing her eyes, then covering her ears. A starry sky is overhead. And, as if heard by the inner ear, the freedom fanfare from *Fidelio*. Close-up of the child's face. The face of the child that went through this world. Fade-out. (*Hitler*, 247–51)

Critics take this to be a hopeful resolution to an otherwise pessimistic film.[23] Syberberg himself gives modified support to a line of interpretation that would see the utopian connotations of the Ninth prevail.[24] But a reading finding this ending far more ambiguous would tally with the rest of the film, and it is a reading to which the configuration of the music lends itself. The Ninth is left in suspension, in its highest register, at a point which cries out for musical resolution (the end of the passage just before the breaking of the double fugue). After this epic pilgrimage the viewer, who throughout the film has also been addressed and activated as a listener, is brought to the very threshold of contemplating the Divine and left

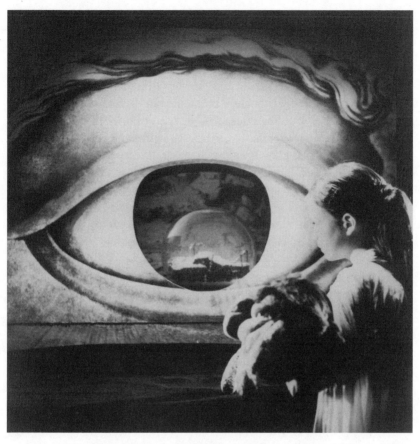

The mind's eye of cinema history; the inner ear of the child,
and of Beethoven—*Our Hitler.*

Courtesy TMS/Solaris/BBC/WDR / The Kobal Collection.

suspended, denied the cadence, the final exultation. The music
overlaps with a return to "one of the film's principal emblems, Le-
doux's ideal theater in the form of an eye"[25] plus the Black Maria,
"the black mother of our film imagination" (*Hitler,* 250), the whole
composition evoking a Gesamtkunstwerk of the Utopian.

Admittedly the freedom fanfare from *Fidelio,* which had also
briefly prefaced the beginning of the Ninth's chorus, is heard. Certainly the opera represented the phoenix of postwar German and
even European musical culture, its performance in many cases "re-

opening Germany's opera houses"[26] (and most famously, Vienna's). Almost exactly a year after the reinstatement of the "Deutschland-lied" as the "national" anthem of the Federal Republic of Germany (with the third strophe supplanting the first), Deutsche Welle on May 3, 1953, ushered in its task of reestablishing German credibility with the musical motto "Es sucht der Bruder seine Brüder" from *Fidelio*. For Furtwängler, this opera became "the linchpin of his effort to redeem German culture in the eyes of the world."[27] But mention of Furtwängler, let alone other names indelibly associated with particular productions of the work (Klemperer, Wieland Wagner, von Karajan) grounds any such redemptive aspiration in the historical context of cultural politics. Even at a purely dramatic level, the paean to freedom that has been the view of *Fidelio* in reception history is no longer unchallenged: "Suddenly this great opera of jubilant certitude appears fraught with considerable doubt. And such doubt also seems to undermine the confident brashness that Wagner discovered in the *Choral Symphony* and on which he built his own aesthetic. Both Wagner and Beethoven stake their operas on the humanizing effects of drama conceived as rescuing society from the devastations of politics and history."[28] To Syberberg, society's redemption is a far less certain matter, one not broached in the film. The director attempts to rescue musical drama itself "from the devastations of politics and history," after these have saturated it ideologically.

As background to the dramatic structure of Syberberg's musical tableau, it is worth noting that Goebbels requested the same sequence of Beethoven works for performances honoring Hitler's birthday in the last two prewar years. In 1937 Furtwängler conducted the Ninth, and in 1938 von Karajan and his Aachen orchestra marked the occasion with a performance of *Fidelio*. "Goebbels would link these compositions with the Führer's birthday to the bitter end."[29] So something of the fate of Haydn's *Emperor* Quartet movement must attach to these iconic Beethoven extracts, too. There no longer exists a "purely" idealist tradition for them to exemplify. At the very end we are returned to the music with which the film began, the Mozart concerto whose slow movement brings this part, like each of the other three, to a conclusion. Its sense seems to be to shore up the outer shell of the film against ideological penetration. The overall effect of the quotations from the Ninth, on the other hand, seems to be one of fragmentation, of a goal never quite attained. Thus it parallels the unconsummated quest for the Grail that underpins the film, which opens and closes with the word *Grail* on the screen. And in Syberberg's view this quest seems to underpin the spiritual history of Germany.

Why the switch to *Fidelio*, as a sort of alternative release of tension built up in the passage from the Ninth? Catherine Clément reminds us that "in Austrian productions of the 1930s, 1940s, and 1950s, Hitler was represented as either Fernando or Pizarro, depending on the changing political climate."[30] The one historical figure was thus represented as either liberator or oppressor in the "timeless" musical work, reflecting the vicissitudes in contemporary perception of the object of allegory. In a broader dramatic sense, this seems to be the crux of Syberberg's reference. His purpose is served precisely by the ambiguity of the quintessential freedom opera of the German tradition staging the restoration of liberty from outside, not ultimately through the revolt of the one in chains.[31] In the dramaturgy of Syberberg's film the threshold of the Divine (in the Ninth) is succeeded at the level of ideas (the plot of *Fidelio*) by the advent of the Messiah.[32] But in the political and historical context of the film, this figure masks the all too human redeemer, the false Messiah, the devil Hitler (who is also, according to Syberberg, "in us"). To recapitulate: Syberberg leaves us in suspension at the highest register of the Ninth, contemplating the Divine beyond the stars, and follows this with the pivotal fanfare from *Fidelio*. Bearing in mind the full title of Syberberg's film and the potential allegory of the opera scene, it is more than tempting to see the actual descent from the clouds, the grounding of the Ninth's ecstatic upreach, to be Hitler's descent to the adoring masses of Nuremberg at the beginning of Leni Riefenstahl's *Triumph of the Will*.

Within the dramatic framework of his own film, we are confronted by Syberberg's revoking of the Ninth akin to Leverkühn's in Mann's *Doktor Faustus*. But the retraction is present, too, at the levels of political history and the history of ideas. The union of the Enlightenment and the French Revolution (Beethoven/Schiller) yields to *Fidelio* filtered through Syberberg's title figure. Hitler's betrayal of Romanticism expands the film's subtitle. It is no longer simply a film from Germany. Via the soundtrack saturated with

Wagner, it also becomes an opera from Germany, culminating in a freedom opera whose compromised political hope proves to be a mirage.

The cyclical principle of the last movement of Beethoven's Ninth then seems to correspond to Syberberg's view of German history. James Webster's formulation expresses a common view when he speaks of an "avoidance of closure," of "its gestural character: its constant urge to move forward, to avoid coming to rest," and of "its striving for deliverance."[33] Inasmuch as this characterization can be paraphrased as restlessness and quest for redemption, the central German myths of Faust and Parsifal would seem to converge. But also, in terms of the relevance of these descriptions to the narrative of Syberberg's soundtrack, musicology would seem to meet film studies. This site alone would seem adequate for the role of a fertile mythmaker like Syberberg in straddling art forms with the pointed narrative use of art music in film.

Coda

If "conscious theatricality makes a film . . . a typical 'German' film,"[34] then Syberberg's already theatrical, studio-bound film is still more "German" in style through integrating so much from musical theater and particularly from Wagner. Part 3 opens with Goebbels's voice intoning, "Faith can move mountains," but the timing of this broadcast, January 30, 1943, is the eve of the capitulation of the Sixth Army. And so, reinforced by the acoustic framing of this part by Siegfried's Funeral Music from *Götterdämmerung*, Syberberg again seems to be recasting myths into his individual slant on German history.

With a single exception, all the art music mentioned has acquired layers of significance that document German history, particularly the reception accorded it during the Third Reich. The exception proving the rule is the Mozart Piano Concerto in D Minor, but the appropriation of "Üb immer Treu und Redlichkeit" shows that even this composer was not totally exempt. Alongside Syberberg's attempts at aesthetic restitution, the only gesture capable of resisting the acoustic scarring is the silence of the child. At the very end of the film she again closes her eyes, as at the end of earlier parts. But this time she also covers her ears, in an act that returns

The silenced child of *Our Hitler*.

her to a sort of acoustic subconscious paralleling the visual one but also as if to summon forth the deaf Beethoven. Both aspects, child and silence, are crucial to the iconography of the film. The child— particularly in the choice of the director's own daughter for the role, the director (b. 1935) belonging to a generation that experienced the war without adult responsibility—is symptomatic not of regeneration but of a Utopia such as that enshrined in some of Mahler's music. Indeed, when his *Resurrection* Symphony first appears in the film, the script blends in "Mahler himself at the piano, playing the part about Celestial Life from his Fourth Symphony" (*Hitler*, 96).

The silence has dramatic significance. Unlike the "Hitler in us," capable of acting as ventriloquist to the Hitler puppet even when ostensibly opposed to his/its arguments, the child remains an acoustic tabula rasa throughout and hence uncompromised by this sign system. The *Fidelio* fanfare registered by the inner ear is a Mahler-like offstage effect opening up vistas of acoustic spaciousness. It also accentuates the inner wellsprings of creativity, evoking the logic-defying capacity of Beethoven to reach the zenith of art music despite outer deafness. Syberberg's vindication of an inner emigration is not located in the Third Reich, but reacts to its continuing aftereffects, which cannot otherwise be exorcised. The inwardness he extols is designed to be the last bulwark against power. The ambiguity of his final narrative example, *Fidelio*, demonstrates the utopian nature of his own project. At the visual level a huge tear hangs down a fissure through the landscape of Ludwig's Winter Garden, and at the acoustic level the historically scarred cultural markers prevail amid the assembled utopias of the canon, whether by Beethoven, Mahler, or the Wagner of *Parsifal*.

5

Alexander Kluge's Songs without Words
Die Patriotin *(1979)*

The Unconventional Patriot

The narrative structure of Alexander Kluge's film is only marginally more traditional than Syberberg's in the previous chapter. No one person, including the title figure, is strongly profiled. The "patriot" is a history teacher named Gaby Teichert, and her history lessons fail to cover the curriculum as her quest for positive materials in German history becomes ever more diffuse. Her nation's history is itself full of fragmented subject matter in the twentieth century. The film's nonlinear path is determined partly by that and partly by its forays into the past and even the future.

In a surreal touch, the most lively narrative voice is that of a Knee, based on a nonsense poem by Christian Morgenstern ("Ein Knie ging einsam durch die Welt" [A knee wandered alone through the world]). The Knee belonged to Corporal Wieland, whose senseless death came just two days before the capitulation of the Sixth Army at Stalingrad, which sealed the military end for Germany in World War II. In chapter 4 we saw the crucial place of this battle in the German psyche. But the history that emerges in Kluge's film belongs to the everyday and to alternative forms of documentation, not to grand narratives. One of those alternative forms is music, largely nineteenth-century music. Like Syberberg, Kluge uses it

89

prominently, although his choice of composers ranges beyond what might be expected of a film nominally about patriotism (see table 1).

Kluge's film is a fantasy-driven essay on German history, from the narrative voice of the knee of a dead corporal through to a bit part in a World War I newsreel for an elephant called Jenny. It is simultaneously a roving approach to the history of fantasy, charting wishes and visions across the centuries. The corresponding musical form, the fantasia, emphasizes extemporization, and this characterizes the surface of Kluge's film far beyond the freewheeling musical examples themselves. Fantasy is not simply a balance to the chronicling side of historical documentation but a scattering of the trajectory of history, with past, present, and future coexisting. To attempt this in a narrative, let alone a visual narrative, is ambitious indeed; among rare examples, George Roy Hill's 1972 film based on Kurt Vonnegut's novel *Slaughterhouse Five* shows the problems involved with blending a sci-fi future, a haunting past, and a paler present.

Oskar Negt and Kluge view such simultaneity as fantasy's "specific movement, as described by Freud."[1] Simultaneity is a given of any historical moment, in its relationship to the past, embodiment of the present, and presaging of the future. (And, to preempt, it is a given of any conventional narrative moment.) Narrative drive is absent at the visual level in Kluge, with visuals accumulating within sequences rather than progressing horizontally. The same applies largely to the use of music, always preexisting music.

The three overlapping time levels nonetheless contain a balance, a quality of being in synch, which does not obtain for German history in the first half of the twentieth century. Nor does it apply to the arts in the postwar period, with a coming to terms with the past [*Bewältigung der Vergangenheit*] as the compelling concern of literature, and renewed confrontation, at least in film, with national identity issues during the assaults on the state from 1968 into the 1970s.[2] Approaching history from below is present from the outset with the title of Kluge's film: "The Female Patriot." Beyond the foregrounding of gender, this further challenges conventional notions of patriotism in being applied to a history teacher, that is, to someone more typically viewed as an intermediary for patriotism. Like many of Kluge's substantial writings, his film is concerned with restoring some degree of temporal authenticity to German history. It attempts this from a series of positions whose "presentness"

Table 1. Music in *Die Patriotin*

Musical example	Scene number	Source	Length
1	3	Eisler, *Night and Fog*	0 40″
2	4	Pachelbel Ciacona/Chaconne in F minor (for organ)	0′19″
3	4, 6	Beethoven, String Quartet op. 132, 1st movement	0′25″
4, 5	6	Skryabin, Prelude op. 11, no. 15	0′12″; 0′45″
6	10–13	Sibelius, *Swan of Tuonela*, op. 22	2′26″
7	21	?	1′00″
8	39–42	*Swan of Tuonela*	2′13″
9	45	*Swan of Tuonela*	0′50″
10	47	*Swan of Tuonela*	0′43″
11	48–49	?	1′24″
12	63	Skryabin, Prelude op. 11, no. 13	0′12″
13	68	von Suppé, *Poet and Peasant* Overture	1′10″
14, 15	75–77	?	2′07″; 0′28″
16	78–81	Schumann, Piano Quartet op. 47, 3rd movement (Andante cantabile)	1′30″
17	82	See text, pp.102–103	1′03″
18	51–52 (NB: scenes 50–60 follow scene 82)	Skryabin, Prelude op. 11, no. 13	1′09″
19	57	Skryabin, Prelude op. 11, no. 15	0′16″
20	57–59	Schumann, Piano Quartet op. 47, 3rd movement	1′36″
21	60	Brahms, Intermezzo, op. 116, no. 6	0′08″
22	83–86	Mendelssohn, Piano Trio no. 1, op. 49, 2nd movement	1′37″
23	88	Haydn, *Emperor* Quartet, op. 76, no. 3 in C	0′19″
24, 25	89	presumably original newsreel sound-track	0′11″; 0′17″
26	116	Mendelssohn, Cello Sonata no. 2 in D Major, op. 58, 3rd movement (Adagio, piano chords only!)	0′12″
27	116	Mendelssohn, Cello Sonata (as in ex. 26)	0′40″
28	117	Skryabin, Prelude op. 11, no. 15	0′08″
29	118	Eisler, "Solidaritätslied" (Solidarity Song)	0′10″

Continued on the next page

Table 1. *Continued*

Musical example	Scene number	Source	Length
30	119	Eisler, *Night and Fog*	1'27"
31	125	"Zehntausend Mann, die zogen ins Manöver"	0'33"
32	126	Tartini, Trumpet Concerto in D Major (slow movement, originally composed for violin)	2'22"
33	127–30	Beethoven, Symphony no. 9, 4th movement	2'43"
34	131–32	Sibelius, *Swan of Tuonela*	1'30"
35	133–34	Skryabin, Etude op. 8, no. 12	1'42"
36	137	"Leise rieselt der Schnee"	0'22"
37	138	piano music [?] plus ex. 36	0'13" in combination; piano continues for 0'35"
38	140	Skryabin, Prelude op. 11, no. 15	0'18"
39	144–45	Schumann, Piano Quartet op. 47, third movement	2'02"
40	147	Skryabin, Prelude op. 11, no. 15	0'24"

is retained, not crushed by the perspectives of hindsight. His is a position of extreme risk taking, as witnessed by reservations voiced by Eric Rentschler, Anton Kaes, and, most strongly, Omer Bartov.[3]

When accepting the Fontane-Prize (awarded in 1979, close to the release date of this film), Kluge spoke of the practical disparity between belated emotion at the Holocaust and what such a reaction could have meant to the internees of Auschwitz if exhibited by German families in the year 1942. Such emotion in the present cannot be "used," for it has become timeless, by which he clearly means that it is no longer anchored to its historical cause.[4] He sees this asynchronicity as the result of separating out the domain of the political instead of appreciating it as "a degree of intensity of our own feelings."[5] Kluge admired this in the late-nineteenth-century writer Theodor Fontane, who recognized at the time the political significance of what seemed to be unpolitical. This is both homage to a master of connectedness [*Zusammenhang*] and an indirect profession of Kluge's own artistic credo. His works, not least *Die Pat-*

riotin, provide an approach from below to ideological history, stripping it of grand narratives and prominent figures.

The "Deutschlandlied" and
Other Music in Kluge Films

A brief excursion to selected films preceding *Die Patriotin* will create a context for the focus of this chapter. The final scene of the Kluge/Reitz film *In Gefahr und größter Not bringt der Mittelweg den Tod* [*The Middle of the Road Is a Very Dead End,* 1974] has tango music accompanying a scene where two children hold string across a pedestrian crossing. At this improvised finishing line a VW hurtles through the tape (roughly at the driver's eye level), and then clouds are seen crossing the moon before the end credits come up on the screen. Going back beyond Kluge's own use of the tango in earlier films, most notably its virtuosic treatment in *Abschied von gestern* [*Yesterday Girl,* 1966], the effect clearly alludes to the infamous eye-slitting scene in Buñuel's *Un chien andalou,* updated to the Economic Miracle stage of German history. And what Kluge does in the way of "estranging" music in this film, in orchestration, tempo, and transfer of context, is nothing short of acoustic surrealism.

In relation to issues of music and ideology, the most fertile example is Kluge's input to *Germany in Autumn.*[6] Eight teams, including leading talents from the West German film industry such as Fassbinder and Schlöndorff, each produced a segment. Kluge headed one team and coordinated the whole project, by far the biggest domestic box-office success of any film he was involved in.[7] This lends particular resonance to musical choices for the film, music for cultural insiders, not pitched at a global audience (as Wenders's always is).

Both text and melody of the "Deutschlandlied" recur in various parts of the film. In Kluge's segment the text (written by Hoffmann von Fallersleben) is scrutinized, presaging the scene in *Die Patriotin* where Gabi Teichert submits Schiller's *Ode to Joy* to a similar close examination. The music is the melodic source for what came to be known as the German national anthem, Haydn's *Emperor* Quartet. Even it is not quite the original source, as Haydn had taken this motif across from his own earlier forging of a national anthem with

"Gott erhalte Franz den Kaiser," conceived as "the Hapsburg answer to revolutionary France's 'La Marseillaise.'" This combination creates a supreme irony surrounding the Austrian-born Hitler, which Kluge is almost certainly playing with. It also provides a parallelism akin to the use of Verdi, with all his Risorgimento resonance, to fantasize about national unity in postwar Italian Cinema: von Fallersleben's selection of music to accompany his text "demonstrated his vision of a united Germany inclusive of Austria."[8] Nearly a century beyond the yearning for democracy and unity of the 1848 liberals, this was a vision shared and implemented by Hitler.

In *Germany in Autumn*, the melody is blended in over the funeral of Rommel (poisoned in 1944) and grisly shots of people being hanged, including Rosa Luxemburg. Kluge dwells on the innate contradiction in the reception of this music, with the one melody both widely known through the ("absolute") chamber music of a Classical composer but also serving as national anthem for a nationalism run amok. It was in fact one of those nationalistic tunes accorded "a special level of sanctity," a 1940 order prohibiting "musicians from playing the 'Deutschlandlied,' the 'Horst Wessel-Lied,' and several other nationalistic tunes in dance halls, cabarets, and other locales that lacked 'solemnity.'"[9] This is the thrust of an early postwar scene in Fassbinder's *Marriage of Maria Braun*, where an unheeded back alley organ grinder—the carnivalistic inversion of a locale with due solemnity—plays the erstwhile national anthem.

Haydn's 1797 composition "Gott erhalte Franz den Kaiser" was dedicated to the last "German" emperor of the Holy Roman Empire of the German Nation. His original conception was to raise Austrian morale in the wars against the French, the same wars which spawned German nationalism. The integration of Austria into a unifying Germany was a distinct historical alternative up until the 1860s. These various layers of historical irony are restored, as is the original context of an anthem that became indelibly associated with the German nation at a time when, under its Austrian-born leader, it "reclaimed" Austria by annexing it (the Anschluß).

The Haydn version is a perfect example in the musical sphere of the positive materials Gaby seeks in Germany's history if we are momentarily prepared to carry out the enshrined collapsing of not just Austro-German musical history but also political history. Being text-free, the Haydn quartet movement also circumvents the problem of the words "Deutschland, Deutschland über alles," however much their original concept differed from their later connotations.[10] But at the same time this example illustrates the dilemma of such solutions: How is it possible to restore to this melody the original context, innocent of ideological connotations (at least of the retrospective irony mentioned above)? Is it possible to remove the patina of Hitler from this work of Haydn, a composer otherwise spared Nazi appropriation? In particular, what national symbol might be capable of postwar resurrection, in view of the blighted history of this one? The "Deutschlandlied" survived the transition to Nazi rule, having been "the one uncontested symbol of the Weimar Republic . . . a national symbol claimed by all and thus above party politics." The Nazis reduced the song to its first verse, now inflammatory rather than idealistic/utopian. What had been "the first national song for all of united Germany," originally in a respectable sense, had by war's end become a hated symbol of German self-aggrandizement.[11] In the most arresting frames of *Die Patriotin*, Kluge translates this cluster of questions into audiovisual terms.

A later stage of German history and German film history illustrates the fluctuations in all identity politics. Toward the end of Schlöndorff's *Die Stille nach dem Schuss* [*Legends of Rita*, 2000], a former West German terrorist, long harbored in the East, finds herself in no man's land once the Wall falls. Her growing disorientation is accompanied by a parodic version of the "Deutschlandlied," now no doubt questioning the "Einigkeit" extolled in the third strophe, the anthem text of post-1950s West Germany, and then of the new Federal Republic from 1990 on.

Music in *Die Patriotin*

Some idea of the range and dramatic integration of music into this arabesque of a narrative emerges from table 1.[12] "Digging for Germany's buried history"[13] yields some unexpected musical treasures, not just German music, alongside a few familiar presences whose layers of sedimentation via their historical reception are in turn stripped back.

While the significance of music in Kluge's films is widely acknowledged, I am aware of no detailed analysis of just how it might function in the entire soundtrack of a film like *Die Patriotin*.[14] The accompanying table indicates the range and the sheer amount of music in this film. As with all features of Kluge's work, neat categories are not possible: not listed is the "music" of a singing doll being displayed in a shop, or that of a busker. In relation to the other components of the film, music exerts a strong dramatic presence, with the soundtrack being otherwise sparse in many places and unexceptional in others (little dialogue, much use of voice-over spoken by the director himself). Roughly one-third of the film has music, and a further quarter consists of two long sequences with no music at all, scenes 22-38 (the Social Democrats' party convention) and 90-115. Simply statistically, then, music plays a very prominent role in the bulk of the film.

Thematically this is not surprising. It is, after all, a film whose central quest is for a more positive version of German national history. The presence of the nation's greatest cultural achievement, at least for roughly 250 years leading up to the Nazi takeover of 1933, is itself a partial answer. This answer, though, simply raises more questions, the nineteenth-century tradition of a nation of poets and thinkers [*Dichter und Denker*] failing to equip Germany for the political rigors of twentieth-century history. Even within the ideologized "Deutschlandlied" and the Ode to Joy section of Beethoven's Ninth Symphony, the attempt is made in *Die Patriotin* to pierce the accrued layers of reception history and recuperate the original tradition of the music or at least a historically viable alternative. The "methodological innovations" of this film provide not just "an alternative version of visual history"[15] but an alternative *to* visual history, to perceptions of historical elements in film that are confined to the visual plane.

There is a further dialectic between the cultural tradition of music and the primary channel of its communication earlier in the century, the radio. As Hitler conceded in 1938, "Without the loudspeaker, we could never have conquered Germany."[16] In *Die Patriotin,* as elsewhere in Kluge's work, the "used" quality signals a scratchy presence of the technology behind early recordings and their commodification. But Kluge is not only working to reclaim an ideologically usurped cultural tradition. He also seeks to initiate new channels for its broadcasting and consumption, namely, as borrowed music used in film, a form of film music that holds dialogue not just with the visual track of the particular film but with the historical traditions of production, reception, and dissemination that it also embodies. Of the directors considered in this book, Kluge is the main exponent of this dialectic, with music not just present in some of his films but outright permeating them.

Music and Dramaturgy

Examples of art music in this film are confined to the offscreen space and in that sense to superimposition by the mind (of listening viewers, addressed as educated citizens, *Bildungsbürger*). This music is contemplative, dramatic, and ravishing by turns, but it remains a background presence. With Kluge, the prior existence of non-diegetic music is not subsumed by the film's images. The immateriality of this music also releases the power of fantasy, deemed by Kluge to be nothing less than the most important form of human labor.

Typical of the density of this film's musical examples is no. 36, which underscores scene 137, the only occasion when the source of the music can (just) be established within the frame of the visuals. The music is a well-known German Christmas song, performed on the trumpet by a guest worker, as the text clarifies. This is a telling instance of Kluge's complex dramaturgy. Conceptually it functions as something of a negative after-image in the wake of the closing words of the preceding scene, relating to Corporal Wieland: "(He) wanted to live, but found himself in the wrong (hi)story (*Geschichte*)." In the new context, this verdict could be applied aptly to the guest workers as a social constellation in Germany.

Over against the many examples of art music stands this single example of folk music, the trumpet melody (plus example 31, a barely audible hummed melody). The person playing it is a member of the *Volk* by social class, but not by political rights or national citizenship, and least of all from a continuity of centuries canonizing the song within his adopted (but not always adopting) homeland. In the immediately following scene the raucous trumpet tones are joined by piano music, and both musical tracks are overlaid with the sounds and images of the inner-city bustle of traffic. Musically the result is a cacophony, and yet folk music, art music, and the sounds of real life (in this context functioning as a kind of *musique concrète*) manage to coexist. Is this an acoustic gloss on the bearers of these different levels, the guest worker,[17] the *Bildungsbürger,* and their juncture in the German yet also international city of Frankfurt?

Such are the open-ended constellations created within this film. Music with Kluge can function in a similarly associative way to images. Sound and image interact within each visual sequence, as each cluster of images (plus soundtrack) in turn interacts in succession. Kluge's "stage directions" to example 20 specify music's binding function, the way it is to bridge images that are disparate both in the story they tell and in their source (typical for the film are photograph, painting, documentary film clip, scene shot in a studio). The director in turn "binds" disparate musical sources through editing that tallies with musical logic.

The evolution of his dramaturgy can be traced through the first four examples in the film, involving quite different musical styles. Immediately after the title fades from the screen, late Romantic (almost Mahler-like) tones accompany images from an earlier film, Curtis Bernhardt's *Die letzte Kompanie* (1930). So to evoke the Empire's dead (51), Kluge uses borrowed footage from one film and quoted music from another, for the music is Eisler's score to Resnais's *Nuit et brouillard* [*Night and Fog,* 1955]. But *Empire* in the singular is belied by the combination of the subject matter of the film clip (the Wars of Liberation against Napoleon), the date of the film itself (identifiable at least as pre–World War II), and the postwar music for a French director's reckoning with Auschwitz. The spoken text emphasizes the roving across history, saying that we're either in the Seven Years' War or the Wars of Liberation, but also drawing attention amid the shadowy images to an antiaircraft gun from 1943. This opening tableau, with "shots of unknown soldiers fallen in battle," forgoes "the accompaniment of coherence within a particular time and place (an indispensible [*sic*] requisite of official histories)."[18] Technically, it is also something of an attempt to rewrite/revisualize history musically, to do more justice to the complexity of history by challenging the dominating role of the word or the image. Kluge reinstates the vertical axis of harmony, of historical chords in a musical sense. This coexists with the conventionally narrative axis of melody, corresponding to more linear history, with its horizontal motion. Or as Kofi Agawu puts it: "A musical segment . . . exists in two interdependent planes, the plane of succession ('melody') and the plane of simultaneity ('harmony'). Language lacks the place of simultaneity."[19]

In this opening example, the duality of visuals and soundtrack in itself opens up the historical frame to embrace different wars in German history. And these wars are at opposite extremes: the liberation of home soil from a foreign occupier (Napoleonic Wars), and the denial not just of home soil but of a place on earth for those condemned to genocide (that aspect of World War II evoked by the soundtrack). The word *patriotism* itself arose in the German language in the first context.[20] What could it still mean in the second? Any answer is still further complicated by the fact that Bernhardt, the director of the clip in question, emigrated to France upon the accession to power of the Nazis in 1933.

The citing of Eisler, one of the composers of music deemed degenerate [*entartet*] by the Nazis, opens up alternative perspectives on patriotism. The film's own choices, for which Kluge has been criticized, are also signaled from the outset. The most terrible chapter of German history will be left to a non-German film (Resnais's), which in turn is present through its soundtrack only. But German music, albeit by composers disowned during the war or else needing reappropriation after it, survives as an aesthetic and as a potentially political text. The history of this music also accords with Kluge's own resonances of theme and visuals. The opening string melody of the Eisler excerpt was entitled "A la funèbre," a reference to the Funeral March from Beethoven's *Eroica* Symphony, while it had been "originally composed in 1954 for Johannes R. Becher's *Winterschlacht*, a stage piece dealing with the German attack on the Soviet Union." Those rehearsing the staging had been mystified as to Eisler's aims in his music, until he explained them in the following sense: "After all, there had been both victory and defeat at Stalingrad. During the prelude to Becher's drama, a few soldiers are shown scattered on the stage. The music then suggests that these solitary figures are part of a collective, the remains of a gigantic defeated army. The orchestral prelude to *Nuit et Brouillard* serves a similar dramaturgical function: the music is a reminder that these now deserted landscapes pictured had once been popu-lated by millions of people."[21] The background of this music is a perfect instance of Kluge's desire to trigger associations, a possibly utopian desire in terms of the actual accessibility of all this within a brief viewing time. But just consider what comes together here: (1) Kluge's own obsessive theme of Stalingrad; (2) the forerunner to Eisler's score, whose staging sounds like the scene we, Kluge's viewers, see from the Bernhardt film; and (3) perhaps even the allu-sion in tempo designation to the *Eroica,* originally dedicated to Na-poleon, whose own army suffered similar conquest by the Russian winter. None of this relativizes or obscures the ultimate reference point—Eisler's, and surely Kluge's, too—namely, Auschwitz, but it does position it within a spectrum of German history. It instances those "parapraxes as mourning work"[22] located by Thomas Elsaes-ser in the New German Cinema.

The Eisler music returns once, much later in the film (scene 119, example 30). Plans for a waterway through the Alps, linking the North Sea with the Adriatic, are seen to be the negative reduction of fantasy, a fanatical notion of organization, linking up with scene 123 where the Alfred Edel figure "plans" the logistics of war opera-tions right down to orchestrating the weather. At the level of the natural world such trust in superrationality is exposed as folly, as the opening images show rivers flowing from melted ice and ice floes.[23] But still more telling is the elegiac return of the *Night and Fog* musical excerpt. The most obscene example of organizational capacity imaginable, the superrationality of Auschwitz marked the greatest irrationality of modern history. But, typical for Kluge's method, none of this is stated in such terms. It is there by associa-tion, via the viewer's/listener's combination of the kaleidoscopic crystals.

In example 32, the ice imagery of example 30 takes on historical shape, and the commentary speaks of the winter campaign of 1942 (159). Having circled round much of the mentality that made it pos-sible, we are thus returned to Stalingrad. Even it is not allowed to clinch the historic progression. After mention of lifeboats in prepa-ration for World War III (160) comes a tale of a man whose house, built on the ice, sank when it melted. Historical documentation is returned to the realms of fantasy and their broader historical span. Throughout the rich texts of this sequence (scene 126), a trumpet sound accompanies the images (anticipating the combination of this instrumental sound with "snow" imagery in example 36). Its lament orchestrates the only stage in the film where Gaby breaks down completely, weeping inconsolably at all the associations aroused by the simple tale. The emotional zero point of the film is reached, before the ice-motif thaws with the final section: "New Year's Eve. 'Ode to Joy.'"

These byways into territory well into the film have been designed to tease out its narrative technique; they also reflect its own erratic chronology. In keeping with this, we can return to the beginning of the film and to what follows the Eisler example already discussed. In example 2, "absolute" music, played on a Baroque organ, succeeds the functional quality of Eisler's music. The images here run a further historical gamut within a matter of seconds: the Brandenburg Gate in 1870, the moon revolving around the earth, and then what the text describes thus: "A nightmare image recurring in German myths: a castle on the mountain, below it a glacis, like a slippery border of ice. A person is trying to climb up the slippery wall to the castle" (53). With mention of myths and nightmares, the timelessness of the subconscious is addressed alongside frequently interpolated documentary footage; here the following scene shows soldiers trudging through snow in Russia. Functioning almost like montage in Eisenstein's sense, the two levels then suggest a third as the real focus—Stalingrad as the fulfillment of a recurring nightmare in the nation's collective subconscious.

Example 3 is a particularly energetic section of late Beethoven, its tones continuing first over Caspar David Friedrich's "Landscape with Grave, Coffin, and Owl," and then over a static wedge of soldiers, positioned almost like tenpins, before this fades out over a blank screen. Combinations like this rely primarily on the power of their suggestiveness and defy concrete analysis. The coffin assuredly is meant to prefigure the fate of the men. But not only is this dénouement offscreen within Kluge's film; it is also historically offscreen, so to speak, inasmuch as artwork as augur and the event it might foreshadow are over a century apart. In examples 2 and 3, history emerges almost as the concretization of fantasy, while throughout the film the historical resonances of (largely nineteenth-century) music relate to the music itself in similar vein.

Examples 4 and 5 then bring the first entry of fragments of piano music that collectively are to make up the major contribution to Kluge's score. These particular instances are simple, contemplative, evocative of Romanticism, and yet not quite identifiable, at least as a German composer.[24] Yet that would be the expectation, given the studding of the surrounding text with the words *deutsch* and *Deutschland*. The visual subject comprises a beautiful, intact landscape; we see a picturebook, preindustrial Germany and hear music that is a kind of summation of the nineteenth century, a combination of acknowledged influences in a style that is nonetheless not reducible to pastiche. The fact that this proves to be the Russian composer Skryabin, accompanying images of Germany, might give a crazy skew to the (owner of the) German knee falling at Stalingrad. Even without this matching, the mood, as elsewhere, is perfectly gauged, the dramaturgy masterly, and further associations are invited without being required.

This particular Skryabin prelude is heard again in examples 19, 28, 38, and 40, its ruminative tones accompanying a vast range of visual subject matter. But beyond creating a certain dramatic unity, the music is presumably meant to carry forward some of its initial context, namely, a meditation on what was, and what still is, "German" and "Germany." The piano functions altogether differently in the Skryabin etude of example 35, restless, even revolutionary in tone. There we see the Social Democrat Egon Bahr, a close colleague of Willy Brandt and synonymous with his Ostpolitik. And then on the cover of Clara Viebig's 1904 novel *Das schlafende Heer*, Barbarossa's army awaits the clarion call to restore the Reich, which will allow it to emerge from slumber. But if the object of a myth like this can remain dormant for so long, reawakened as a symbol of national aspirations in the early Romantic era,[25] then Kluge's ploy in eliding Hitler from this film seems not irresponsible. The Führer is then the drastic end point of long-standing national hopes, and given the historical antecedents, this end point could well have been different. The music captures something of the swirl of these dense historical cross-references, as well as musical protest—the Knee keeps emphasizing its own energy and capacity for protest—at Hitler's false appropriation of the Barbarossa legend. Operation Barbarossa could only ever lead to Stalingrad, the nadir of German nationalism and of history from below.

Example 17 stands out from this catalog of classical music. It comes from a scene that was the only response to Kluge's invitation to other directors to contribute to his film, which would have made it more of a collective venture akin to *Germany in Autumn*. Margarete von Trotta shot a scene of a lucky draw for a television set in a casino belonging to the Bundeswehr. The winner, clearly not knowing how to react, is regaled with a rendition of a song that was a 1942 composition for the Wunschkonzert, a request program. In this musical link between the war front and the home front, a woman croons to her husband of the joys awaiting him on his return. Von Trotta here gives a very clever twist to the title of the film, illustrating how "die Patriotin" as a designation might have been understood in the war years. Her own sketch is estranged from the original in every sense. Not only is it sung by male voices, but there is not a woman in sight, and the recipient of song and prize is in civilian clothes. Within Kluge's overall dramatic conception, then, this song belongs with a handful of other examples of popular music (especially song). They testify to its power as a seismograph for the collective subconscious, a feature of the films of another unconventional documentary filmmaker, Marcel Ophüls (see chap. 1).

Sibelius: Classical "Mood" Music or Nordic Patriotism?

Featured in examples 6, 8, 9, 10, and 34 is the elegiac tone poem by Sibelius, *The Swan of Tuonela*. In the first, extended example, it accompanies some of the film's ruminations on time, and eventually moves from the archetypal to the historically bound as the background to a bombing raid. It begins over time-lapse photography of a city profile (Frankfurt), and continues behind a shot of windmills turning by a riverside, and then the lights of army vehicles traversing a dark forest, the setting for the kind of legends featured in much of Sibelius's program music. (But this Sibelius piece had also been used over Bundeswehr autumn maneuvers in *Germany in Autumn*.) After iris-type close-ups of faces, the music is joined by the sounds of bombers flying in formation, creating an additional drumroll effect.

Sibelius's music is characterized by the simplicity of its motifs. This resonates with the miniaturist approach of Skryabin in much of his piano repertoire, particularly in many of the op. 11 Preludes, which only enhanced his music's elusive quality of memories of the seemingly familiar (via the strong influence of Chopin and echoes of Wagner and Liszt—not the bombastic Liszt of the Nazi signature tune, *Les Préludes*). Kluge's Skryabin excerpts function as a distillation of (and narrative gloss on) the nineteenth century.

Another link between the two non-German composers that may have influenced Kluge's choice is their early contact with Germany (in fact, some of the Skryabin preludes were composed there). In this sense, too, they provide an alternative to the directions that German musical history took. In a film from whose soundtrack Wagner is absent, Sibelius further seems to be functioning as an alternative direction for the integration of nationalistically colored Nordic myth.[26] Kluge opts for Sibelius's *Swan* over Wagner's in *Lohengrin* and for Skryabin's synthesizing miniatures over the original models they reflect.

But in a film seeking a positive version of one's own history, a visual and acoustic essay on patriotism rather than chauvinism or even nationalism, Sibelius's prominence is not exhausted by the effectiveness of his compositions as classical mood music. The time span of Finland's war with the Soviet Union between 1939 and 1944 saw the USSR initially the signatory of a nonaggression pact with Germany and then at war with the Axis powers. This in turn shifted Finland's relationship to the Axis powers between 1941 and 1944.[27] Far from unique in Europe, this is an intriguing case in relation to patriotism: Was this a struggle against Soviet imperialism, or support of Hitler Germany, or both? And what of musical patriotism, from *Finlandia* to the pursuit of Nordic mythology in tone poem settings of the national epic, the *Kalevala*? Predictably the Nazis were attracted to notions of Sibelius as Nordic, but well before Finland became a transitory ally. Howard Pollack reports: "Hitler awarded Sibelius a Goethe Prize in 1936, and Nazi minister Joseph Goebbels founded a Sibelius Society in 1942. Although Germans by and large had never thought all that much of Sibelius, performances of his music continuously increased during the Third Reich until, by the war years, he emerged as the most often performed non-German in symphonic concerts."[28] The "open, dialogic, discursive form"[29] attributed to this film thus applies to the soundtrack as well. The premier musical example, occupying by far the most time in this film about patriotism, is not German. But its composer's context within Nazi cultural politics raises intriguing questions about political patriotism and musical nationalism.

Examples 8–10, all accompanied by the same Sibelius work, further link Kluge's essay on Time with themes of fantasy and the imagination. Parallel to the arc in example 1 between the Wars of Liberation and Auschwitz, one is drawn in example 8 between 1813 and Stalingrad. As in the sort of moral reckoning of the scene(s) behind example 1, the German perspective on the two historical events makes the second all the more senseless. In contrast to a successful war expelling Napoleon, an invader, the Russian campaign of World War II proved a disastrous defeat at the hands of a nation treacherously turned upon.[30]

In example 10 the camera briefly pans a poster for *Bridge on the River Kwai*. Just as Gaby Teichert seeks alternative materials for teaching German history, this is the mainstream film type rejected by Kluge, historically based romance, however well done. If one compares that film's musical theme, the cheery whistling by the prisoners, with the Sibelius permeating this part of Kluge's film, the alternative use of film music is in turn exemplified.

In the final entry of the *Swan of Tuonela* (example 34), marked by the plaintive return of the cor anglais, indistinct battleground images yield to a shot of a pensive, unhappy Gaby, as the music fades out. The lapidary commentary informs us that the Hessian Ministry for Culture intends watering down history as a school subject into the amorphous Social Studies. The Sibelius has accompanied wide-ranging images meant to evoke both ambiguities of concrete history and history in the abstract, the latter a capacity probably denied any German music.

Music and Ideology

Directors of the New German Cinema, with Fassbinder and Kluge at the helm, had been strongly influenced in their dramatic technique by Brecht. Brecht's colleague Eisler, at least in examples like the "Solidarity Song" (see example 29), was the equivalent in music. Kluge's use of Eisler in *Kuhle Wampe* (a film scripted by Brecht himself) reflects Eisler's own conception of film music as critical commentary, not as acoustic underpinning of the visual track. In this example, snatches of a tinny old recording render music that is heard over shots of miners emerging from their lifts. Such direct documentation via both visual and soundtracks is unusual in Kluge, and the short example is succeeded by the symbolically complex example 30, which returns us to the film's opening music.

Commentary of this kind is not confined to originally composed music. In a brilliantly evocative tension between visual and musical associations, the "Deutschlandlied" theme is heard in its Haydn embodiment as the Reichstag building is viewed from a car window (example 23). The "Deutschland über alles" sense prevails inasmuch as the visuals show the more recent historical context, until the music breaks off abruptly as scene 89 (with the dark chords and dramatic, high-pitched strings of examples 24 and 25, a formulaic accompaniment to newsreel footage) shows retribution for the excesses of this brand of patriotism, with Germans deemed terrorists being shot in the closing stages of the War.

In keeping with his overall aim and style, his archaeology of visual and acoustic layers, Kluge's conjunction gives rise to a welter of possible associations.[31] The Reichstag building takes us back to early days of the new German Reich, founded under the aegis of Prussia, which like all but one other German state used a melody identical to the British national anthem. This transferability of melody to a number of expressions of nationalistic sentiment is a further facet of the search for national identity by the Female Patriot herself. It further sifts elements that only threaten to harden into ideological trappings through the prevailing ideology and not through any intrinsic aesthetic qualities. What could easily become the imposition of ideological uniformity, such as Nazi-era associations of the "Deutschlandlied," is fragmented by Kluge in the arresting juxtaposition of visual (Reichstag) and sound (a maligned melody in the original instrumentation). The effect is to release layers of historical consciousness, rather than suffering the music to fossilize as acoustic freeze-frames.

Ode to Joy: Spark of the Gods amid the Twilight of the Gods

The final section of the script to *Die Patriotin* is headed "New Year's Eve. 'Ode to Joy.'" It is framed musically by sections of the final movement of Beethoven's Ninth Symphony, first in a collage of musical excerpts, and then as the last musical statement in a film in which music has played such a key role, fading out over the final credits. Along with her colleagues, Gaby Teichert is working through the Schiller text (including stanzas not in common usage) in example 33, an extension into the semantic realm of her archaeological work. The music continues as acoustic backdrop to a sequence of shots showing New Year's Eve celebrations, a Christmas tree with lights, Cologne Cathedral with fireworks lighting up the sky, and a suburban train crossing a bridge over the Rhine. Then the screen is filled with the Karl Kraus text, with the last word added by Kluge: "The closer you look at a word, the more distantly does it look back. GERMANY."

At the very end of the film, with the text of a Brecht poem the only image,[32] the last movement of the Ninth sees out the film, no longer the choral section, but an entry for cellos and double basses at measure 92. Its continuation as the credits roll up sees this music functioning almost as conventional film music. But not quite. The history teacher is after all searching for a positive variation to her country's history, so blighted in the century she lives in, and the hope and idealism of that quest are embodied in Beethoven's setting of Schiller, or at least what convention has made of it. Amid a welter of examples that have not all been German and have not all come from the canon, the final musical statement is reserved for the Ninth. It reestablishes the German core of a film which has examined what genuine patriotism[33] might mean, as against the uncritical adoption of thought from the past.

The Beethoven excerpt is an inspired choice to complete the film's intellectual and musical fabric. The on-screen Brechtian text avoids direct reference to Germany, although mention of a millennial period unfailingly conjures up the Nazi period. The real signature of German-ness is the music, which answers the challenge posed by the Kraus plus Kluge inscription. The word *Germany* in capital letters positions the viewer as executing the preceding line, looking at the word ever more closely without penetrating the veil of its meaning. With the Brecht text accompanied by Beethoven's Ninth, the old/new utopian associations are evoked of a borderless German/universal identity, without that being synonymous with Nazi expansionism. Above all the last "word," no longer constrained by the inadequacy of words, is left to music. And Kluge's

Brecht-Beethoven combination proves more tenable than Syberberg's Brecht-Wagner symbiosis.

This order of music (as opposed, say, to Wagner) functions as expression both of the spiritually and intellectually ineffable, as well as of that German art which has largely survived from the nineteenth century through the false millennium of the Third Reich, without being swallowed up by the latter's ephemeral social context. This is not a plea on Kluge's part for aesthetic autonomy, a concept with a baneful ideological history in Germany. His rhetorical question mark of the Reichstag juxtaposed with Haydn shows that the danger is diverted simply by historical consciousness. His plea is for the demystification of art, a process which does not exclude a positive, future-directed thrust for music that had once been propagandized.

In this sense such music emerges alongside Gaby Teichert as a true, if unconventional, patriot. What Kluge chooses from the Ninth is also a microcosm of the dramaturgy of his own film. The passage follows the instrumental recitative of the opening bars of the movement, in which various orchestral voices essay a series of tentative false starts and retracings of preceding material. The central theme emerges in its least adorned form, establishing a basis for a whole range of variations. This reinforces the film's narrative progression and its theme of a hard won but understated brand of patriotism, seeking to regain the original impetus of the Ninth's idealism.

This seems to be Kluge's "take" on the work, bypassing all hackneyed overtones and all extension into the realms of a European Union national anthem or of world music. He wishes to reestablish its roots within both revolutionary and humanistic German traditions, as embodied by the younger Schiller and the older Beethoven. The further connection is the timing of the broadcast, New Year's Eve. This accords in a more general sense with Gaby's position by the end of the film, assessing the past and simultaneously formulating resolutions for the future. But beyond that, Kluge reinvokes an earlier Social Democrat tradition of performances of this work on New Year's Eve.[34] The amalgam sees this far from innocent example of film music aptly crowning the film's narrative.[35] In the final musical statement the visuals reinforce the note of quiet hope. Just after Gaby has been seen looking out expectantly through her window, the Ode to Joy melody enters over a shot of an illuminated, snow-swept tree in the courtyard.

In Benjaminian terms, Kluge tries to reinvest the aura of music that was subsequently ideologized. He does this not through a total depoliticization but through a return to a pre-Nazi era. (With Beethoven's Ninth, he even embraces an alternative historical path, whose twentieth-century course was eclipsed by Third Reich "values.") In using this music in the first place as film music, he (and, of course, not he alone) also gives an alternative setting for its dissemination in "the age of technological reproducibility." Politically he salvages Beethoven's Ninth from the bourgeois concert hall and the false socialism of the Nazis, regaining it for the "proletarian public sphere."[36] And in so doing he overlaps Gaby's quest for a positive version of German history with positive wellsprings for the Left, which according to Kluge in an interview was threatening to self-destruct in 1977.[37] Inasmuch as film history is "a history of collective wishes and repressed desires,"[38] Kluge's deployment of Beethoven's engagement with the utopian is a classic instance of an approach to history denied written texts and unique to film via its soundtrack.

6

Fassbinder's Compromised Request Concert
Lili Marleen *(1980)*

Overture

In a chapter entitled "Mapping the Postmodern," Andreas Huyssen locates Fassbinder as a pivotal figure for that map: "It was only in the 1970s that artists increasingly drew on popular or mass cultural forms and genres, overlaying them with modernist and/or avant-gardist strategies. A major body of work representing this tendency is the New German Cinema, and here especially the films of Rainer Werner Fassbinder, whose success in the United States can be explained precisely in those terms."[1] Crucial for German identity issues, Fassbinder's output has been mined for gender politics, specularization, and ideology. Typical is the following appraisal by Thomas Elsaesser: "It is as if all secondary identifications were collapsed into primary identification, and the act of seeing itself the center of the narrative." He insists on "Fassbinder's commitment to the primacy of vision and the representation of interaction and action in terms of fascination and specular relations."[2] But frequently Fassbinder films also feature a rich soundtrack; *Lili Marleen*, lavish (and suspect) visual spectacle that it is, translates the above claims into the acoustic realm as well.

To contextualize Fassbinder's treatment of music in *Lili Marleen*, the core of this chapter, earlier films of this prolific director will be considered briefly. *In einem Jahr mit dreizehn Monden* [*In a Year of*

110

Thirteen Moons, 1978] is commonly regarded as his most personal film, grappling as it does with issues of transsexuality in the wake of the death of Fassbinder's lover, Armin Meier. *Die Ehe der Maria Braun* [*The Marriage of Maria Braun*] was his first major international breakthrough, a success that also financed the opulent *Lili Marleen*.

In a Year of Thirteen Moons (1978)

In a Year of Thirteen Moons begins with such a low lighting level that it is hard to see exactly what is going on until dawn breaks and pale light picks out the city that is the secret hero of the film. It is a film about passion across conventional sexual boundaries, and its soundtrack opens with the Adagietto from Mahler's Fifth Symphony. So far, this description could apply to Visconti's *Morte a Venezia* [*Death in Venice*, 1971]. In Fassbinder's film, the story involves the transsexual Erwin/Elvira, who years before has undergone a sex-change operation in Casablanca [!]. This was in response to her bisexual lover, who claimed he might have been able to love Erwin, were Erwin a woman. In the opening sequence Elvira, who had once been Erwin, is beaten up after an abortive sexual encounter with three youths by the river Main in Frankfurt. Fassbinder's use of Mahler, which as a film opening simply has to evoke Visconti's film, is supremely ironic; the process of inversion we shall see operating in *Lili Marleen* indicates bitter disillusionment. Visconti's film, with the decadent beauty of Venice as its ever present backdrop, told of the love of an elevated artist for a beautiful boy. The Mahler, repeated throughout the film, functioned very much as highbrow mood music. One acerbic critic even claimed, "The Adagietto is used like the thick sludge of string tone composed in imitation of Mahler by the various Central European refugees who worked in Hollywood in the 1930s and 1940s."[3] Fassbinder signals from the outset that he is constructing his own drastic counter-example to Visconti, in a film that could well have been called *Death in Frankfurt*. The seedy underbelly of life in the singularly ugly German city—at least as Fassbinder depicts it—breeds the desperate attempt of the main figure to find a love that is anything but Romantic.

In all these cross-references, the quotation of the music in this parallel yet totally different setting raises complex issues. It both evokes the earlier film and strips it bare of all pretence. It shows the reality—the vulnerability of the sexually different—behind the lofty intellectualizations of Thomas Mann and Visconti. It shows the impossibility, in any narrow sense, of reclaiming Austrian music from the "German" symphonic tradition for a German film, when another European director has made it so indelibly his own.

In Visconti the visuals, the narrative theme, and the use of the music all complement each other in the direction of an unfulfillable Romantic longing. The music as used never actually cadences, so the enormous musical tension generated is never released. Fassbinder at the outset seems to duplicate the music, while constructing his own variations on the visuals and theme. But this combination is at odds with the acquired overtones of the music—he shows how it doesn't have to accompany ravishing images of Venice. In Visconti, the Mahler operates as conventional film music, complementary to the mood, whereas in Fassbinder it functions as a counterpoint to the visuals, a radical extension of the Eisler/Adorno view of film music which then approaches Eisenstein's classic theory of montage. Both images and art music are defamiliarized by their conjunction, and that in itself can be a powerful narrative device.

But beyond this there is a mise-en-abîme effect, with layers of significance going beyond the music itself. All this accords with the weighting of the soundtrack in Fassbinder's films, for here the cultural reference is not to the Mahler score itself (which is without the ideological thrust of a work like Beethoven's Ninth) but to the acquired significance of another film soundtrack.[4]

The Marriage of Maria Braun

Amid a welter of other sounds at the beginning of this film there emerge strains of the third movement of Beethoven's Ninth Symphony. The music is undoubtedly a dirge for the destruction of the other Germany, for a tradition of humanism at whose pinnacle stands this work. It possibly stands, too, for the exclusivity of German preoccupation with the mind at the expense of political maturity throughout its history.[5] The two aspects telescope with a picture of Hitler followed by the music of Beethoven, which modulates back to the world of Hitler via a siren signaling the all clear after an air raid.[6] At first this sounds like an instrument of the orchestra in a different key, so that within the context of the film it functions as a bizarre example of musique concrète.

Such a weighted musical reference is far from gratuitous in its elaborate cultural coding. Its subsequent identification by a radio announcer reinforces the emphasis away from any notion of theme music in the direction of historical (and cultural) framing. He interrupts Beethoven's Ninth to read out a list of names of soldiers missing in the chaos of the immediate postwar period. Coming in the wake of the (acoustically and historically) severed link to the tradition of Beethoven's Ninth, this announces the main theme of the film, the quest for the identity of immediate postwar Germany.[7]

The work's national/international status is made still more complex by a propaganda sign picked out by the camera. Brilliantly reappropriated by Fassbinder in this, his first major success at home and abroad, it admonishes, "Feind hört mit," a warning that the enemy is listening, the walls have ears. But rather than listening to the barely audible dialogue, Fassbinder's contemporary generation of the "enemy," by then the triumphant occupier and ideological ally, heard strains of the third movement of Beethoven's Ninth. Its function denies any trend toward world music and locates it as a lament for the violent passing of the culture to which it originally belonged. A direct parallel is created between past and present, between the Nazi propaganda sign and the hearing activity of Fassbinder's international audience. Only the latter "realistically" hears the Beethoven, whose significance in turn has changed since the war setting, a setting from which it simultaneously looks backwards. To vary the stated aim of Edgar Reitz in his first *Heimat* series, Fassbinder here reclaims German acoustic history (like Syberberg and Kluge in films just analyzed, and other New German Cinema directors elsewhere).

Historical reference points proliferate still further with the strong visual similarity between the registry office papers blown everywhere by the bomb blasts in Fassbinder's film and a scene near the end of Fritz Lang's *Dr. Mabuse, der Spieler* [*Dr. Mabuse: The Gambler*, 1922]. Before hurling forged money in the air, Mabuse has attempted to gain world domination through hypnotism and blackmail. He is ultimately unmasked as a maniac—prescience perhaps in Lang, but outright referentiality with Fassbinder. Within his own film, Lang's scene in turn echoes an earlier image of papers flying in the air at the stock exchange, signaling the manipulated economic boom. What is being claimed here for Fassbinder films at the level of the soundtrack[8] accords then with the director's layering at the visual level.

The nonmusical soundtrack can itself be a highly complex citation. Immediately following the scene in which we learn Maria has lost her own child by Bill—now a "little black angel"—she makes her way through a throng of travelers in the direction of the train's first-class compartment. Her ruse to force her passage is to call out five times the name Leni, while insisting on her right to search for her daughter. While not a precise echo, her intonation strongly evokes Elsie Beckmann's mother calling her own daughter, five times, about ten minutes into *M*. As with the *Mabuse* example above, cinema history predominates even in a film that allegorizes contemporary history. But as a process, the parallels are not totally far-fetched, for history provides its own examples—the 1954 World Cup soccer match which reestablishes a German self-image at the film's conclusion was played out on July 4. So the celebration of Germany's recovery of a sanctioned profile "borrows" from the independence declaration of its erstwhile enemy and contemporary liberator/occupier.[9]

With this weighting and virtuosic juggling of the Fassbinder soundtrack in mind, we may return to the music in the opening scene. The Beethoven third movement has been described by Susan McClary as "arcadian recollection, the imaginary sublime, or a dream of utopia. . . . But it can never be reality, as its infinite regress through a spiral of flat-six relationships indicates."[10] The abstract terms at the beginning almost read as a gloss on Fassbinder's film, where Maria is sustained throughout by the memory of her marriage. Her husband had been immediately called up to the Eastern front, returning only to be imprisoned, and then emigrating when released. When they come together after separation for most of the film, Maria's construct is impossible to sustain, as her lover turned philistine eats sardines from a tin, while listening to the soccer broadcast. Beyond the plot, the unreality of the music is established with Fassbinder in the way it is assailed on all sides by the totally alien sounds of the bombing raid and then of a railway station.

A further reference point for Fassbinder, who admired Douglas

Sirk, may well have been Sirk's film *Schlußakkord* [*Final Chord*, 1936]. What we see at length in Sirk's film is a performance of the fourth movement of Beethoven's Ninth. But when a transatlantic listener thanks the conductor for saving her life through music, she specifies the third movement, whereupon they both imagine the realms of hope onto which its vistas open.

For Fassbinder's postwar Germany no such vistas exist, and the movement's overtones accord with McClary's reading. It is worth noting how Fassbinder combines here the unsourced music of his own opening to *In a Year of Thirteen Moons* with sourced music (as in *Lili Marleen*). We start with the first (music superimposed on nonrelated images), but it blends into the second (the announcer acknowledging the performance), and hence we're uncertain of the status of Beethoven's Ninth as cultural artifact—is it part of a film score, or is it supposed to be an authentic concert hall transmission, somehow bridging a number of years of the narrative? This sort of continuity between what is usually irreconcilable we've already witnessed with a siren signaling the all clear after an air raid, as it seems to soar out of the orchestra pit. Here the transition effects two levels of historical reception of the symphony, from a nineteenth-century bastion of culture surviving the air raid, to a product that can be switched off or interrupted at will. Art's aura is compromised by its function in the age of technological reproducibility, as Fassbinder acknowledges his own lineage from Walter Benjamin.

Music and Melodrama in Fassbinder

In his classic article on the family melodrama, Thomas Elsaesser stakes out the broad background of American cinema as "determined . . . by an ideology of the spectacle and the spectacular . . . essentially dramatic (as opposed to lyrical—i.e., concerned with mood or the inner self) and not conceptual (dealing with ideas and the structures of cognition and perception)."[11] By contrast, this study has been at pains to establish the virtual impossibility of bypassing the conceptual, of dealing with ideas arising from one's national history and particularly recent history, in films of the New German Cinema. That holds even for the melodrama, Fassbinder's home genre via his model, Douglas Sirk. But Fassbinder converts this into historical melodrama. *Lili Marleen,* for instance, is certainly not lyrical, as witnessed by the weakness of its love strand. It is beholden to the spectacular; indeed, its critics claimed that it outright pandered to Fassbinder's Hollywood aspirations. But it is still a long way from any Hollywood melodrama formula,[12] retaining a concern with the conceptual that this chapter seeks to dredge to the surface.

The past that Fassbinder dissects includes the musical past as well, often invested with an ideological overlay and still shaping his contemporary cultural climate. This, to my mind, is the subversive aspect of many of the musical quotations in Fassbinder, whether from art music or popular music. In *Angst essen Seele auf* [*Ali: Fear Eats the Soul,* 1974], the Arab tones that draw Emmi to the guest workers' pub promise an escape from the familiar. Everything is loaded with associations extending back well before the issue of the assimilation of guest workers: Emmi was a member of the Nazi Party ("like almost everyone," she claims), and of all the restaurants in Munich her wedding feast (a dinner for two shared with Ali) takes place in Hitler's favorite haunt. The counterpoint to the Arab melody is a German song on the jukebox whose text intones: "Du schwarzer Zigeuner, komm, spiel mir was vor" [Come, you black gypsy, play something for me]. "Black" is transparently applicable to the Moroccan Ali, whose subsequent restless wandering— back to the much younger pub owner—matches the stereotype of "gypsy." In a film invoking the Nazi shadow cast on the present, this just might create a continuity of attitude between the forced labor of concentration camps (for which Sinti and Roma were as predestined as Jews) and the ostracized guest workers. This line of thought becomes ever more compelling once we realize that the composer of this and other popular 1920s songs was Fritz Löhner-Beda (Friedrich Löwy), an Austrian Jew who believed his music would find him favor with Hitler. He perished in Auschwitz.[13]

The choice of song further alludes to a solidarity of bourgeois rejection. So strongly does the unlikely pair feel their pariah status that at one point in the film both become "gypsies" and simply flee. But the nineteenth-century topos of retreat into a private idyll can no longer be represented, and this stage of the narrative remains a dramatic gap. Whatever simple affect the song's text might once have had, it has lost, and any momentary immersion of Emmi's self can only come through totally unfamiliar music.

Early on in *Chinesisches Roulette* [*Chinese Roulette*, 1976], the viewer hears a section close to the end of Mahler's Eighth Symphony. The lush fullness of the music, nearing its long-delayed finale, contrasts starkly with the barrenness, the lack of visual or emotional opulence, of the film's opening frames. The emotional void is sustained to the end by coruscating camera work and virtuosic mise-en-scène (including a glass case strongly reminiscent of the opening scene of *Laura*). Without an emotional referent, these emphasize the void all the more strongly. There may be tenuous connections to the plot of Fassbinder's film—his characters are called Angela and Gabriel; the text to the Mahler is the end of *Faust II* complete with angelic hordes—but basically this is music distanced from its "earlier contexts, identities, or fantasies."[14] It is used here substantially as (ironically totally inappropriate) mood rather than as cultural marker.

Fassbinder claimed this was his most personal piece of music, the music which best expressed himself,[15] which might support a totally eclectic view of his use of the classics. Certainly Fassbinder does use music across films—for example, the final duet from *Der Rosenkavalier* both in *Angst vor der Angst* [*Fear of Fear*, 1976] and *The Marriage of Maria Braun*. But in both cases the libretto ("Ist ein Traum, kann nicht wirklich sein" ['Tis a dream, it cannot be real]) is factored in with poisonously satirical effect. A similar sense of the utopian attaches to the second movement of the *Emperor* Concerto in *Wildwechsel* [*Jailbait*, 1972], entering at different stages of a teenage relationship (as it does, with similar utopian import, in Weir's 1975 film *Picnic at Hanging Rock*). But the illusory quality is present from the music's first appearance over the film's titles, as we see a gray riverbank and church steeple, markers of the small Bavarian town which will ultimately frustrate the main players totally.

Fassbinder can use more gesturally melodramatic art music as "mood," e.g., Peer Raben's Schubertian "Waltz of Longing" in *Katzelmacher* (1969), or the Bruch Violin Concerto no. 1 in *Martha* (1973) and *Die Sehnsucht der Veronika Voss* [*Veronika Voss*, 1982]. Character constellations are sketched through musical tastes, as with Helmut's imposition of Orlando di Lasso (here seemingly equated with bloodlessness) on his wife as part of her unsentimental education in *Martha*, and the title figure's preference for *Lucia di Lammermoor*, which also takes on narrative significance in presaging her own mad scenes. Once non-German music is used, especially from a pre-Romantic era (as with di Lasso), subjective slantings have far more scope than with the common body of connotations implied by music used as a cultural marker.

Further instances defy searches for other than contrapuntal connections between music and film action. In *Rio das Mortes* (1970), a conversation between two women is underpinned by the celebrated Albinoni Adagio, and the sole appearance of a landlady asking for the rent sees her go back to warbling Puccini with unabated gusto, once her mission has proved unsuccessful. But in a context like the plot of *Lili Marleen*, whatever the degree of conscious programming by Fassbinder and/or Peer Raben, the Mahler Eighth takes on additional overtones, which will now be explored. As cultural spectacle it sets up a high art parallel to the song "Lili Marleen," while as continuation of the film's ironies, it belongs to the postwar corpus of Germanic music, within its "most German" genre, the symphony, despite its composer having fallen afoul of Nazi racial politics.

The Bilateral Request Concert: *Lili Marleen*

> At the end of the North African campaign, in May 1943,
> when the 7th Armoured Division, on its way to the Allied
> victory parade in Tunis, passed the German 90th Light
> Division marching into captivity, both columns were sing-
> ing it ["Lili Marleen"].
> *The Oxford Companion to World War II*, 718

Lili Marleen (1980) traces the love between the heroine, Willie, brought to fame by her rendition of the popular song of the title, and Robert Mendelsson, who ultimately succumbs to family pressures in marrying a fellow Jew and embarking on a career as a conductor. The story is set largely in World War II, and the provocative feature of Willie's song (a feature historically vouched for) is that it is a huge success with both German troops and their enemies. This historical constellation ghosts through Fassbinder's construction: to the Axis powers the song was identified with Lale Andersen, to the Allies, with Marlene Dietrich. The battle lines separate audiences on both sides, as well as singers who originally came from the same side. Fassbinder's ideological balancing act sees him basing his film loosely on the memoirs of Lale Andersen and styling Hanna Schygulla loosely on the Marlene Dietrich of Josef von Sternberg's *Der blaue Engel* [*The Blue Angel*, 1930] and Billy Wilder's *A Foreign Affair* (1948). The song was composed by a German (Norbert Schultze); its ambiguous status extended across the dividing lines of high and low culture. It was the view of German musicologists in the mid-1930s "that entertainment music . . . which would have been considered low culture and hence the music of the masses, was in fact mostly the work of alien races, was degenerate, and was to be excluded from any program of Volksbildung."[16]

Ideologically the film has attracted considerable criticism and been viewed as part of a new discourse (not confined to Germany) which aestheticized fascism and reflected its fascination without critique.[17] The film also inverts its historical background by portraying the mysterious Jewish clique as perpetrators, or at least successful agents, and the central German, the apolitical, good-hearted Willie, as victim. Robert, the Jew, is not allowed to marry an Aryan woman, instead of the real state of play viewers are all too aware of. But in the final minutes of the film, Robert is seen in his role as conductor, feted by an audience extending well beyond the Jewish community of Zurich.

This analysis will attempt to engage with the film as a whole more than was possible with the films of chapters 4 and 5, where musical examples proliferate. The use of art music as narrative and ideology can then be viewed more clearly in its interaction with other elements of the film. There is in fact but little art music performed in *Lili Marleen*, although its presence, it will be argued, is implied beyond the few concrete instances. The film's central theme of the cultural politics of Nazism is approached via the relationship between entertainment music [*Unterhaltungsmusik* or *U-Musik*] and serious music [*ernste Musik* or *E-Musik*].[18]

The musical soundtrack itself is prominent, even overbearing. It reaches maximum intensity in an acoustic torture chamber scene, where Robert Mendelsson is confined to a cell with a musically unresolved section of the title song repeated indefinitely, as if the

Water torture of the eye and the ear—the hapless musician/lover in *Lili Marleen.*
Courtesy Waldleitner/Roxy/Cip / The Kobal Collection.

needle were perpetually stuck in the groove. The singer is Willie, whom he has just disowned for their mutual safety. Fassbinder's saturation technique brings strong viewer/listener identification with Robert, hammering against the walls. The ritual of the song's regular nightly performance has become compressed into a perpetuum mobile of history, or rather history itself stuck in a groove. The model for this scene was surely Wilder's *One, Two, Three* (1961), in which the lyrics "It was an itsy bitsy teeny weeny yellow polka dot bikini" are meant to soften up a man under interrogation before the accusing question (in German) implying he's an American spy. A further model was Lang's *Scarlet Street* (1945). Last but not least, one is reminded of similar treatment meted out to Alex in *Clockwork Orange,* causing him to hurl himself from an upstairs window to escape Beethoven's Ninth. Beyond this parallel to acoustic torture in *Lili Marleen,* we shall see how Beethoven's Ninth finds a phantom counterpart in Fassbinder's film.

Wilder and Lang, as émigré directors, link well with Fassbinder's theme of the transportability of "national" art. But the homage also links social critiques of German history to other artists' (originally compatriots') approaches to related moments of that history. Such film references in *Lili Marleen* (we shall find one to *The Great Dictator* as well) thus also stake out an alternative path for German film history, both in provenance and in themes. In addition, Fassbinder's renowned cinephilia is shown to embrace not just visual references but also soundtrack elements of earlier films.

Before the opening "action," where Willie and Robert are surprised in bed by a knock at the door, a brief introduction confounds viewer expectations and alone qualifies those critiques which read the following parade of illusion and excess as their glorification by Fassbinder. After a few inconsequential bars of Peer Raben's music behind a darkened screen, we are further denied movement by a landscape painting in nineteenth-century Romantic vein.[19] With strange detachment and uncompromisingly Anglo "r" sounds in a German text, a voice locates the start of the story in Zurich and the date as "seven years before the end of the war." We have then an inversion of an establishing shot at every possible level: visuals that do not correspond to the setting, a time frame that leaps to the end of an event yet to begin (or is this a dig at Swiss neutrality during the war?), and a dematerialized voice of mixed linguistic credentials. Thus is the story of Willie and her song set in motion by a shadowy show compere of a narrator.

The song itself sustains these augurs of a fractured narrative throughout the film.[20] With a text emanating from World War I (whose original musical setting was eclipsed by Schultze's), its fate is to be a chance hit thanks to airspace on Radio Belgrade. It becomes a unifying force across enemy lines, a favorite with troops from both sides, and ultimately an item on the Nazi banned list. It comes with a consignment of records from Radio Vienna that, to the dismay of the Radio Belgrade announcer, is full of forbidden musicians such as Offenbach and Kálmán. Although its source distinguishes "Lili Marleen"[21] from these, they prove to be its fitting companion pieces with its later fall from grace.[22] It brings the war to a momentary stop each night at 9:57, yet this same war impinges dramatically on successive renditions of the song and the career of the singer with whom it becomes indelibly identified. In the film, a brawl breaks out after its first performance (1938) in a Munich

A song conquers Europe.

cabaret, a fraught recording session overlaps with the proclamation of the Polish campaign (i.e., the outbreak of World War II) on the radio news, the Führer's birthday in 1942 is disregarded by a massed audience that only wants to hear more of the song, and the final Sportpalast performance is succeeded by the announcement of Germany's total capitulation, as the glazed stare of a heavily drugged Willie bores directly into the camera.

Via Peer Raben's musical variations of each successive entry of the title song, the film becomes a one-song musical. Performances momentarily halt not just the immediate dramatic action but, according to the film's conceit, the world stage of conflict. The recurring incidences of popular culture are interspersed—and link up here with my central concern—with examples of high culture. Directly before her first performance of the song, Willie has a loud phone conversation with Robert, bizarrely magnified to the audience. She congratulates him on his own forthcoming Beethoven concert, establishing from the outset the constellation of U- and E-Musik as parallel paths. While the film explores primarily the first strand, the second is there throughout, and the fusion of the two is ruled out by the impossibility of union between Willie and Robert.

This narrative outcome reflects a hardening of the barriers to their individual love, not the historical progress of the two cultures. As Thomas Elsaesser claims: "Nazism was that period in German history when, paradoxically, the division between high culture and mass culture began to seem less definite."[23] And light music, already claiming nearly half of the musical airwaves in 1938, became even more dominant during the course of the war. Musical energy was focused on the highly popular Wunschkonzerte [request concerts] for the German armed forces. Fassbinder's film is partly modeled on *Wunschkonzert* (1942), the second most successful film of its day.[24] The original radio programming mix of classical and popular music yielded to the overriding consideration of propaganda: "The escapist qualities of popular music were of more immediate benefit to the war effort."[25] But before this stage was reached, popular or explicitly Nazi music was increasingly allied with classical music in broadcasts, as part of the Nazi realigning of culture. Immediately after the outbreak of the war, military and cultural mobilization were equated by none other than Peter Raabe, president of the Music Chamber, the principal National Socialist music organization.[26] While in *Wunschkonzert* the progression was from the icon "Beethoven" to the kitsch of a male voice rendering "Goodnight, Mother," Fassbinder foregrounds the kitsch and repeatedly implies Beethoven in the background.[27] In Fassbinder's film it is the Jewish community which, underground, arrests this downward slide and keeps the fires of classical musical culture burning for its postwar reemergence (although it is the German Jew Bernd who first brings the fateful record to Radio Belgrade, thereby ensuring a musical pincer movement).

References to High Culture and Film Culture

A number of pointed literary references permeate this film. Early on, Willie and Taschner are ruminating on a railway platform about the song's lack of success. Willie flicks through a magazine, and we glimpse images of Gustav Gründgens in his stage role of Mephistopheles. This actor had been the butt of Klaus Mann's dissection of art and morality under the Nazis in his novella *Mephisto* (1936), a work still not available in the Federal Republic at the time Fassbinder's film was made. Its banning is a historical mirror image of the fate of "Lili Marleen" at different stages of World War II.

Toward the end of the film, as von Strehlow and Willie walk through a forest, he mentions a murder in the woods that was documented by a writer in 1928–29. And so Fassbinder's long-standing preoccupation with Döblin's *Berlin Alexanderplatz,* his television project concurrent with this film, spills over into another work.[28] A further literary reference is Fassbinder himself playing the leader of the Resistance group, Günter Weisenborn, who appears in Andersen's memoirs and belongs to the contemporary "reality" of Fassbinder's film. For Fassbinder, hounded by claims of anti-Semitism,[29] this must have been a piquant role reversal, as the figure persuades Willie to help inmates of Polish concentration camps. Finally, the rendezvous leading to Robert's arrest takes place in Oswald Spengler Street during a bombing raid. The decline of the West, or at least the German West, is indeed nigh by this stage of the film's narrative.

But of central interest here are film references, which go beyond the oft cited general allegiance to the UFA style of the 1930s and

1940s.[30] At one point the rather bumbling figure of Henkel, via his roots in the Nazi cultural functionary Hinkel, alludes to Hynkel in *The Great Dictator.* His twiddling with a world globe, initially in the background and then in ostentatious close-up, draws on a celebrated Chaplin scene which Syberberg's *Hitler: A Film from Germany* had also restaged. Rather than being just a cinematic homage, Fassbinder seeks to embed the reference in his own tale: Henkel informs Willie that some people wish to ban her song, whose morbid aspects hardly express the National Socialist struggle (Goebbels calls it "diese Schnulze mit dem Totentanzgeruch" [this tearjerker with the stench of the Dance of Death]). To the historical Goebbels, the fourth verse was the source of offense,[31] possibly an implied subtext with Fassbinder referring to the postwar restoration of the "Deutschlandlied" as national anthem after the fluctuating fate of its first stanza.

Film references also extend well beyond visual allusions. Earlier in the interview with Henkel, Willie is told that six million German soldiers listen to her song each night, a figure she repeats with naïve incredulity, but one which Fassbinder does not, cannot, repeat naïvely. This transfer of the estimated number of Jewish victims of World War II to any other context, let alone that of German soldiers, is one that understandably makes Fassbinder's critics most indignant of all. Fassbinder's twist would make the song effectively a *Symphony of Six Million,* the title of a 1932 film with a score by Max Steiner. The title, plus its advent in the year before the Nazi takeover, would alone seem to make it an irresistible reference point for Fassbinder, and when an expert describes Steiner's as a score "which drowns the viewer/listener in a flood of Semitic musical stereotypes,"[32] then Fassbinder's chameleon aspect seems boundless.

After Henkel has mentioned the theme song's suspect qualities as morale booster, a choir sings words encompassed by Henkel's spinning globe: "tomorrow the whole world." This tune had rung out after the announcement at the railway station of the fall of Belgrade to German troops. But the convolutions of Fassbinder irony create a further level here: for the song "Lili Marleen" to conquer the world it took the fall of Belgrade for the different Nazi regulations applying to occupied countries to come into effect. (Jazz was another classic example. Driven underground but never entirely out of town by Nazi cultural politics, jazz was propagated in occupied

Europe with Nazi lyrics replacing the original, through recordings of "Charlie and His Orchestra." The band's head, Freddie Brock-sieper, was freed from enlistment for his musical services.)[33] Again there is a mirror image situation in the realm of high art and ethnic exclusivism, with the Berlin Philharmonic's "Kraft durch Freude" concerts for soldiers in the field. "Outside Germany, these concerts were strictly reserved for German nationals, especially when they included a performance of the Ninth Symphony. . . . Live concerts of the Ninth were forbidden to the populations of occupied areas, particularly Eastern territories."[34]

There are irresistible points of contact between *The Great Dictator* and Fassbinder's film as one of many inversions in *Lili Marleen*. For example, the first appearance of Bernd is set to duly crass music by Raben. Assisting the Jewish cause, he is dressed in soldier's uniform. Overlap includes the slippage between the roles of Jew and dictator and, above all, the total debunking of the false glory of dictatorship (compare Willie's admission to an audience with Hitler, effaced by a flash of bright light when the portal opens).

In this last example, Hitler's stylization by Fassbinder as a *deus absconditus* means that the central point round which the whole film revolves is missing (as in Kluge's *Die Patriotin*), indicated only by a gap in terms of visual presence, whether documentary or enacted.[35] Or rather it is confined to "artistic" representations: aesthetic disagreements between Goebbels and Hitler are conducted by the camera ranging from a painting, photograph, or bust of one to the other. Instead of a dark portrait of Hitler, he emerges as the ineffable, as a radiance without substance, akin in the latter sense to Willie's song. Hitler then becomes the end point of kitsch, whose representation is no longer possible, though in an aesthetic rather than a moral sense, precisely what disturbs critics like Saul Friedländer about "the new discourse."[36] In this particular aspect, however, Fassbinder is simply extending the original to suit his own purposes: "As a desired object beyond narrative representation, Hitler does not play a diegetic role in any Nazi feature film."[37]

And in a further vanishing point, the Führer is replaced by the Verführerin [seductress], the spectacle and ritual of fascism by that of state-sponsored popular art. Here, too, Fassbinder is not being simply irresponsible but is playing with historical givens, with the "mystical emotional captivation of the ritual participants"[38] in rela-

Mass rallies for a song, "just a song."

Courtesy Waldleitner/Roxy/Cip / The Kobal Collection.

tion to Nazism as ersatz-religion. This applies to Willie's audiences at the Sportpalast (as opposed to the earlier, uninhibited brawl following her first appearance, and the barely concealed contempt of her throwaway rendition of the title song on Hitler's birthday), but above all to the trancelike troops in the trenches, immobilized by the "emotional captivation" of a song. The musical pivot, however, defies straightforward approaches to ideology and art, inasmuch as its mysteries transcend national allegiances and extend the fascinations of fascism beyond its glitz for a target audience.

Music: Neutral Art, Partisan Reception

Aesthetically speaking, Willie is right when she claims that what she sings is no more than a song. The attributes it gains reflect its social context, not any innate musical qualities or aesthetic fluctuations in artistic tastes. But her chosen art form is innately subversive. As Edward Said reminds us, the "transgressive element in music is its nomadic ability to attach itself to, and become a part of, social formations, to vary its articulations and rhetoric depending on the occasion as well as the audience, plus the power and the gender situations in which it takes place."[39] Fassbinder plays on this nomadic quality and simultaneously on the fluid international boundaries of once national(istic) music, with the warning "Feind hört mit" [The enemy is listening] in *The Marriage of Maria Braun* and *Lili Marleen*. In the latter film the sign is visible in front of the official who reminds soldiers singing in the troop train headed for the Eastern front that the title song is now on the banned list.

The treachery of this nomadic quality is shown when Taschner leads his men in the direction of a broadcast of the song, assuming it must be compatriots who are listening, only to be mown down by Russian troops. The border-hopping capacity of the song has taken on concrete form. But again there was a historical parallel to high art. While Taschner's charge into death is staged as melodrama, it had indeed been a Soviet practice on the Eastern front to broadcast both propaganda and Beethoven, mightily amplified, to encourage defection. Just how subversive this approach is in terms of film dramaturgy may be seen in a comparison with a black-and-white case like *Casablanca*'s antiphonal use of "Die Wacht am Rhein" and "La Marseillaise" (see chap. 1). There the positions are counterpointed with no ambiguity possible, whereas in *Lili Marleen* both political sides of the ideological divide collapse in the one musical text. In both world wars the "Deutschlandlied" had functioned as a "signal song" in combat, preventing deaths at the hands of one's comrades. When such an anthem function can no longer be localized, and once friendly fire becomes enemy fire (the betrayed non-aggression pact with the Soviet Union), Fassbinder's otherwise ludicrous scene becomes charged with historical and cultural markers.

Nor does the parallel between "Lili Marleen" and Beethoven end there. In Fassbinder's film, Radio Calais announces toward the end that even if Radio Belgrade is banned from broadcasting the song, (German) listeners will still be able to hear it from the "enemy" station. Again we have a reflection in the sphere of U–Musik of the historical situation of E–Musik, in this case the BBC broadcasts of Beethoven's Fifth. This monument in German music history had been recast for many listeners through the Allies' appropriation of the rhythm of the opening bars as Morse code for "V" for victory. This triumphant undermining even provided a glimmer of light in the darkest possible situation for members of the Mädchenorchester at Auschwitz when required to perform the work for the SS.

Said's verdict above applies all the more to the Mahler examples late in the film, to the parallel strand of art music. Much German intellectual history, and certainly the defining stages of the Nazi era,[40] deemed music to be "the most German art," "die deutscheste Kunst."[41] At stake was nothing less than the nation as defined by culture, "since one of Hitler's main objectives was to renew national pride, and since full rehabilitation of German identity would have to draw on the rich history of German music."[42] Fassbinder endows the title song of his film with signifiers of both the "Deutschlandlied" and of Beethoven's Ninth, not as a synthesis of these markers but as a celebration of their contradictions.

Comparing music with painting, Deleuze and Guattari speak of its power in terms similar to Said's: "Music seems to have a much stronger deterritorializing force, at once more intense and much more collective, and the voice seems to have a much greater power of deterritorialization. Perhaps this trait explains the collective fascination exerted by music, and even the potentiality of the 'fascist' danger . . . : music (drums, trumpets) draws people and armies into a race that can go all the way to the abyss (much more so than banners and flags, which are paintings, means of classification and rallying)."[43] This reads as the theoretical underpinning of Said; it also reads like a gloss on Fassbinder's film, with the combination of the voice, the potentially fascist element of music's collective pull, and total war drawing in both sides of the combat (united by the song). It also implies a capacity for film music to usurp film visuals, another subtext of this film and part of Fassbinder's inversion of Hollywood even in this, his glossiest work. Beyond Fassbinder, it partly explains the power in the New German Cinema of the "Ode to Joy" and the "Deutschlandlied," whether with direct or implied voices, as a reminder of their power in the reterritorializing quest of Nazi Germany.[44]

Of art music there are but few examples in *Lili Marleen*. The catalog comprises a motif reminiscent of *Pagliacci* whose intentionality Peer Raben contests;[45] some strains of Saint-Saëns's *Samson and Delilah* are briefly superimposed on Raben's original score; and two examples of Mahler occur toward the end, the first with Robert at the piano amid his clan in Zurich, the second when he is seen conducting before a full house (with visual allusions to the concert near the end of Helmut Käutner's *Romanze in Moll* [*Romance in a Minor Key*, 1943]). The Saint-Saëns appears in the scene where Willie is walking around the palatial villa that is her endowment from the Führer himself. Over a gentle drum rhythm that styles her survey as a kind of march, a phrase is recognizable that just precedes the words "softly awakes my heart" in the opera libretto. This commentary on Willie's state of mind is ironized by the soap-operatic arrangement for strings that blends in with the orchestration of Raben's own score. It also involves a non-German musical text based on an Old Testament story, so that in context even this instance of musical (at least in this arrangement) and narrative schmaltz has a subversive element that depends purely on politics contemporary with the story.

With the positioning of the conclusion to Mahler's Eighth, the "Symphony of a Thousand," Fassbinder stages a complex finale to the film's intertexts of German cultural history. In the final minutes Robert the conductor is feted by an audience extending well beyond the Jewish community of Zurich. At the level of melodrama that the film also embodies, true love loses out, and popular art, too. But awareness of the identity of the music Robert is conducting opens up cultural associations that extend the film's tensions well beyond World War II. In this context, this Mahler movement encapsulates the film's ideological minefield. It is one direction of the innovation begun with Beethoven's Ninth Symphony in concluding with a choral setting of a text (not, of course, the only instance of voice plus orchestra combinations in this or other Mahler symphonies). The alternative direction, the one appropriated by the Nazis, was what Wagner saw as the logical extension of Beethoven's trailblazing in his own *Gesamtkunstwerk*. The further advantage of Mahler for Fassbinder is undoubtedly the counterpoint that, as high art, it provides to "Lili Marleen." But Mahler's idiom also softens such counterpoint toward the accommodation of a bridging function. Referring to Russian musicologist Ivan Sollertinsky's view of Mahler's symphonic output, Michael Chanan writes of how "the conventions of classical style are confronted by musical material derived from popular genres. Here too, then, the symphony is double-voiced and expressly dialogical."[46]

If the mythologizing of Wagner is absent from the soundtrack, the myths of German high culture are not, with the hegemony of German music, itself an integral part of German ideology, allied with *the* uncontested German contribution to world literature. The text to the Mahler movement is the last scene of Goethe's *Faust*.[47] So the combination emerges of a high watermark of German culture, incorporated into his own work by the Jewish-born Catholic convert Mahler, in a performance conducted by the fictitious Jew Robert. It is this amalgam which crowns a narrative that has been punctuated by renditions of "Lili Marleen," whose reception has in turn fluctuated between endorsement and then proscription by the Nazis.

This is the final, definitive inversion of the film. Throughout the dark years of World War II, the *Jewish* family has maintained true German culture against the inroads of the sentimental kitsch of the pop song "Lili Marleen."[48] The song's fortunes are framed at the beginning by a musician named Mendelsson and at the end by the music of Mahler. And yet the carnivalistic approach to history is not all the film director's invention but partly his elaboration of history's own ambiguities. Hans Hinkel, Fassbinder's historical model for Henkel, was an indefatigable Nazi functionary as state commissioner. He had supervised the apartheid of non-Aryan and Aryan culture,[49] which led to the founding of the Jewish Cultural League. The triumph within Fassbinder's plot of the Jewish clique in Zurich is only an extension of the extraordinary vigor of the League, even beyond the Kristallnacht of November 1938. But disagreement also existed within the Jewish groupings over the question of assimilation, and to those seeking characteristic Jewish strains in music (and thereby in a bizarre sense accommodating Nazi claims), Mendelssohn and Mahler were suspect inasmuch as they were "too German."[50]

In this light the postwar performance of Mahler's Eighth in *Lili Marleen* becomes a cultural melting pot rather than an unqualified triumph of the old cultural order. The Jewish Cultural League, piloted in Berlin in 1933, expanded into the Reich Association of Jewish Culture Leagues in 1935, before this umbrella organization was replaced by the Jewish Culture League in Germany in 1939.[51] Despite the suppression of their activities with ever harsher persecution up until September 1941, beyond which no activity was possible, the League(s) produced a host of names of composers of E-music. But next to none of these was performed after the war. Goebbels, on the other hand, seems to have abandoned hopes of a distinctively Nazi brand of serious music by 1936, and thereafter Nazi Germany progressively encouraged an escape into popular/mass culture. After the war both German and Jewish components in the sundered identity of German or Austrian Jew were again combined, as much as that could ever be possible after the caesura of the Holocaust. With Fassbinder's choice of concert music, Germany in the immediate aftermath of World War II—the so-called Year Zero—retreats culturally to the first decade of the twentieth century.

The Politics of Culture

The complexity of the Mahler example (which dramatically seems swamped by the numerous repetitions of the title song) is exceeded only by a gap in the text which Fassbinder has consciously, to my mind, factored in. It comes in what David Bathrick views as "the most interesting and historically important" among the many reversals in the film, the scene of the first rendition of "Lili Marleen" after Willie's encounter with Günter Weisenborn.[52]

Concreteness of place is often treated by Fassbinder with sovereign disregard (compare comments at the beginning of this piece on the "Zurich 1938" setting, but also the occasional disorientation of the viewer in *The Marriage of Maria Braun*). The setting of the *Lili Marleen* scene in question is a beer hall, which the script requires to be at the Polish front, and the prime significance of the ambience really seems to be a rehearsal for the bordello-style lighting of *Lola* (1981). But the time setting is quite explicit. It is the birthday of the Führer, April 20, 1942, and Henkel proposes a toast. The rowdy mob ignores his invitation to join in three ideological cheers (a "dreifaches Sieg Heil"), a response so inconceivable in terms of its danger in the "real" situation that the consistently nondocumentary register of this film borders on a total recasting of events. Instead of even token reverence to their leader, they all clamor for "Lili Marleen." Alongside all its other attributes, the song then comes to be the unofficial birthday tune for Hitler.

The other main music in the scene conceals Fassbinder's barb beneath the conscious banality of its performance, as a dancer whips up the audience to the tune of "Veronika, der Lenz ist da" [Veronica, the spring is here]. This was a signature tune of the Comedian Harmonists, as featured in Joseph Vilsmaier's 1997 film about their rise and fall in late 1920s and early 1930s Germany. We hear, then, a song whose reception fluctuates according to the lavishing or withdrawal of political favor, just like that of "Lili Marleen." The entertainment function is submerged beneath ideological debate, and in Fassbinder's context the song cannot ultimately be "just a song," as Willie pleads for her own. In his archaeology of film history and film as history, Fassbinder's allusions extend to the soundtrack, too, as he bridges the height of the Weimar Republic with the early Nazi years through the vicissitudes of this song, known to his 1980s audience.

This then is the prelude to the frontline performance of "Lili Marleen," a performance located in a historically precise setting. Now there was indeed music performed for Hitler's birthday in 1942. With the request coming not from an ineffectual Henkel-type but from the guest of honor himself, it was a summons that could not be ignored. The music was Beethoven's Ninth Symphony, and the conductor was none other than Wilhelm Furtwängler.[53] To recall the context: we have seen how Beethoven was the first composer Jewish musicians were no longer allowed to play under the Nazi regime, and how Beethoven's Ninth was performed more frequently than any other work in the concert season of 1941–42—coincidentally the apogee of "Lili Marleen." Extending the parallel between U- and E-Musik, we have then, in reception terms, something of a high art equivalent of the film's centerpiece. The presence of this work in New German Cinema, the focus of chapter 3, is here the acoustic equivalent of a negative after-image, present in its absence and with inverted (tonal) colors, implied by the most throwaway of all the versions of the title song in the film.

As for the reluctant performer/conductor, still a controversial case study in the intersection of art and morality under the Nazis, there were certain parallels, at a far more sophisticated level of debate, with the role of Lale Andersen/Willie. Just as Willie attempts to do at this stage of the film, the historical Furtwängler did help some Jews escape further persecution. And while his emphasis would not have been on the "only" of Willie's defense that "it's only a song," his self-styled mission was to preserve the traditions of German art music, however politically compromising his continued residence in Germany might have seemed to the outside world. Bathrick's gloss on Lale Andersen's presentation of her own story could easily be one of Furtwängler's critics: "an extraordinarily naive and steadfastly apologetic version of the artist as morally and aesthetically transcendent, and in that way resistant."[54] Moreover, this particular birthday performance for Hitler was marked by Goebbels's announcement of his leader's new role in personal command of the Wehrmacht in Russia.[55] The parallel between high art public history and low art private history—Lale Andersen's Eastern front performance, in turn reworked in the direction of fiction by Fassbinder—becomes ever more irresistible.

This is the only wartime performance of the song where we see the adulatory masses in motion, rather than as a hushed Sportpalast audience or a frozen trench tableau, as history stands still just before 10 o'clock each night. The precise dating of this extended scene seems to demand consideration of simultaneous (cultural-) historical events, in keeping with Fassbinder's meshing of fictional performance and documented history elsewhere in the film. The double musical strand also tallies with one of the main themes, which via this aesthetic war on two fronts looks at issues of national identity at a deeper level. The scene in question, alongside the Henkel/Hynkel connection discussed above, supports Bathrick's claims for "historical specificity" in the film, but also significantly extends them. The scene furthermore expands to the realm of high culture Bathrick's location of the film's importance in "the extent to which its depiction of popular culture and media in the Third Reich participates in a historiographical discourse."[56]

It's Not Only a Song

At its inception, a work like Beethoven's Ninth might once have been, as Willie claims for her own signature tune, "just a song." Like Willie's song in the course of the film, it has long lost that innocence. It was the moment of that realization that crushed the spirit of Alex in *Clockwork Orange,* with the will of the state momentarily triumphing over his protests that Beethoven just wrote music. Once the audience of Willie's song extends from German to

Allied troops, and from "Henkel" to Goebbels to Hitler (where its reception vacillates),[57] she can no longer hope for control over it, even though she is held accountable for it. The parallel to filmmaking is obvious, particularly to a filmmaker still smarting from accusations of anti-Semitism. But Fassbinder's juggling acts in *Lili Marleen* provide far more than "sardonic treatment of the Nazi war as only another face of show business."[58] The film is a metatext about art and (moral/political) responsibility. Drawing on some of the historical reception of both the "Deutschlandlied" and Beethoven's Ninth, the song's own history unmoors their signifiers. This is not postmodern chic on the film's part but an unmasking of the ironies and the ideological sidesteps of that reception.

Both as ideology and in a more general dramaturgical sense, the use of art music in film is a powerful narrative tool indeed. It can generate a triad of historical referentiality, superimposed on the visual level. Whether "Lili Marleen" or Beethoven's Ninth, music, in its contemporary reception, can embrace the time of the fictional setting as well as the time of the film's realization. A third prong of outreach can be added when the work has a founding myth like that behind the *Eroica* Symphony. Fassbinder's film, as well as the reception it has generated, is a key document in this project, as it is in the historically compromised setting of German art from 1933 up until . . . ? At the very least, up until its agonized reappraisal by the New German Cinema.

7

The Great Eclecticism of the
Filmmaker Werner Herzog

Wenders, Herzog, and
Different Uses of Music

Among the most prominent of the New German filmmakers, Wim
Wenders and Werner Herzog stand out as exceptions to the strand
pursued so far of ideologically weighted music from the Classical/
Romantic canon used as a cultural marker. If we view issues of national self-representation as the hallmark of this body of films, the
extension of these issues to the soundtrack takes an inverted form
with Wenders and is a nonissue for the surface at least of Herzog's
films.[1]

In his earlier work, Wenders does indeed negotiate the cultural
landscape of postwar West Germany, but for him military occupation by the Western allies is overshadowed by the more pervasive
presence of U.S. popular culture. "For Wenders, . . . even classical
music seemed to have been compromised by the fact that the Nazis
used the German musical tradition for ideological aggrandizement.
. . . The void created by the contradictions and hypocrisies of German culture was filled with the ready-made products of American
pop culture."[2] In *Alice in den Städten* [*Alice in the Cities*, 1974] a
brief section of Verdi's *La traviata* is heard on the airwaves at low
volume. In *Der amerikanische Freund* [*The American Friend*, 1977]
one scene creates a cinesonic global movie, as piped music emits in

the corridor of a Japanese-style hotel in Paris a snatch of Mendelssohn's *Italian* Symphony! Otherwise the music in Wenders's films remains an earline match of the visuals of jukeboxes, Canada Dry, and Coke signs. Where a genre like the road movie is transplanted to German soil, as with *Im Lauf der Zeit* [*Kings of the Road*, 1975], the music is not, could not convincingly be, a homegrown equivalent. The soundtracks of later global road movies like *Bis ans Ende der Welt* [*To the End of the World*, 1991] help obscure the distinctiveness of any geographic setting, and thereby echo the mise-en-scène and narrative of these films. With the visual transfiguration of Berlin in *Der Himmel über Berlin* [*Wings of Desire*, 1987] it is easy to overlook the way this central site of German history is devoid of recognizably German music, with the counterpointed appearances of two imported rock bands and Jürgen Knieper's somewhat ethereal original score (in the direction of a Herzog soundtrack).

With Herzog, matters are different again. He is uninterested in the historical concerns of Fassbinder, Kluge, or Syberberg, perhaps remaining closest to the latter's reevaluation of Romanticism, though without the further component of nationalism. Herzog is the New German director most dependent on the power inhering in his images. Unlike Wenders, who seeks to salvage visions from the demands of Hollywood, Herzog seeks to dredge them from the subconscious. His pronouncements on this area consistently echo the following: "I believe, or rather I am certain, that I have particular images, images I can see on the horizon and can articulate, which may be relatively new to the cinema, something that has never been seen before."[3] The monumentality of this claim relates not just to the unique niche staked out within cinema history, but perhaps even more boldly to its sidestepping of the perennial subject matter of twentieth-century German history, whose layers penetrate into a more socially malleable subconscious. Herzog's project is one of liberation, self-deception, hubris, or all three combined.

With such a weighting of the visual, what can be the role of music on the soundtrack? At its best, as in the opening of *Aguirre* (1972), it is a fully equal partner in the dramatic sense. The eye of God perspective of the opening images is complemented by an ear of God soundtrack, an ear attuned to the music of the spheres simulated by the music of Popol Vuh. Gravity-laden images and cinematography (extreme low followed by extreme high angle shots of the procession) then pull screen figures and viewer down to the point where the plummeting cannon explodes, completing the arc of descent. Simultaneously, the hieratic music drops in register and takes on a fully developed bass line rather than soaring above a grounding rhythmic pulse.[4]

Herzog certainly takes responsibility for decisions about his soundtracks, and in relation to art music he also seems less versed than some other West German directors, notably Kluge and Syberberg. He confesses to unfamiliarity with the music prior to the invitation to direct *Lohengrin* at Bayreuth. And since German history is effaced by his output, so too is German(ic) music robbed of the overtones of its historically layered reception. In a revealing program on Austrian television, he analyzed the two possible musical choices he considered for a film about Jean Bedel Bokassa, ruler of the Central African Republic from 1966 to 1979. In *Echos aus einem düstern Reich* [*Echoes of a Sombre Empire*, 1990] there is a scene, grotesque even within Herzog's œuvre, in which a caged chimpanzee smokes a cigarette he's been given. Not content with capturing the animal's nonchalant finesse, albeit from behind bars, Herzog superimposes the cantilena of Schubert's *Notturno*. In this choice he overruled his editor's preference for Bach's *Jesu, Joy of Man's Desiring*, while conceding that musically, either would have fitted admirably. Describing both excerpts simply as "wunderschön," he gives no further analysis or explanation, let alone discussing the decision to underscore this scene with music in the first place.[5] The director's own perception of mood seems the sole criterion for musical choices, and the whole narrative thrust behind Syberberg's lament for the sellout of cultural history is absent.

The quality Herzog seeks in music seems to be one that complements the "sacral" in his mountain films, *Gasherbrumm der leuchtende Berg* [*The Dark Glow of the Mountains*, 1985] and *Schrei aus Stein* [*Scream of Stone*, 1991]. Thus for the latter he ultimately chooses Heinrich Schütz to complement camerawork that almost caresses mountain peaks. Similar aesthetics seem to have dictated the more perfumed musical incense of Fauré's *Pie Jesu* over the opening images of *Wo die grünen Ameisen träumen* [*Where the Green Ants Dream*, 1984]. At the conclusion of *Nosferatu* (1979), similarly conceived music underpins the shimmering plains traversed by Jonathan Harker as the reincarnated vampire, namely, the Sanctus from Gounod's St. Cecilia Mass.

Herzog's approach as counterexample to the general thrust of this book is a salutary reminder of the context-driven capacity of art music to embody historical commentary, no more nor less than that. From the rarefied social connections within Herzog's films, different combinations emerge. The point to remember with the first example below is that it stems from the golden years of the New German Cinema and is synchronous with West German films and filmmakers whose soundtracks have yielded very different results.

Woyzeck (1978)

Somewhat surprisingly, this acoustically sensitive film does not attempt to convey Woyzeck's point of view/hearing by making audible the cosmic subterranean voices he claims to perceive.[6] The voices of nature are simply there as an unheard given, a subjective world defying what we hear on the soundtrack or see suggested on the screen. Herzog's film opens with what is probably his only scene totally outside the script of the Büchner play it is based on, an establishing shot of the small town where Woyzeck's garrison is stationed. A slow pan takes in an uncannily still tableau. The camera angle shifts to a position looking out over town and countryside, beneath a silvery grey sky. The impression of unreality is filtered into one of a highly fragile reality by the soundtrack, a glockenspiel-type effect, akin to a child's music box still playing once the child— like this town—has gone to sleep. The simplicity of its tones is modified if the tune is recognized, for this is no decorative salon piece but the slow movement ("Absence") of Beethoven's Sonata op. 81a, *Les Adieux*,[7] that is, a complex intellectual expression behind the artless façade. The disembodied sound, the lifelessness of the town, and the steady path of the camera all add up to an equivalent of the image evoked much later of the world being dead, with not a living soul left. The film's opening is a metaphor for this tale. It is tempting, though more suggestive than in any sense a direct parallel, to relate the title of Beethoven's movement (framed by the "Farewell" and the "Reunion") to the state from the outset of the relationship of Woyzeck and Marie, or else to the town's lifelessness as discussed above.

At the end of Herzog's film, a Vivaldi mandolin concerto is blended in over the play's line: "a good murder, a beautiful murder." The serene quality of the music is ironic balm on the wound in the social order, the murder for which this one wretched man is held accountable, but which reflects on the very fabric of the society that torments him.[8]

The final images of the film use slow-motion shots to very different effect to that of the murder of Marie, in the direction of caricature. While musings on the "beautiful" nature of the murder appear on-screen like the intertitles in a silent film, absurd, spindly figures move about on a lush meadow on which lies the coffin. The background is washed out in definition, so that it seems to be a painting rather than a real-life image. The anonymous figures' ghostly movements are complemented first by a return to the disembodied tinkling of the glockenspiel and then by the Vivaldi discussed before, music Alex North definitely had an ear to when composing the soundtrack to *Who's Afraid of Virginia Woolf?* The coffin seals the end of the main dramatic strand, leading to the crime of passion, but the final ballet creates a sense of open-endedness. The society that has driven Woyzeck to his actions survives, unenlightened, closing ranks with the dangerous euphemisms of the titles on-screen. This is the core of the pessimism of both play and film, a feature captured strikingly at the end of Berg's opera *Wozzeck* (1925), with the alternation of two adjacent notes that could have continued indefinitely, tapering off arbitrarily on the upbeat. Without the musical "logic" of a cadence, Berg creates an open-ended work, with the perpetual motion of the quaver rhythm conveying more eloquently than any word setting the cyclic quality of human life. Something of this transcendence of the socially specific is captured by Herzog's choice of art music, with the non-German Vivaldi and the "estranged" and (in film at least) underexposed Beethoven excerpt. Both advance the film's dramatic narrative, but not historic memory.

Fitzcarraldo (1981)

Fitzcarraldo, rambling companion piece to *Aguirre*, also features the music of Popol Vuh. But the soundtrack differs notably in that it includes art music, the film being virtually framed by opera performances for a start. The "action" is also punctuated by Caruso performances issuing forth from an old-style gramophone, the mellifluous tones accompanied by a duly scratchy record surface. Two brief passages from Strauss's *Death and Transfiguration,* with images of the riverboat at sunset, are virtually the only nonoperatic examples of art music.

In this film Herzog does not foreground the soundtrack, but thematizes the crossovers between film, opera, and mythology, in artificiality, audience involvement, and self-reflexiveness. The element of artifice in music is best caught by Italian opera, with a counter-example being mentioned once toward the end, when the rubber baron reports that a touring European opera company has arrived to perform Wagner. Fitzcarraldo's eyes light up at the thought of a purer fool, his fellow pilgrim Parsifal. But the music is in fact Bellini's *I Puritani,* and Herzog's film dissolves on a note of light unreality rather than the weightiness of Wagner. In a film whose realization took many turns, Wagner was planned up until nearly the end. In Herzog's script version published in 1982,[9] the opening opera house performance is of Verdi's *Masked Ball,* while Wagner's *Die Walküre* is the opera he brings to the jungle at the end. This was likely to have derived from Coppola's famous use of the "Ride of the Valkyries" in his take on Conrad's *Heart of Darkness,* the point of convergence with Herzog.

In the final cut of the film, the opening performance is of the conclusion of Verdi's *Ernani.* Ostensibly sung by Caruso (for whom Fitzcarraldo has traveled 1,200 miles—to experience the last few minutes!), and with the role of Elvira acted by Sarah Bernhardt, this segment of the film was in fact directed by Werner Schroeter, whose own films have strong ties to opera. The link to cinema history is undoubtedly the opening scene of *Senso* (see chap. 8), with the performance of Verdi setting the stage for the film. Visconti repeatedly intercuts stage with audience, and emphasizes the incendiary potential of music both through the historical context of the performance and the reception of his fictional audience. Nothing could be further from the effect achieved by Schroeter within the Herzog film, this directorial framing alone creating a level of artifice before even considering the staging of the music.

By operatic standards, *Ernani* has probably no less verisimilitude than many companion pieces, certainly within the early Verdi repertoire. But Schroeter compounds the very elements that point away from an anchoring social reality. Indeed at a later garden party

Fitzcarraldo tells his detractors scornfully that the reality of their world is but a rotten caricature of great opera, and these remain the coordinates of reference within the film. The mise-en-abîme possibilities of performer and role are explored to the confusing hilt if we absorb the credits for the performance at Manaus:

Soloists:
 Ernani—Singer: Veriano Luccheti
 Ernani—Actor: Costante Moret
 Silva—Singer and Actor: Dimiter Petkov
 Elvira—Singer: Mietta Sighele
 Singer in Orchestra Pit—Lourdes Magalhães
 Sarah Bernhardt—Jean-Claude Dreyfuss

In Schroeter's staging, Ernani has no evident voiceover. In the time frame of Herzog's film, the character is performed by Caruso; the first silent film appearances of Caruso were mimed performances, silent onstage (in that respect like Sarah Bernhardt here), but synched to a recording of his own voice. The Ernani figure, considerably shorter than Schroeter's Elvira and remarkably like Caruso in appearance,[10] upstages her by remaining in frame (even though with back to the audience—of Schroeter's opera and of Herzog's film) during Elvira's erratic descent of the staircase. He also seems oblivious to her acknowledgment of teamwork as the final bows are taken.

Silva combines both actor and singer in the only unified performance among the principals. The last three listings in the credits quoted above all relate to the one stage figure, with the celebrity Bernhardt being acknowledged, unlike Caruso to whom, under Schroeter's direction, she is dramatically subservient. Acknowledgment of two singers for the part of Elvira is enigmatic, unless we assume that the person listed as "singer in the orchestra pit" is in fact only acting there, and that the voice (on Herzog's soundtrack) is sung by the singer listed alongside the role. Elvira, then, is ostensibly acted by Sarah Bernhardt, as played by Jean-Claude Dreyfuss. The gender ambiguity of the figure is a winking inversion of the historical situation of Bernhardt's fame, alongside "straight" roles, in male parts (e.g., Hamlet).

The role of Elvira is sung by a vocal source present on Herzog's soundtrack but not, it seems, within the performance staged by Schroeter. Inasmuch as the singing capacity of the figure is crucial to the opera's narrative, a Russian doll effect is set in place of ever greater removes from the source of musical communication. Elvira nearly stumbles down the stairs into the arms of Ernani, but less through the distractedness of the emotional moment than, we sense, through the technical unfamiliarity of the male actor negotiating the long train of "her" apparel and "her" different footwear. The impresario mentions crowds flocking to see an actor who can't sing and who has a wooden leg. This held for Sarah Bernhardt as of 1915. The notion of this anachronistic feature being in turn mimed by a presumably uninjured male lends a further contortion to the layers of unreality here. Elvira gestures with flamboyant extravagance and is acoustically demystified for Herzog's cinema audience as the camera draws back to focus on the "actual" singer ("Singer in Orchestra Pit"). But according to the logic above, this is in turn an actress. Less conspicuous at the side of the stage/frame in the opening shots, she is foregrounded near the orchestra pit in one extensive shot, while the stage actor is eclipsed in the background.

But no distancing has any effect on the totally smitten Fitzcarraldo, whose name in turn is a stylization of the humble (Brian Sweeney) Fitzgerald. The dying but still melodically loquacious Ernani points out in the direction of the audience; for Fitzcarraldo this gesture is the finger of fate, singling out him alone. Along with the feigning of spectator involvement at various levels (Fitzcarraldo's with the Caruso figure, ours as spectators with both), the scene represents the passing on by the operatic figure of the legacy of an artificial but grand endeavor. And the self-styled successor lives up to the challenge, again at various levels, when the ship is successfully dragged up and over the mountain.

This adopting of tradition's mantle in turn relates to Herzog's self-positioning within cinema history. For Herzog, the profilmic event is film, including film music. Beyond the clear homage to Huston's *African Queen*, the documentation of the feat of Herzog's own crew (e.g., the natives' pulley systems) at times resembles an epic in the style of the Babylon episode of *Intolerance*, or a Cecil B. DeMille film, without access to a studio. And historic recordings of Caruso evoke not just the era of the silents but also the function of music in such films, as the crackly technical rendition of the masterful voice is allowed to hold sway on Herzog's soundtrack, often without competing sound elements. If Fitzcarraldo feels chosen by Caruso, Herzog interprets the challenge posed by the synchronous beginnings of film in similarly monomaniacal vein. The Schroeter opera production at the beginning is a miniopera within a film. In a less trivial sense, the disembodying of the voice of Elvira evokes features of a silent film. We are partly positioned as viewers not just of an opera but of an opera film.

This complex production of an opera scene is clearly relevant for a film bearing Herzog's signature. Dialogue, never the forte of Herzog's silent, enigmatic types, is more extensive and yet more preposterous here, while the missing three-dimensionality of Herzog's characters is the perfect complement to the amalgam between opera and life. Far beyond its name, the *Molly Aïda*, the boat itself is configured to be suggestive of an opera house. Its railings and their surrounding framings create phantom opera boxes, the effect heightened by the boat's diagonal inching across the screen as it is hauled up the hillside, shot through veils of mist. When Caruso's voice issues forth on deck, the ventilators are like an assembly of gramophone horns and, when viewed singly, like a prompter's box. As a further inversion, such prompting as takes place is from above to below, as orders are issued to the engine room. The fusion of vessel and operatic arena is total by the end, when Fitzcarraldo does indeed bring opera to the jungle, but in a less primitive setting than envisaged. The touring company momentarily transforms his boat into an opera stage, its future as a tool of commerce assured through its reacquisition by the rubber baron.

In this sense, his goal is reached. His intention to turn the natives' myth to his own advantage is checked when they seemingly comply with his wishes, only to undo and rescript his whole project. In similarly fatalistic fashion we are told at the opening of *Aguirre* that El Dorado is a myth invented by the natives to lure the white invaders to their doom. But *Aguirre*, while baroque, is not operatic. *Fitzcarraldo*, on the other hand, evaporates in insubstantiality, technically a disaster matching the main figure's scheme to build a railway across the Andes. But unlike that project, it is magnified by music. There is probably no grander gesture testifying to the power of music in the age of technology than the moment—of incredulousness, hilarity, and reverence—when the natives' pulsating

Music's charms to soothe a savage colonial breast—the
acoustic visionary in *Fitzcarraldo.*

Courtesy Herzog/Filmverlag Der Autoren/ZDF / The Kobal Collection.

drumming is routed, the natives themselves no doubt totally bemused, by the voice of Caruso cranked up on a gramophone. Historically perhaps the last film of the New German Cinema, Herzog's mock epic dissolves that Cinema's favoring of ideologically
laden music (and would have even with the original ending, far from
Syberberg's Wagner). In returning to *I Puritani* at the end, it es-
pouses an ideal for images and for narrative weight whose aesthetic
is similar to the bel canto ideal of opera.

But the epic, while mock, is never farcical. Amid the sounds of
the orchestra warming up, the camera picks out the horns, not rehearsing Bellini but breaking away with a few bars of their accompaniment of the soloist in Beethoven's *Emperor* Concerto. This brief
moment of private homage seems addressed to their benefactor, the
would-be emperor of the jungle, rather than to the musical tradition of Herzog's background. Simultaneously, it seems to invert
the horncall that meant death for Ernani—here the horns signal a

non-Wagnerian acclamation of the hero—just as Bellini's radiant bride Elvira seems a symmetrical resurrection of Verdi's eponymous figure.

The libretto of Bellini's opera is all about the couple being united, a further irony in Herzog's context, as Claudia Cardinale's Molly waves enthusiastically from the shore but remains physically distant from the main action, as she has been throughout the adventure section of the film. The only unity seems to be that between Fitzcarraldo and his beloved opera, and the scene fades out visually (as the soundtrack continues into the darkness) on the central figure, with his mini-Zeppelin of a cigar.

Except for the opening landscape shot, Italian opera then accompanies the first and last curtains in Herzog's film. The conspiratorial element of *Ernani* at the beginning leads only to the natives' concealed conspiracy, as they seem to realize Fitzcarraldo's vision but in fact subvert it. The political overtones of this opera from its Risorgimento reception, drawn upon by Bertolucci in *La Strategia del ragno* [*The Spider's Stratagem*, 1970],[11] is defused. Operatic national politics yields to an internationalized opera as fantastic vision, as pure artifice. Herzog has remodeled reality to bypass restraints on the imagination. At the end of the film Wagner, whose reception embodies the confluence of opera and ideology, is retracted at the levels both of Herzog's plot and of cinema history embracing Herzog.

The retraction of Wagner is itself retracted in Herzog's film of a decade later.

Lessons of Darkness (1992)

The following verdict captured an outside view of the flux within West German self-representation in early 1989, the year in which the Berlin Wall unforeseeably fell: "In West Germany today, national self-understanding and cultural self-fashioning are marked by a number of striking contradictions which play themselves out in various kinds of cultural representation. In political culture, in consumer culture, in pop culture, and in film culture, the new nationalism competes with a new internationalism; a generalised sense of post-modernity manifests itself as nostalgia for pre-modern society."[12] A few of the paradoxes inherent in the post-'89 situation of

Germany's European aspirations were spelled out at the beginning of this book. Some of the analysis that follows needs to be seen in this context, rather than solely that of the eternal outsider, Werner Herzog, on whom the fall of the Wall might have been expected to have least effect among surviving New German Cinema filmmakers. (But whom *has* it affected?) In the film under discussion, a co-production with Paul Berriff with finance from a number of European channels, the tensions observed within this book along the axis of nationalism and internationalism become an amalgam of Western political and cultural histories. In the combination across Herzog's own output of an idiosyncratic ethnography and mythmaking, this film represents a new synthesis. It captures images far more telling than the CNN footage sampled within the film, but transmutes those images into ahistorical myth (rather than virtual reality), not least through a prominent soundtrack, whose musical examples function narratively as a threnody for the West.

As is so often the case, the list of source music acknowledged by the end credits tells us nothing about the manner of its use or the interplay between visuals and soundtrack. (Nor even the sequence, with the end credits citing composers alphabetically.) The list comprises

Grieg, *Peer Gynt*
Mahler, Symphony no. 2
Arvo Pärt, *Stabat Mater*
Prokofiev, Sonata for Two Violins, op. 56
Schubert, *Notturno,* op. 148
Verdi, *Requiem*
Wagner, *Das Rheingold, Parsifal, Götterdämmerung*

These musical examples play a far more prominent role than spoken commentary, absent for over half the film, and in places yield only to the greater volume of "natural" sound effects, such as jets of water in a fire-extinguishing operation. With the exception of the Schubert, which clearly hasn't given Herzog peace since *Echoes of a Sombre Empire,* and the Prokofiev, a fittingly "abstract" accompaniment to the clinical presentation of the torture chamber, all are theatrical. They are taken from operatic, sacred, or stage music or, with the Mahler example, a (vocal) symphonic rendering of a highly theatrical program. Their national provenance, so major an issue in most film examples considered from the 1970s and early 1980s, seems secondary, and the prevailing sense is of spectacle, to match the slanting of the breathtaking images. A closer look at the original theatrical contexts reveals a certain carryover of contents, but these in turn are not the most important markers.

The Wagner examples alone form a striking contrast to their deployment by Syberberg as seen in chapter 4. The film's opening images are accompanied by the *Rheingold* prelude, appropriate in dramatic and possibly in narrative terms, with the archetypical lust for gold conceivably matched by the contemporary greed for oil. Far less obvious, unless cynically equating the Grail with the West's obsession with oil, is the choice of the *Parsifal* prelude in the section "After the Battle." It accompanies footage of bones in a desert landscape, belching smoke, and images reminiscent of Herzog's early film *Fata Morgana* (1968/69). The weak link between the earlier and later films, *Where the Green Ants Dream,* also features Wagner over a desert landscape, this time the *Wesendonck Lieder,* which establish nothing more than an antithetical relationship to the imagery in a *reductio ad absurdum* of the Adorno/Eisler view of film music.

The citing of *Parsifal* in *Lessons of Darkness* brings an absolute discrepancy between image and sound at a narrative level. The camera alone is "questing" as it tracks a static, battle-scarred landscape, which suffers the Wagnerian sound to wash over it until some sense of the nonaestheticized origin of these images is restored, as wind swirls and blends with the music toward the end. The longest Wagner excerpt, Siegfried's funeral music, ushers in the commentary-free bulk of the film. But the kind of connotations that it carried with Syberberg have gone; neither a mythical nor a false hero is dead, but a civilization. And the fires burning on-screen function as opera sets, with Kuwait transformed into Bayreuth, above all the pit, for Herzog's film uses footage of the Gulf War. But this profilmic event is merely the pretext for his own private apocalypse.

The Bayreuth connection is foreshadowed elsewhere in Herzog. In the first of three appearances of the prelude to *Das Rheingold* in *Nosferatu,* the musical shape of the sustained E-flat chord crystallizes to visuals of a stationary Jonathan Harker on a rock, silhouetted from behind like a figure on a parapet, and intercut with clouds rolling in over the mountains in synch with the swirling of the music.[13] The two-dimensional quality of the visuals, to which the music lends the third dimension, is most striking with a silhouette of ruins that emulates a Bayreuth mise-en-scène. The music stops suddenly as doors open for the Count to greet Harker, signaling not just the beginning of a new scene but also the necessity to break the (purely instrumental) operatic flow, for to be consistent, the dialogue between Harker and the Count would need to be staged as a kind of recitative.

The Germanic songlines of war-tarnished Wagner still permeated his staging by Syberberg. But in Herzog, at the latest with *Lessons of Darkness*, these have been overhauled by Wagner as world music, as harbingers of doom, but without strongly Nordic overtones.[14] Whether consciously or not, the breadth of the original *Ring* myth is reinstated after the straitjacketing of its reception by, and in the wake of, Nazi Germany. Along with German films of the 1990s eschewing the "Deutschlandlied" and Beethoven's Ninth, both so prominent in the 1970s (with directors other than Herzog), this association of Wagner with obsequies for the West, in a war that signaled debate about Germany's military obligations under its return to the world stage, marks the end of the arc of this project. The rainbow bridge transporting these gods to Valhalla bears the hues of the nations of the Western alliance and no longer just the colors of Germany.

The sparseness of commentary within the film is complemented by two brief interviews with women, one carrying her muted son, the other bereft of her two sons. The second mother commends the inexpressible to Allah, and the dearth of spoken language in Herzog's film plus the succession of intertitles points it in the direction of silent cinema. This functions not as homage to an earlier artform, as for instance in his *Nosferatu*, but as a cinema of the silenced, as a narrative vindication in itself of the extensive use of music in this film. But the music also points in this historically earlier direction, both dramatically—for long stretches it supplies the only sound—and in the particular selection, at least with that warhorse of the silents, *Peer Gynt* (here the "Death of Ase"). Cultural memory is also cinematic memory, which in turn involves musical memory. Herzog's sound montage locates this film somewhere between a dirge for the old, mostly nineteenth-century Europe and the impossibly weighted Philip Glass soundtracks for *Koyaanisqatsi* and *Powaqqatsi*.

The music overlaying the film's final images comes from Mahler's *Resurrection* Symphony, but there is no indication of the imminence of a resurrection with Herzog. The text speaks of "der Mensch," still with its Enlightenment trappings.[15] But the on-screen figure intercut in perfect synchronization with these words has a recognizably human shape, and no more than that, with the whole body shielded against the intense heat of the firefighting operation. A similar mismatch applies to Verdi's *Requiem* in a section called "The Banquet of the Dinosaurs." Its melodiousness and measured quality counterpoint the apocalyptic imagery, and the landscape devoid of humans features dredging equipment looking like prehistoric monsters.

The ultimate irony is that Herzog's wonderful images obscure the political reality not for political purposes (like those of CNN used in the film) but for apolitical purposes. Therein lies perhaps a kinship with the self-defense of that other great but suspect image-maker of German cinema, Leni Riefenstahl. But overshadowing even them in the stakes raised by issues of art and politics, Wagner demonstrates in his profoundly different roles in the films of Syberberg and Herzog the fluctuating sense of music as cultural marker in German film.

8

Pivot Chords
Austrian Music and Visconti's Senso (1954)

Curtain Call

Throughout this book, comparisons have arisen between U.S. and European Cinema traditions in the course of their development. This final case study concerns Austro-German music within a non-German film. The director, Luchino Visconti, was Italian, with a particular eye and ear for German culture. His use of Bruckner in *Senso* is but one indication of that. The time frames of this film's setting and its making are quite different from those analyzed in detail to this point. But beyond a highly effective, dramatic use of Bruckner's Seventh Symphony, at times even verging on the operatic, it will be argued that Visconti factors in cultural weightings of its reception history and myths attaching to that history.

For Italian Cinema the issue of art music as cultural marker looks somewhat different than choices facing the New German Cinema. This was simply because, as a figure in Leto's *La Villeggiatura* [*Black Holiday*, 1973] puts it: "In Wagner there are too many irrational myths, but Verdi is ours." Verdi, an unproblematic cultural, political, and above all popular identity, and Wagner, none of the above. Indeed, where there is a strand of popularity in nineteenth- or twentieth-century Austro-German music, it takes an Italian film to draw on it unselfconsciously, as with the swirling Strauss waltz in the Taviani brothers' *Padre Padrone* (1977). This admittedly

151

yields to the greater sophistication of the Mozart emitting from the radio later in the film, signaling the by now unbridgeable cultural gap between father and son. The so-called Euro-Cinema may bring further liberation: certainly Szabó's *Meeting Venus* (1991) manages to make the *Tannhäuser* overture sound simply like European rather than pan-Germanic music. Looking at German classical music in other European films can then yield different perspectives, and this is what is sought in the bulk of this chapter, devoted to a close analysis of *Senso*.

Bruckner and Drama

In Visconti's film the historical feud in Austrian-occupied Italy in the 1860s is briefly bridged by the relationship between an Italian countess, Livia Serpieri, and an Austrian officer, Franz Mahler. This constellation is established musically by a stage performance of *Il trovatore* at the beginning,[1] giving way to excerpts from the first two movements of Bruckner's Seventh Symphony, used throughout as nondiegetic music. The dramatic potential of the Verdi is usually acknowledged by critics in terms of the film's dramaturgy and the politically incendiary role it plays.[2] But the role played by Bruckner's music has been largely ignored,[3] despite its prominence on the soundtrack. Less central, but still crucially positioned and furthering the Austrian "counterpoint," are folksongs sung by Franz's fellow soldiers. These, too, have been disregarded.

So far we have seen how classical music in film can generate the narrative, and how it can profitably be read as text, enabling ideological comment, as in West German cinema of the 1970s. It can also function simply as mood, and the lush Romanticism of Bruckner undoubtedly creates mood. But the narrative and ideological functions are what we might expect of a director as musically versed as Visconti, and both hold for the Austrian music chosen for *Senso* and are crucial to the film's overall design. "Operatic melodrama"[4] the film undoubtedly is, but it is also symphonic drama.

The fact that Visconti (contrary to his source, Camillo Boito) elects to call the Austrian officer Mahler, and to accompany Mahler, or at least the countess's image of him, by music of Bruckner, surely arrests attention. When the future lovers cross a Venetian bridge, it proves to be the beginning of a relationship that will consume her

The intact Romantic heroine, with Verdi yet to yield to Bruckner—Visconti's *Senso*.

Courtesy Lux Film / The Kobal Collection.

and destroy him. Musically a turning point is also reached here, as after some twenty minutes dominated by Verdi, Italian music is supplanted. The opening strains of the Bruckner first movement signal the symphony's first entry, the shimmering water in the visuals matched by the shimmering string sound.

The second entry jumps to the second movement, and it accompanies Livia's words to Franz: "I'm like my cousin . . . a true Italian." But the music says otherwise: we hear not Verdi but Bruckner, signaling the gradual erosion of both her personal and national allegiances. Four days later, the strains of Bruckner accompany Livia as she crosses the square, full of a lover's anticipation she has yet to acknowledge. The arches of the music parallel her progress up the staircase, until there is a total change at the aural and then the visual level. The Bruckner yields to the whistling of a figure, initially offstage but emerging into the frame, and to a snatch of the same melody whistled by a second Austrian emerging from a doorway. The dramatic effect is immediate, the grounding of yearning, dramatic art music by a jaunty, uncomplicated tune (paralleled in the visuals with the officer's feet being the first we see of him). This is reinforced by the camera movement, which in turn grounds Livia's ascent after an extreme low angle shot, just as the soldiers' nonchalance bears down on her exalted state. She is in one blow reduced from aspiring Romantic heroine to supplicating courtesan. The Bruckner is seen as her Romantic construct of Franz. The man behind this acoustic mask is to be defined neither by the simple, folklike tones of his comrades nor as the Romantic hero Livia would have him be.

In a later scene, Livia's maid announces the visit of an unknown messenger who entreats her to go at once to a given address and ring three times. Pursued by her husband, she rushes off, the Bruckner first movement proclaiming her conviction and seemingly the perspective of the narrative, that the summons has come from Franz. She rings three times, but before the door is opened her husband apprehends her and she reveals: "It's true: I have a lover! I love him! I want to live with him, do you understand?" Both she and the viewer are totally disoriented when the door is opened to reveal not Franz but the return of her cousin. When he speaks of raising funds for his political movement, and the need to subordinate everything to the national revolution, there is no return to the Verdi but a continuation of Bruckner, foreshadowing her later betrayal of the funds entrusted to her for the sake of buying Franz out of his military service on fabricated medical grounds.

Many strands converge here. Within Livia, her personal Austrian alliance has eclipsed her public Italian allegiance. As narrative commentary, the choice of music possibly provides dramatic anticipation of Austria effacing Italy at the 1866 Battle of Custoza. It is also a critical point in the fragmentation of Livia's self, as the three men in her life are present simultaneously, her husband and cousin visibly, her lover as an unexpected absence, and yet he exerts the strongest presence of all. And this foregrounding of Livia's subconscious is conveyed entirely by the music.

She seemingly makes the required break in the Serpieri family villa, but Franz visits her there and gradually breaks down her resistance to sheltering him. The first theme of the Bruckner second movement is repeated as he gains the upper hand, and this shifts to the major key of the second theme, an illusory haven from chromaticism, as they contemplate the approaching dawn. There follows a long stretch without any music, even though they're alone, as she hides him in the granary. Their sense of relief when her husband signals his intention to be away for lunch one day is matched by the next Bruckner entry, a lush musical release, and shortly after comes a famous climax in the second movement, marked by a clash of cymbals. This accompanies her resolve to betray the funds entrusted to her earlier by Ussoni, by buying a medical release for Franz. As Livia sees her lover off, the opening of the work is restated, creating the illusion Livia simply has to sustain, that a fresh start is possible.

First movement excerpts accompany the arrival of a letter from Franz, announcing that he has been exempted and is now safe in Verona. A peasant carrying an Italian flag links up with the Italian colors raining down on the Austrian audience at the opening performance of *Il trovatore* (a scene echoed with Japanese occupying forces at the Beijing Opera in Chen Kaige's 1993 film, *Ba wang bie ji* [*Farewell My Concubine*]). But for Livia the private now totally dominates the public, and her earlier political leanings are swamped by her consuming passion. She makes a trip to Verona to see Franz, and the excerpts at this stage are crosscut far more than elsewhere, signaling perhaps her ever more tenuous hold on the stability of her construct.

The construct is shattered when she finds Franz supporting a

Sumptuous decors and surging passion, made for Verdi, but scripted for Bruckner.

Courtesy Lux Film / The Kobal Collection.

prostitute with her, Livia's, money, and he mocks her: "I'm not your romantic hero!" Snatches of the second movement accompany this scene; an elegiac section of the first underscores her denunciation of Franz to the Austrian authorities. The final Bruckner entry in the film narrative is a surging strings passage in the second movement, as drunken Austrian soldiers stagger near Livia, and she breaks away to scream "Franz" repeatedly, before his execution completes the film's action.

Only the music remains of the "romantic hero" notion. She is surrounded by inebriated soldiers, his military persona always having been problematic for Franz, and her humiliation in front of his mistress has demolished Franz the lover. The music behind her screams for Franz had been left in suspension, but over the end credits, Visconti shows his musical hand one last time. First we hear the cymbal clash climax already mentioned in connection with her betrayal of the patriots' funds, and then directly following on—as of course is not the case in the symphony itself—the end of the first movement, an exhilarating conclusion which achieves the cadence that has both dramatically and musically been denied the narrative and the lovers.

This analysis has not taken into account all the Bruckner entries, but the catalog here should suffice to demonstrate their reinforcement of the story's dramatic structure, their leading, and in one notable case misleading, of Visconti's characters and viewers. But there is a further dimension to the choice of this particular symphony by this Austrian composer.

Bruckner and Ideology

In 1939 Wilhelm Furtwängler spoke of the restriction of Bruckner's reception to German-speaking cultures. He himself had conducted Bruckner symphonies in America, England, and Italy and encountered the same lack of appreciation everywhere.[5] The war would not have helped this situation. As Bryan Gilliam has documented, "For much of Europe, especially occupied Europe, Bruckner's music would inevitably recall German occupation, especially throughout the late 1940s and 1950s."[6]

This is illustrated by a film not released until 1964, though started in the 1950s: Kevin Brownlow and Andrew Mollo's *It Hap-*

pened Here. A remarkable investigation of what could have happened had the German invasion of England been successful, it uses not only visual but also musical icons to brilliant effect. It is framed by march music over the opening credits before the film's title fills the screen, and Liszt's *Les Préludes*, again functioning as a signature tune for the Nazis, fills the auditorium. At the end, with the Germans in disarray, the radio emits a few bars of the new victor's acoustic trademark, an Elgar *Pomp and Circumstance* march. In a crucial scene early in the film the central figure, a nurse, is seen in long shot against a desolate urban landscape, a kind of British equivalent of early images in Rossellini's *Germania anno zero* [*Germany, Year Zero*, 1948]. The camera follows her uncomprehending walk past signs of devastation, panning across homeless figures and their possessions, rubble, and above all counterpointed placards. These alternately attack "American Culture" (with images of bombs raining down) and encourage the enterprising to "Work in Germany," with duly Aryan faces setting the scene. Throughout this walk there are no natural sounds, say, of footsteps on the pavement, but only an eerie music that gradually builds in volume. The musical climax is reached with a turning point in the film's thematic evolution, a close-up of a sign indicating the Jewish ghetto, leading on to a truly arresting image of an identifiably English street with haunted looking figures on the other side of barbed wire. The passage of music functions tellingly as mood music alone, but it is undoubtedly more than that, given the iconography at the heart of this film's effectiveness. It comes near the end of the first movement of Bruckner's Ninth Symphony, the only film music example of a symphony by this composer that I am aware of outside Visconti.[7]

Visconti is undoubtedly aware of Bruckner's reception of the immediate postwar years—alongside the travesty of Wagner in *The Damned*. A single piece of classical music is used there (alongside an original score by Maurice Jarre plus various German military tunes or folksongs). One of the characters turns on the radio, and the music playing at this early stage of the Third Reich is by Bruckner. Bruckner shared with Hitler his Austrian birth, his reverence of Wagner, and what Goebbels called their "undamaged peasant roots,"[8] and in June 1937 a bust of the composer was installed in Walhalla, the pantheon of Germanic demigods near Regensburg

in Bavaria. He was the only Germanic composer accorded such ele-
vation during the Hitler era. The original versions of his works,
celebrated by their editors in the 1930s, substituted a "genuine,"
reclaimed Bruckner for a creative renewal vainly sought by the Nazis in the present.[9] In Goebbels's historical "consecration" speech
given in Hitler's presence at Walhalla, Bruckner's Austrian birth
was emphasized as part of the outreach of the "German" influence,
uniting the German people beyond existing national boundaries, as
something of a rehearsal for the Anschluss of Austria in the following year.

This background seems relevant for *Senso*, which experienced
problems with the censor and the Italian Ministry of Defense precisely because it was read as a film with thinly veiled historical allusions. Ussoni's patriots provided an uneasy reminder of Italian
partisans in the latter stages of World War II, when both patriots
and partisans were thwarted by the regular army or the national
government. Even at the first historical level of the film's immediate
narrative, Bruckner is an apt choice, for his position in the Austrian
cultural heritage has been seen as nothing less than "a vast sum-
ming up, a final passionate outpouring of a long and hallowed tradition."[10]

In a Viennese musical journal of October 1932, one critic takes to
task the New York Bruckner Society for spreading propaganda for
Mahler alongside Bruckner. He sees this as an affront to European sensitivities, and he counterpoints the two composers as "the
Aryan Bruckner, our German composer, and Mahler, with the dis-
integration attendant on his Jewishness. . . . On the one hand edification, on the other a destructive tendency, even modernism!"[11]
This, too, makes interesting reading when approaching the sundered character of Visconti's figure Mahler, who appears to the
strains of Bruckner.

Bruckner was working on the Seventh Symphony in 1883—the
year, incidentally, when Boito's *Senso* was first published. Myth has
it that Bruckner was preoccupied with a sense of the imminent de-
mise of Wagner, his own Romantic hero. Bruckner ultimately dedicated the work to Ludwig II, but the second movement ended with
funeral music for Wagner, an elegiac fadeout. News of the master's
death, of his death in Venice, reached Bruckner at a point in the
second movement where there is a contentious climax involving a

clash of cymbals. As well as recalling Livia's momentous decision to betray the patriots' funds to Franz, this climax appears over the word *Fine*, in the immediate wake of the death of the man who has said to Livia: "I am not your Romantic hero." But for her, that was what he represented from the time of their first nocturnal walk through Venice. The musical progression in Visconti has to evoke the myth, attached to Wagner, following on directly from the death of his own figure, Franz. But with the end of the film's narrative separating the hero's death from the musical allusion to it, Visconti sets up a further disjunction in the Romantic myths that he unmakes. This same adagio had been heard in April 1945 on German radio immediately after the news of Hitler's death, in a performance conducted by another broken Romantic hero, Furtwängler.[12]

Folksongs

The Verdi and Bruckner examples are offset by folksongs. The first, sung by Franz's comrades intercepting his first visit from Livia, is "O du lieber Augustin," billed by Hans Weigel as an unofficial national anthem of Austria.[13] Augustin was a strolling singer who was thought to be dead and thrown into a common grave with real corpses during a plague. However, he had actually been in a drunken stupor, from which he awakes. He sings of everything having gone, his money, even "'s Mensch," the human being, as he addresses himself as if another. The cheerful melody leavens the mock-tragic catalog of woes. Is there more to it than the function of bringing down to earth the notions of Livia and the strains of Bruckner? It is tempting to see a connection to the issue of the purse entrusted to Livia being emptied later for Franz, further to the inglorious death that awaits Franz without an unexpected resurrection, and perhaps even to the divided self of Franz. On this reading, the soldiers are functioning not only as an opera-style chorus but also as a Greek chorus, commenting on dramatic developments. And the distance created by their commentary further deromanticizes the hero.

The second song comes when Livia again "invades" the barracks, this time without finding Franz. He has wandered and is described as a perpetual wanderer by his former roommate. The soldiers sing "Am Brunnen vor dem Tore," a song by Schubert that has achieved folk status. It depicts the central figure of the song cycle *Die Winterreise* resisting, without firm conviction, the temptation to commit suicide. In a German context the linden tree of the song's title is a traditional lovers' meeting place, but the song itself is also on the lips of Hans Castorp when at the end of Thomas Mann's *Magic Mountain* he and his militarily naive comrades launch themselves onto the battlefields of World War I. All this would seem to have resonances for *Senso*, the German Romantic tradition and its aftermath, and the elements of love and restless wandering addressed by the text of the song. Dramatically, the scene is a mirror image of the first. There we saw the Bruckner/Livia constellation submerged by "Augustin" as rendered by Franz's colleagues. Here the repeated stanzas of the *Lindenbaum* dominate the scene, but toward the end more Bruckner is faded in above the words "That's the way he is!" uttered by Franz's ex-roommate. And it continues as Livia finds a medallion she had given Franz is missing. She momentarily sees him for what he is, but the music continues to say otherwise, and the music has the last say.

When Livia emerges from her final meeting with Franz, she is accosted by drunken Austrian soldiers singing "Alle Vöglein sind schon da," a Lower Austrian folk melody. Here the text proclaims the arrival of spring and its merry celebration, a sense of freshness and rebirth that the lovers have never achieved and that they have just forfeited forever. Finally, as Franz meets his death at the hands of the firing squad, and drumrolls proclaim the ritual, soldiers' voices carry from offstage as they sing "Viktoria, Viktoria." They mean the victory over Italy, but the chorus also seals the victory over Franz's insubordination, the affirmation of the body (politic) over the transgressing member.

How might all this adjust perceptions of *Senso*? Critics make stylistic references to opera and melodrama, paying some attention to the Verdi and also much to aspects of color and allusions to Italian painting.[14] Angela Dalle Vacche writes of Visconti's "teas(ing) out conflicts in the Italian identity" in this film.[15] This chapter has made a case for a bifocality to foreground Austrian, alongside Italian, identity. And the third player, the completion of the constellation, is Germany, at both historical levels of 1866[16] and the 1940s. Certainly there is a strong sense in this film of German presence at the second historical level: as the tide of the war turns, we are told that Garibaldi has sent a message praising the patriots but that he has done so from his position at Salò. This loaded reference catapults the story into the 1940s; for Visconti's audience, the place would be synonymous with the Republic of Salò, where the Germans installed Mussolini as head of a puppet government after Italy had changed sides.

For Austria, the first time frame witnessed its exclusion from the dynamics of German unity, the so-called *kleindeutsche Lösung*. The latter period inverts that process with its inclusion, its Anschluss, in the entity that was the historical successor to Bismarck's Reich. Whether this inclusion was enforced or welcomed, or both, is a question belonging to the annals of Austrian mythology. The historical position of Bruckner, and his own Anschluss by Nazi mythmaking, reflect perfectly this split in identity and this historical duality.

Visconti went on, after all, to make a German trilogy—*The Damned, Death in Venice,* and *Ludwig II.*[17] An examination of Austrian identity through its history is an important subtext of *Senso,* and via the counterpointing of the Italian against the Austrian, the Italian does gain focus, simply in a dramatic sense. The blend of popular and aristocratic tastes in Verdi gives way to the split into high art late Romanticism and folk or military songs, in the Austrian music cited. These function dramatically in directing what might be called the acoustic gaze of the spectator.[18]

But the Austrian music in *Senso* also operates extramusically, via the weighted references explored here.[19] And concealed in the Austrian elements, particularly the range of resonances found in the music, lies much of the richness of Visconti's film. Just as the approach adopted in this book could be applied to the use of Verdi and Puccini in postwar Italian Cinema, for a start, the cultured European director Visconti is capable of using music of the Austro-German symphonic tradition both in a more Hollywood sense, as inspired mood, and also as European cultural marker. Alongside the non-German films considered in chapter 3 in relation to Beethoven's Ninth, *Senso* as interpreted here opens out the body of evidence and demonstrates how cultural markers can, with informed empathy, be culturally transferred.

Conclusion
Film Music and Cultural Memory

Mieke Bal has lamented the "linguistic, visual, and aural domains that blend so consistently in contemporary culture but remain so insistently separated as fields of study in the academy."[1] This book may be considered an approach to redressing that imbalance. Beethoven's Ninth Symphony, the first to blend linguistic and aural domains in its final movement's incorporation of Schiller's *Ode to Joy*, enters the visual domain when used on film soundtracks. A work with such a rich reception history of its own, of course, primarily is quoted in film not for musical values or dramatic effect but for the cultural memory it brings, particularly to a German context. The sound-image mix in any German film comes from "a national-cultural tradition in which the very concept of music (specifically, musical high culture) was laden with extraordinary cultural-historical and ideological baggage."[2]

At the cinematic site of "the cultural negotiation of memory and identity in the aftermath of fascism,"[3] a quest common to controversial artist Anselm Kiefer and a disparate array of directors from the New German Cinema, Beethoven's Ninth serves as a key text. It establishes a degree of continuity amid the discontinuities of twentieth-century German history, while simultaneously, via the suggestiveness of its reception history, stressing the century's ruptures. However paradoxical that might seem in relation to the me-

163

dium of film, it furthermore signals a shift from cultural consumerism to reactivated listening, given its "estranged" new setting.

The New German Cinema director with the richest examples of classical music, Alexander Kluge, repeatedly stressed his desire to activate the film in the spectator's head, rather than tie the viewer to a concrete set of images on the screen. His complex soundtracks are undoubtedly designed to set in motion the soundtrack in the viewer/listener's inner ear. Like images, this is a soundtrack that is culturally conditioned. If the Yanks had colonized the subconscious of Wenders's postwar German viewers, then the Nazis had colonized their acoustic subconscious. For this reason Wenders avoided the classical musical repertoire that Kluge, Fassbinder, Syberberg, and others used to enact and interrogate cultural memory within national consciousness.

Alongside Mieke Bal in *The Practice of Cultural Analysis*, Routledge publishing director William P. Germano claims, "The interdisciplinary appears to be the high-culture loser in the high-low market wars."[4] But there is no inherent reason why this prognosis should hold in the future. To rearrange Germano's players, high culture may well have been the interdisciplinary loser in the high-low market wars, but that has been a loss for cultural studies. And a combination like Beethoven's Ninth (or more accurately, in most cases, fragments of its fourth movement) in commercial film is a perfect melting pot for confounding high-low distinctions.

Even during the heyday of the New German Cinema in the 1970s, an element of self-legitimation of cultural status was sought through cinematic renderings of canonic music. Employing Beethoven, Mahler, or Wagner on the soundtrack complicates cultural validation by inevitably evoking cultural politics.[5] A Haydn melody, which at a significant stage of German history was better known in its military band incarnation as the "Deutschlandlied," exemplifies still better what is at issue. Jonathan Culler reminds us that in the United States "national identity has often been defined *against* high culture," whereas British "national cultural identity was linked to monuments of high culture."[6] How much more does the latter hold true for German culture and within German culture for "die deutscheste Kunst," the most German art of all, music.

Nineteenth-century German music was the central component of that cultural tradition, which went largely unchallenged until appropriated by the Nazis. It was retained, as was seen in the first film by Makavejev (see chap. 3), as part of the cultural (albeit bourgeois) heritage in former East bloc countries. All this is alien to the register of music largely used for "mood" purposes by classical Hollywood. It enabled a European director to shore up a film acoustically against the penetration of Hollywood.

The examples throughout the book of German film and preexisting German music identify a historical stage of an ongoing debate about national identity. As a soundtrack component, Beethoven's Ninth largely disappears from German films of the 1980s, except for parodistic treatment (as a bastion of the patriarchy) in *Felix*, or as an implied presence in Fassbinder's *Lili Marleen* (see chap. 6). In the 1990s it seems to disappear at a time of quite different reflections on national identity, now no longer sundered. At the same time this work, above all others from the once "Germanic" canon, experiences irresistible globalizing tendencies. A more embracing European Cinema framework is established first by *Clockwork Orange* and then by the end point of the Ninth as European humanism—of a necessity reached outside Germany—in Tarkovsky.

The ideal of this project would be to illustrate the answer Michael H. Kater supplies to his own rhetorical question: "Why should historians of modern Germany be concerned with books on the performance of music in the Weimar Republic or on music in the Third Reich? Because such studies today are part of the interdisciplinary and, I would add, crosscultural pursuits that ideally inform the historiography of any country in any period."[7] The aesthetic, dramatic, and above all cultural performance of music in films of the New German Cinema also belongs to those pursuits. And while this artistic mix is especially rich, there is no reason to stop at German music and German cinema: film studies, German studies, and musicology are challenged far more broadly. Marc Silberman concludes his important article already cited in chapter 2 thus:

Germany's historical trajectory in this century during which the cinema has come of age may strike many as extreme and therefore unrepresentative for the general issue of national cinema history. Yet its encounter with modernism through the cinema brings into high relief a set of factors and contradictions which bound together the discourses of cinema and nation, of global interest and national identity. Tracing the way in which these discourses sought to make sense of a specifically historical and national development sheds light on the categories which constitute national cinema histories.[8]

When music is factored into these discourses, especially music when used in cinema, Silberman's conclusion must meet with even fuller endorsement. Film studies has stressed the importance of engaging with the cultural specificity of scopic regimes. The present study has achieved its purpose if it has staked out the claims of acoustic regimes and the need for film studies, musicology, and cultural studies to engage with them. In that sense this book may be taken as a case study which will hopefully challenge those areas to undertake a much broader and necessary project.

The picture emerging reflects dominant tendencies, but it must not be overstated as uniform. Within music contemporary with film directors considered here, Stockhausen compressed stages of reception history. Even in his project of "writing not 'my' music, but music of the whole world,"[9] the electronic transformation of a wide range of national anthems in *Hymnen* (1966–67) included the Nazi Horst Wessel-Lied alongside the anthem of Germany. So cultural memory is not to be denied within a conscious attempt to achieve world music. World music is a different stage of "music as history" to that exemplified by the soundtracks of New German Cinema films. But both realize "the function of musical memory in a given culture."[10]

At the October 2001 Day of Unity celebration at the German embassy in Canberra, as no doubt in all world capitals with a German embassy, the German national anthem was played. An eighty-year-old German, unaware of my project, confided that in his mind the music was still coupled with the Horst Wessel-Lied. Even when in some future generation this is no longer a living memory, treating it as more than a museum piece of cultural memory will be an important part of understanding much larger issues of national identity, not confined to Germany. For even the seemingly permanent changes. In July 2001 Daniel Barenboim and a German orchestra emulated Holocaust survivor Mendi Rodan, who conducted the Israel Symphony Orchestra the year before, in breaking the long-standing taboo on the live performance of Wagner in Israel.[11] In the

year 2000, on the highly symbolic date in German history of November 9, Federal president Johannes Rau clearly differentiated nationalism and patriotism. It could be argued, I feel, that this is
Kluge's main point, reinforced by his use of music, but a point
made when such a theme was deemed too awkward for Germany.
These indicators of flux and continuity testify to the interplay between images and music in 1970s German film being an important
stage of cultural reception of the music, one from which transferable cultural models can be extracted.

These and other issues of cultural politics, identity politics, and
cultural memory clearly extend far beyond the German focus of this
book. The extremity of the German example makes it ideal for en-
compassing cases beyond Germany, as Silberman points out above.
Unsettling scores can then constructively unsettle disciplines. To
make that point persuasively from the perspective of studies in music, I should like to finish with a long quotation from a chapter on
Wagner's *Ring,* in which the historical layers of the work's reception
are sketched almost like the age rings of a tree. While few of us are
such culturally versed listeners as its author, Herbert Lindenberger,
his reading is highly relevant for the German context at the core of
the present book and, when one adds film to the already potent mix
here, summarizes its issues:

The old notion that art reflects history grants too passive a role to the
work of art, at least to a seminal work such as the *Ring.* Moreover,
the historicity I have sought to locate in the *Ring* lies not simply in
the nineteenth-century image that it conjures up but in the meanings
it has accumulated through more than a century of interpretation
both on the stage and in the study. When I attend a *Ring* cycle I hear
both the voice of an otherwise lost nineteenth-century world as well
as the long succession of later significations that have stamped themselves upon it—for example, Nietzsche's condemnation of Wagner as
"der Künstler der *décadence*" [the artist of decadence] for allowing
Schopenhauer's pessimism to compromise the ending of *Götterdämmerung;* or Adorno's reading of Alberich and Mime as caricatures of
Jews; or Hitler's statement in his notebooks, "Young Siegfried, well
known from my time at the Linz Opera; Wagner's piece showed me
for the first time what blood-myth [*Blutmythos*] is"; or Wieland Wagner's suppression of the traditionally Germanic visual effects in his
Bayreuth *Ring* after World War II; or Chéreau's presentation of the

Rhine maidens as whores prancing about a hydroelectric dam. Even while thinking myself spellbound at a *Ring* performance I confess that I do not erase the photo-images in my memory of Hitler paying his respects to Wagner's descendants at their shrine in Bayreuth. Through an examination of the *Ring*'s many entanglements past and present all these strikingly diverse matters can assume connections with one another—can, in fact, build up a larger image to which we then attach the name *history*.[12]

Notes

Introduction

1. The terms *classical music* and *art music* have their defenders and their fierce critics. The former risks historical fuzziness when used more generally, while the latter risks sounding elitist. While both will be found here, I have tried to defuse the first problem by capitalizing *Classical* when referring to the era to which Mozart and Haydn belonged. What is never meant here is a style of orchestration applied, say, to original Hollywood scores (by Steiner, Korngold, Newman, etc.). As generic and historical senses of "classical" overlap in relation to Hollywood cinema, no such problem arises there.

2. One German critic even refers to it as nonfilm music [*Nicht-Filmmusik*]. See Norbert Jürgen Schneider, *Handbuch Filmmusik I: Musikdramaturgie im Neuen Deutschen Film*, 2d ed. (Munich: Oelschläger, 1990), 202ff. In a book devoted to music in the New German Film from 1960 to 1985, Schneider, himself a composer of film music, devotes but a few pages (266–73) to the use of classical music. He claims, "Mostly a quotation of classical music is only used to create a mood or to accentuate a particular aspect of the piece" (267). This seems to undersell some of his own striking examples.

3. Claudia Gorbman, *Unheard Melodies: Narrative Film Music* (Bloomington: Indiana University Press, 1987); Kathryn Kalinak, *Settling the Score: Music and the Classical Hollywood Film* (Madison: University of Wisconsin Press, 1992); Caryl Flinn, *Strains of Utopia: Gender, Nostalgia, and Hollywood Film Music* (Princeton, N.J.: Princeton University Press, 1992); Royal S. Brown, *Overtones and Undertones: Reading Film Music* (Berkeley: University of California Press, 1994); George Burt, *The Art of Film Music* (Boston: Northeastern University Press, 1994). For sample reviews of these advances of the area, see Claudia Gorbman, "The State of Film Music Criticism," *Cinéaste*

169

21, no. 1–2 (1995): 72–75; James Buhler and David Neumeyer (review of Flinn's and Kalinak's books) in the *Journal of the American Musicological Society* 47, no. 2 (Summer 1994): 372–77. I largely use these books to profile my own concerns, which in no way does justice to the scope of theirs. More general points taken up from one author are rarely unique to that author.

My concerns are closer to the "affiliating identifications" (3) located by Anahid Kassabian in compiled scores of 1980s and 1990s Hollywood. In her terms, my project involves examples of affiliation with a range of identifications that were nationally problematic, in a very different film industry. See Anahid Kassabian, *Hearing Film: Tracking Identifications in Contemporary Hollywood Film Music* (New York: Routledge, 2001).

4. Nicholas Cook, *Analysing Musical Multimedia* (New York: Oxford University Press, 2000). To locate this alongside other recent, relevant books, see Simon Frith's review in *Screen* 41, no. 3 (Autumn 2000): 334–38.

5. See especially Claudia Gorbman's translations of Michel Chion's *Audio-Vision: Sound on Screen* (New York: Columbia University Press, 1994) and *The Voice in Cinema* (New York: Columbia University Press, 1999). Chion's original text for the latter appeared in 1982. To my knowledge, not one of the book-length German contributions to this area has been translated. For an interview with Peer Raben, however, see "Peer Raben: Work without End," in *Chaos as Usual: Conversations about Rainer Werner Fassbinder*, ed. Juliane Lorenz, trans. Christa Armstrong and Maria Pelikan (New York: Applause, 1997), 29–39. Within German approaches, a key text is a translation from the Polish of Zofia Lissa's *Ästhetik der Filmmusik* (Berlin, 1965), unknown here and long out of print. The same applies to what to my mind is the best of the German texts: Helga de la Motte-Haber and Hans Emons, *Filmmusik: Eine systematische Beschreibung* (Munich: Hanser, 1980). Like Jonathan Harker at the end of Herzog's *Nosferatu*, we have much to do.

6. See Royal S. Brown, "Film and Classical Music," in *Film and the Arts in Symbiosis: A Resource Guide*, ed. Gary R. Edgerton (New York: Greenwood Press, 1988), 165–215; Jack Clancy, "Music in the Films of Peter Weir," *Journal of Australian Studies* 41 (1994): 24–34; "Arthouse Cinema and Classical Music" in Russell Lack, *Twenty-four Frames Under: A Buried History of Film Music* (London: Quartet Books, 1997), 296–309; Randall D. Larson, "Classical Music," in *Musique fantastique: A Survey of Film Music in the Fantastic Cinema* (Metuchen, N.J.: Scarecrow, 1985), 347–53. Caryl Flinn is the only scholar I am aware of who has approached the subject of this book in any detail. See her "Music and the Melodramatic Past of New German Cinema," in *Melodrama: Stage, Picture, Screen*, ed. Jacky Bratton et al. (London: BFI, 1994), 106–18; "Strategies of Remembrance: Music and History in the New German Cinema," in *Music and Cinema*, ed. James Buhler, Caryl Flinn, and David Neumeyer (Hanover, N.H.: Wesleyan University Press, 2000), 118–41; "The Legacy of Modernism: Peer Raben, Film Music, and Political After Shock," in *Cinesonic: The World of Sound in Film*, ed. Philip Brophy (North Ryde, NSW: Australian Film Television and Radio School, 1999), 171–88. As I was completing this manuscript, Flinn's latest book arrived: *The New Ger-*

man Cinema: Music, History, and the Matter of Style (Berkeley: University of California Press, 2004). Its strong focus on matters of gender and performance, in particular, provides a perfect complement to the present volume. Obligatory reading for music under the Nazis and in the early postwar period is Lutz Koepnick, *The Dark Mirror: German Cinema between Hitler and Hollywood* (Berkeley: University of California Press, 2002).

7. This study is confined to West German films, to films of the Federal Republic of Germany as that title was used between 1949 and 1990, after which it remained unchanged to designate (re)unified Germany. To supplement the picture emerging here, see Hans Joachim Meurer, *Cinema and Divided Identity in a Divided Germany, 1979–1989: The Split Screen* (Lewiston, Me.: Edwin Mellen, 2000). Meurer quite rightly points out that his book "resists a dominant tendency according to which the term *German* has commonly been attributed to the films produced in the former FRG" (ii).

8. See Bryan Gilliam, "The Annexation of Anton Bruckner: Nazi Revisionism and the Politics of Appropriation," *Musical Quarterly* 78, no. 3 (Fall 1994): 584–604.

1. Establishing a Tonal Center

1. This basic assumption of film music criticism, yet to filter through sufficiently to film criticism, is borne out by empirical evidence in Annabel J. Cohen, "Associationism and Musical Soundtrack Phenomena," *Contemporary Music Review* 9, nos. 1/2 (1993): 163–78. In addition, see the special issue on film music in *Psychomusicology: A Journal of Research in Music Cognition* 13, nos. 1/2 (Spring/Fall 1994), plus Marilyn G. Boltz, "Musical Soundtracks as a Schematic Influence on the Cognitive Processing of Filmed Events," *Musical Perception* 18, no. 4 (Summer 2001): 427–54.

2. Chion, *Audio-Vision*, 5.

3. Ibid., 68.

4. Lawrence Kramer, *Musical Meaning: Toward a Critical History* (Berkeley: University of California Press, 2002), 182.

5. Leo Treitler, *Music and the Historical Imagination* (Cambridge: Harvard University Press, 1989); Lawrence Kramer, *Music as Cultural Practice, 1800–1900* (Berkeley: University of California Press, 1990) and *Classical Music and Postmodern Knowledge* (Berkeley: University of California Press, 1995); Susan McClary, *Feminine Endings: Music, Gender, and Sexuality* (Minneapolis: University of Minnesota Press, 1991).

6. A very different example for a similar plot abstraction is Philip Glass's music for the Errol Morris film *The Thin Blue Line* (1988). The typical qualities of Glass's music, circling without tonal progression, abstract in coloring, almost arbitrarily beginning and ending, and emotionally neutral, provide a perfect mirror for the Texan legal system as portrayed in this film.

7. For more on film music and geographic location, see David Burnand and Benedict Sarnaker, "The Articulation of National Identity through Film Mu-

sic," *National Identities* 1, no. 1 (March 1999): 7–13. For this issue in relation to the depiction of American Indians, see Claudia Gorbman, "Drums along the LA River: Scoring the Indian," in *Cinesonic: Cinema and the Sound of Music*, ed. Philip Brophy (North Ryde, NSW: Australian Film Television and Radio School, 2000), 97–115.

8. As acknowledged by biographer Barbara B. Heyman, *Samuel Barber: The Composer and His Music* (New York: Oxford University Press, 1992), 173. But of relevance for the case of *Wild Reeds* considered below is the whimsical French film *Amélie* (Jeunet, 2001); the sole example of preexisting classical music is this Adagio played over the central figure's vision of her own state funeral. In the French context, the same music accompanied advertisements for the World Cup soccer championship in 2000.

9. Private communication from Julie McQuinn, who approached Téchiné's sound engineer, Jean-Paul Mugel when preparing her paper presented at the Royal Musical Association conference (Southampton, April 2001) on "Filmic Counterpoint: Samuel Barber's *Adagio for Strings* as a Voice in a Time of War."

10. For changing reactions to the hymn and its various verses—noting that the offending stanza is eliminated from the postwar version on official occasions—see Joyce Marie Mushaben, *From Post-War to Post-Wall Generations: Changing Attitudes toward the National Question and NATO in the Federal Republic of Germany* (Boulder, Colo.: Westview Press, 1998), 68.

11. See Robynn J. Stilwell, "'I just put a drone under him . . .': Collage and Subversion in the Score of 'Die Hard,'" *Music and Letters* 78, no. 4 (November 1997): 551–80.

12. Review by Richard Porton in *Cinéaste* 21, no. 1–2 (February 1995): 104. The music is used with feminist overtones by Jane Campion in *Portrait of a Lady* (1996), to resist the inner death of the maiden.

13. Gorbman, *Unheard Melodies*, 17. Matching examples are cited by Flinn, *Strains of Utopia*, 37.

14. Not Gorbman's assumption; she effectively contests this elsewhere and signals it here with the quotation marks.

15. See Udo Rauchfleisch, *Musik schöpfen, Musik hören: Ein psychologischer Zugang* (Göttingen and Zurich: Vandenhoeck & Ruprecht, 1996), 98: "After all, listening represents an archaic, relatively imprecise form of perception, with the aid of which direction, for example, can be calculated precisely, but not distance."

16. Albrecht Riethmüller, "Wunschbild: Beethoven als Chauvinist," *Archiv für Musikwissenschaft* 58, no. 2 (2001): 101. The original, referring to the takeover of his works for the cause of nationalism, reads: "Beethoven als Inbegriff der deutschen Musik, diese begriffen als die Musik schlechthin."

2. Music as Cultural Marker
in German Film

1. Cook, *Analysing Musical Multimedia*, 23, 83. Rejecting approaches hitherto by a range of disciplines, including musicology, other British scholars plead for "discussing a *relationship*, a set of *processes* between music's sounds and music's meanings wherein sounds are significant, but meanings are the consequence of the socially and culturally mediated character of this relationship." John Shepherd and Peter Wicke, *Music and Cultural Theory* (Cambridge: Polity Press, 1997), 16.

2. Brown, *Overtones and Undertones*, 1.

3. Chion, *Audio-Vision*, 68. Elsewhere he emphasizes music's porous quality, speaking of it as "cinema's *passe-muraille*" (ibid., 81).

4. Kalinak, *Settling the Score*, 20.

5. But this, too, is not confined to Germany. *Laura* has an intriguing example, tellingly confined to the script. Shelby Carpenter's claim to have been at a concert featuring Brahms's First and Beethoven's Ninth seems to implicate him in murder, as he is unaware that a last-minute change had seen an all-Sibelius program. When in *Husbands and Wives* (1992) Woody Allen actually goes to a concert with (a few bars only of) Mahler's Ninth, it is almost a self-parody of the director's penchant for European cinema.

6. Cook, *Analysing Musical Multimedia*, 105.

7. Brown, *Overtones and Undertones*, 52.

8. Compare the semantic effects created when "seventeenth- and eighteenth-century theorists compiled charts and tables of musical figures, very much like a bilingual dictionary, so the young composers would have no trouble saying exactly what they wanted to say in their music." Joseph P. Swain, "The Range of Musical Semantics," *Journal of Aesthetics and Art Criticism* 54, no. 2 (Spring 1996): 149.

9. Dominique Nasta, *Meaning in Film: Relevant Structures in Soundtrack and Narrative* (Berne: Lang, 1991), 51.

10. Jerrold Levinson, "Film Music and Narrative Agency," in *Post-Theory: Reconstructing Film Studies*, ed. David Bordwell and Noël Carroll (Madison: University of Wisconsin Press, 1996), 249.

11. Peter Reichel reminds us that "the NS [National Socialist] regime tried to define itself and acquire legitimation via mass culture and the arts probably more than any other ruling system of modern times." See his "Culture and Politics in Nazi Germany," in *Political Culture in Germany*, ed. Dirk Berg-Schlosser and Ralf Rytlewski (New York: St Martin's Press, 1993), 74. See also David B. Dennis, *Beethoven in German Politics, 1870–1989* (New Haven: Yale University Press, 1996), 143–44.

12. See Dennis, *Beethoven in German Politics*, which documents the ideological reception of Beethoven through various historical stages.

13. See Frank Trommler, "The Social Politics of Musical Redemption," in *Re-Reading Wagner*, ed. Reinhold Grimm and Jost Hermand (Madison: University of Wisconsin Press, 1993), 119–35.

14. See Cook, *Analysing Musical Multimedia*, 107: "The existing literature of multimedia suffers, as I see it, from two associated problems: the terminological impoverishment epitomized by film criticism's traditional categorization of all music-picture relationships as either parallel or contrapuntal, and a largely unconscious (and certainly uncritical) assumption that such relationships are to be understood in terms of hegemony or hierarchy rather than interaction."

15. In the introduction by David Neumeyer with Caryl Flinn and James Buhler to *Music and Cinema*, the New German Cinema is credited with the "attempt to problematize a national history that would pass itself off as seamless, teleological, or untroubled" (5). At least the outer adjectives would seem impossible to pass off. Flinn's own assessment of Syberberg's *Our Hitler* seems much closer to the mark: "Music is positioned as an anchoring continuity while everything around it falls to ruin" (ibid., 125).

16. Bernhard Giesen, *Intellectuals and the German Nation: Collective Identity in an Axial Age*, trans. Nicholas Levis and Amos Weisz (Cambridge: Cambridge University Press, 1998), 145.

17. As reported in *Kulturchronik* 5 (1994): 6.

18. Martin Jay, *Downcast Eyes: The Denigration of Vision in Twentieth-Century French Thought* (Berkeley: University of California Press, 1993), 265.

19. This in turn led to more linear artistic traditions: "As far as high musical culture in the era of Romantic nationalism is concerned, one could easily speak in terms of a 'German century' extending from Beethoven to Mahler." Michael Gilbert, "'Ich habe von einem Esel gelernt': Eisler Pro und Contra Schönberg," in *High and Low Cultures: German Attempts at Mediation*, ed. Reinhold Grimm and Jost Hermand (Madison: University of Wisconsin Press, 1994), 63.

20. Kathleen Higgins, *The Music of Our Lives* (Philadelphia: Temple University Press, 1991), 34.

21. Norbert Elias, *The Germans: Power Struggles and the Development of Habitus in the Nineteenth and Twentieth Centuries*, ed. Michael Schröter, trans. Eric Dunning and Stephen Mennell (New York: Columbia University Press, 1996), 123–27.

22. Giesen, *Intellectuals and the German Nation*, 91, 97.

23. See Marc Silberman, "What Is German in the German Cinema?" *Film History* 8 (1996): 303: "Here as in no other country the cinema encountered resistance as a threat and antagonist to 'culture' in its tendency toward standardisation, democratisation and internationalism."

24. Walter Benjamin, "A Berlin Chronicle," in *Selected Writings*, vol. 2: *1927–1934*, ed. Michael W. Jennings et al., trans. Rodney Livingstone et al. (Cambridge: Harvard University Press, 1999), 634.

25. Bernd Sponheuer speaks of "the relative constancy of a notion of the 'German' in music over the last two hundred years," viewing it as "this touchstone for German identity." Bernd Sponheuer, "Reconstructing the Ideal Types of the 'German' in Music," in *Music and German National Identity,* ed. Celia Applegate and Pamela Potter (Chicago: University of Chicago Press, 2002), 36.

26. Silberman, "What Is German in the German Cinema?" 297.

27. Now entitled to German citizenship are children born in Germany to parents who have resided there legally for eight years. For the context of this change, see Donald G. Phillips, *Post-National Patriotism and the Feasibility of Post-National Community in United Germany* (Westport, Conn.: Praeger, 2000), 169–80.

28. For an overview of the evolution of early nineteenth-century Romantic nationalism, see the section "Nationalism in the Wider Context," in Eric R. Wolf, *Envisioning Power: Ideologies of Dominance and Crisis* (Berkeley: University of California Press, 1999), 208ff. For more background to the German situation, see Mary Fulbrook, *German National Identity after the Holocaust* (Cambridge: Polity Press, 1999), 180ff.

29. See Eric Rentschler, "From New German Cinema to Post-Wall Cinema of Consensus," in *Cinema and Nation,* ed. Mette Hjort and Scott Mackenzie (London: Routledge, 2000), 260–77; Hans-Bernhard Moeller, "Zur deutschen Filmkomödie der Generation nach 1968," *Monatshefte* 93, no. 2 (Summer 2001): 196–208.

30. See Anton Kaes, "How German Is It? Probleme beim Schreiben einer nationalen Filmgeschichte," *Filmkunst* 148 (1995): 54–63.

31. In appendix 2 to his *Fassbinder's Germany: History Identity Subject* (Amsterdam: Amsterdam University Press, 1996), Thomas Elsaesser cites as the "major media event in 1978: Günther Rühle, in the (conservative) *Frankfurter Allgemeine Zeitung* accuses West German literature of shunning contemporary topics: 'Only the cinema is still dealing with current issues.' His articles signal the ascendancy of the right over the left in cultural policy (*Tendenzwende*)" (316).

32. See Werner Weidenfeld, "Ratloses Nationalgefühl: Fragen an die Deutsche Frage," in *Nachdenken über Deutschland: Materialien zur politischen Kultur der Deutschen Frage* (Köln: Wissenschaft und Politik, 1985), 13. See the same author's chapter "Die Suche nach Identität: Ein deutsches Problem?" in *Nachdenken über Deutschland:* "Since roughly the end of the 1970s or the beginning of the 1980s, just about all the attributes of a boomtime for the concept of identity can be registered: best-sellers, interest shown by the academies, the engagement of the mass media" (89). There was also a boom in interdisciplinary interest in identity issues at the end of the 1970s and beginning of the 1980s, with prominent German examples alongside figures like Claude Lévi-Strauss. See Jan Assmann, *Das kulturelle Gedächtnis* (Munich: Beck, 2000), 130n1.

33. See Dirk Verheyen, *The German Question: A Cultural, Historical, and Geopoliti-*

cal Exploration (Boulder, Colo.: Westview Press, 1999). Verheyen sets out identity issues with great clarity (e.g., 62–65). He stresses that for "the Germans themselves ["the German Question"] revolves significantly around the issue of *identity*" (7), and prepares the ground for the present work's claims for music in film by suggesting "that the issues of *identity* and *unity* are perhaps first and foremost cultural and ideological in nature" (7). This is historicized, in a passage that further highlights the resonance of nineteenth-century music in postwar films, by a German sociologist: "Only in the nineteenth century did the discourse on national identity itself achieve the rank of an ultimate reference point, around which all other discourses and codes had to be oriented." Giesen, *Intellectuals and the German Nation*, 50.

34. Peter Lerche, quoted by James J. Sheehan, "National History and National Identity in the New Germany," in *European Cultures: Studies in Literature and the Arts*, vol. 1: *1870/71–1989/90 German Unifications and the Change of Literary Discourse*, ed. Walter Pape (Berlin and New York: W. de Gruyter, 1993), 30. For difficulties since unification, see Richard Schröder, *Deutschland schwierig Vaterland: Für eine neue politische Kultur*, 3d ed. (Freiburg: Herder, 1995), 9–16.

35. Schroeter shows the transitory attainment of a utopian cultural *Heimat* at festivals like the one at Nancy that dominates his film.

36. Weidenfeld, "Ratloses Nationalgefühl," 94.

37. For contemporary reflections on the crisis that contextualize it within a broad span of German history, see Elias, *The Germans*, 405–33.

38. The title word alone involved a revaluation of a compromised concept. On the other hand, each episode of the first series is preceded by a stone bearing the inscription "Made in Germany," in English. This internationalization tempers the defiance of the motto, contrary to Reitz's intention, as a German director finishes up speaking the language of Hollywood.

39. Anton Kaes, *From Hitler to Heimat: The Return of History as Film* (Cambridge: Harvard University Press, 1989), 197.

40. See Elsaesser, *New German Cinema: A History* (New Brunswick, N.J.: Rutgers University Press, 1989), 49: "No other European country, it seems, is as unsure of the meaning of its culture as Germany, or as obsessed with its national identity."

41. Elsaesser, *Fassbinder's Germany: History Identity Subject*, 15. See also Robert Picht, "Disturbed Identities: Social and Cultural Mutations in Contemporary Europe," in *European Identity and the Search for Legitimacy*, ed. Soledad García (London: Pinter, 1993), 82: "It is no accident that identity debates have a long tradition in Germany and have flourished again since the 1970s." And Stuart Parkes, in *Understanding Contemporary Germany* (London: Routledge, 1997), writes of "the theme of Germany again bec(oming) an issue of intellectual debate in the late 1970s" (176), albeit debate among the Left.

42. Nor was it confined to the word *Deutschland* among elusive words. Kluge's colleague Edgar Reitz described the more subjectivized form of "home" thus:

"It seems to me that one has a more precise idea of Heimat the further one is away from it." Quoted in *Becoming National: A Reader*, ed. Geoff Eley and Ronald Grigor (New York: Oxford University Press, 1996), 459.

43. Silke Hahn, "Vom *zerrissenen Deutschland* zur *vereinigten Republik*: Zur Sprachgeschichte der 'deutschen Frage,'" in *Kontroverse Begriffe: Geschichte des öffentlichen Sprachgebrauchs in der Bundesrepublik Deutschland*, ed. Georg Stötzel and Martin Wengeler (Berlin: Walter de Gruyter, 1995), 317-22.

44. Ibid., 317. Hahn traces how the CDU/CSU demanded the resignation of Secretary of State Günter Gaus, the first "Ständige Vertreter" of the Federal Republic in the GDR. His "crime," in the course of an interview with *Der Spiegel*, was the formulation "GDR-policy" rather than "Deutschlandpolitik" —policy on East Germany rather than Germany. The very avoidance of *ambassador* or the like with the term *ongoing representative* [*Ständige Vertreter*] further reflects the intellectual juggling acts in operation: for Bonn, East Berlin represented both an internationally recognized regime and a second German state, a second (and, beyond unification, secondary) state within an entity not then in existence.

45. Ibid., 319.

46. Hans-Jürgen Syberberg, *Hitler: A Film from Germany*, preface by Susan Sontag, trans. Joachim Neugroschl (New York: Farrar Straus Giroux, 1982), 58.

47. Fulbrook, *German National Identity*, 122.

48. Fifteen to twenty years after this corpus of films, a German historian's résumé of the century affirms this undiminished shadow: "As polls show, the Hitler era is the most important point of reference for the Germans, and this is the aspect from which they are still viewed from outside." See Eberhard Jäckel, *Das deutsche Jahrhundert: Eine historische Bilanz* (Stuttgart: Deutsche Verlags-Anstalt, 1996), 283-84.

49. Anne Bowler, "Methodological Dilemmas in the Sociology of Art," in *The Sociology of Culture: Emerging Theoretical Perspectives*, ed. Diana Crane (Oxford: Blackwell, 1994), 253, 257.

50. See Dave Morley and Kevin Robins, "No Place Like *Heimat:* Images of Home(land) in European Culture," in *Space and Place: Theories of Identity and Location*, ed. Erica Carter, James Donald, and Judith Squires (London: Lawrence and Wishart, 1993), 9.

51. Silberman, "What Is German in the German Cinema?" 299.

52. The term *depthless culture* comes from Jameson (1984), cited here by Colin Symes, "Beating Up the Classics: Aspects of a Compact Discourse," *Popular Music* 16, no. 1 (January 1997): 90. For inroads from a different direction, see Rob Burns and Wilfried van der Will, "Americanization and National Identity," in *German Cultural Studies: An Introduction*, ed. Rob Burns (New York: Oxford University Press, 1995), 310-23.

53. In the U.S. film tradition, the ancestor is likely to have been the arrangement of Wagner's warhorse in *Birth of a Nation* (1915). The domestic contentiousness of that film, where the Wagner accompanied the Ku Klux Klan, alone

casts a highly skeptical light on the U.S. involvement in Vietnam in Coppola's film.

54. Symes, "Beating Up the Classics," 90.

55. Elsaesser, *Fassbinder's Germany*, 17.

56. For a fuller interpretation of this soundtrack, see my chapter "Narrative, Sound, and Film: Fassbinder's *The Marriage of Maria Braun*," in *Fields of Vision: Essays in Film Studies, Visual Anthropology, and Photography*, ed. Leslie Devereaux and Roger Hillman (Berkeley: University of California Press, 1995), 181–95.

57. The Lacanian term is usually used to address the viewer's interaction with the screen image and the stitching process that creates an illusion of unity.

58. Robert Rosenstone, *Visions of the Past: The Challenge of Film to Our Idea of History* (Cambridge: Harvard University Press, 1995), 44.

59. Annabel J. Cohen, "Introduction to the Special Volume on the Psychology of Film Music," *Psychomusicology: A Journal of Research in Music Cognition* 13, nos. 1/2 (Spring/Fall 1994): 2.

60. Ibid., 5.

61. Berenice Carroll-Phelan and Peter J. Hampson, "Multiple Components of the Perception of Musical Sequences: A Cognitive Neuroscience Analysis and Some Implications for Auditory Imagery," *Music Perception* 13, no. 4 (Summer 1996): 549.

62. Ibid., 555.

63. David Lidov, "Music," in *Encyclopedic Dictionary of Semiotics*, 2d ed., ed. Thomas A. Sebeok (Berlin: Mouton de Gruyter, 1994), 585.

64. V. Kofi Agawu, "The Challenge of Semiotics," in *Rethinking Music*, ed. Nicholas Cook and Mark Everist (New York: Oxford University Press, 2001), 138–60.

65. Lidov, "Music," 586.

66. Agawu, "The Challenge of Semiotics," distinguishes between "pitch-based analytical approaches . . . ('hard' semiotics) and some broader perspectives stemming from a more anthropological view of the musical work ('soft' semiotics)" (154). He applies "hard" semiotics to the melody "God Save the King," whereas the present study is concerned with such questions as how the one melody can be "read" so differently ("God Save the King" and the Prussian national anthem; a Haydn quartet movement and the "Deutschlandlied"): "soft" semiotics.

67. V. Kofi Agawu, *Playing with Signs: A Semiotic Interpretation of Classic Music* (Princeton, N.J.: Princeton University Press, 1991). "A topic . . . may be defined as a musical sign" (128). Examples from his far more extensive list of such signs, applying to works from the period 1770–1830, include "fanfare," "hunt style," "march," "Sturm und Drang," and "Turkish music" (30).

68. Mark deBellis, *Music and Conceptualization* (Cambridge: Cambridge University Press, 1995), 1.

69. Gabriele Brösske, " . . . a language we all understand: Zur Analyse und Funktion von Filmmusik," in *Strategien der Filmanalyse* (= *Münchner Beiträge zur Filmphilologie*, 1), ed. L. Bauer et al. (Munich: diskurs film, 1987), 12–13.

70. As quoted by Robert Stam, Robert Burgoyne, and Sandy Flitterman-Lewis, eds., *New Vocabularies in Film Semiotics: Structuralism, Post-Structuralism, and Beyond* (London: Routledge, 1992), 170.

71. Lucy Green, *Music on Deaf Ears: Musical Meaning, Ideology, and Education* (Manchester: Manchester University Press, 1988), 43.

72. Ibid., 217.

3. History on the Soundtrack

1. Nicholas Cook, *Beethoven Symphony no. 9* (New York: Cambridge University Press, 1993), viii, ix.

2. Andreas Eichhorn, *Beethovens Neunte Symphonie: Die Geschichte ihrer Aufführung und Rezeption* (Kassel: Bärenreiter, 1993). Pages 334–39 are concerned with interpretations of the work after 1918, while mention of Furtwängler, for instance, is confined to the first part of the book.

3. For its reception history preceding the advent of film, see Ruth Solie, "Beethoven as Secular Humanist: Ideology and the Ninth Symphony in Nineteenth-Century Criticism," in *Explorations in Music, the Arts, and Ideas: Essays in Honor of Leonard B. Meyer*, ed. Eugene Narmour and Ruth Solie (Stuyvesant: Pendragon, 1988), 1–42.

4. Heribert Schröder, "Beethoven im Dritten Reich: Eine Materialsammlung," in *Beethoven und die Nachwelt: Materialien zur Wirkungsgeschichte Beethovens*, ed. Helmut Loos (Bonn: Beethoven-Haus, 1986), 210, 218.

5. Dennis, *Beethoven in German Politics*, 158.

6. Sam H. Shirakawa, *The Devil's Music Master: The Controversial Life and Career of Wilhelm Furtwängler* (New York: Oxford University Press, 1992), 481.

7. And this must have been less a change than an afterglow. Richard Taruskin claims Furtwängler's performances "preserved in aspic a century-old tradition of Beethoven interpretation that went back precisely to the great figure the Bayreuth Festival worships. This was no secret in 1951; indeed that anachronistic link with Wagner was precisely what made Furtwängler indispensable to the occasion his performance celebrated." See Richard Taruskin, "Resisting the Ninth," *Nineteenth Century Music* 12 (1989): 244.

8. Dennis, *Beethoven in German Politics*, 162.

9. Ulrich Ragozat, *Die Nationalhymnen der Welt: Ein kulturgeschichtliches Lexikon* (Freiburg: Herder, 1982), 63.

10. For this fascinating chapter of music and ideology, see Caryl Clark, "Forging Identity: Beethoven's 'Ode' as European Anthem," *Critical Inquiry* 23 (Summer 1997): 789–807; Esteban Buch, *Beethoven's Ninth: A Political History*, trans. Richard Miller (Chicago: University of Chicago Press, 2003), 220–42.

Notes to pages 49–60

180

11. Wilfried van der Will, "Culture and the Organization of National Socialist Ideology, 1933 to 1945," in *German Cultural Studies: An Introduction*, ed. Rob Burns (New York: Oxford University Press, 1995), 121.

12. Clark, "Forging Identity," 803.

13. Richard Toop, "Dangerously Romantic," in *ABC Radio 24 Hours*, April 1994, 45.

14. Eichhorn, *Beethovens Neunte Symphonie*, 280.

15. Ibid., 338.

16. See Roger Hillman, "Germany after Unification: Views from Abroad," *Film Historia* 7, no. 2 (1997): 103–12.

17. See Ragozat, *Die Nationalhymnen der Welt*, 61–62.

18. Ibid., 61.

19. Pamela M. Potter, *Most German of the Arts: Musicology and Society from the Weimar Republic to the End of Hitler's Reich* (New Haven: Yale University Press, 1998), 17. The orchestra's financial future was secured by the Propaganda Ministry early in 1934, and it became the "official Reich Orchestra." Pamela M. Potter, "Musical Life in Berlin from Weimar to Hitler," in *Music and Nazism: Art under Tyranny, 1933–1945*, ed. Michael H. Kater and Albrecht Riethmüller (Laaber: Laaber-Verlag, 2003), 95.

20. For a still broader range, see James Wierzbicki, "Banality Triumphant: Iconograpic Use of Beethoven's Ninth Symphony in Recent Films," *Beethoven Forum* 10/2 (Fall 2003): 113–38.

21. Marc Silberman, "Interview with Helke Sander: Open Forms," in *Gender and German Cinema: Feminist Interventions*, vol. 1: *Gender and Representation in New German Cinema*, ed. Sandra Frieden et al. (Providence: Berg, 1993), 164.

22. The film's strange title bitterly inverts a slogan of the East German state: "die allseitig entwickelte sozialistische Persönlichkeit" [the all-around developed socialist personality]. Sander coins *Redupers* as an abbreviation of *"reduced personality."*

23. Gilles Deleuze and Félix Guattari, *A Thousand Plateaus: Capitalism and Schizophrenia*, trans. Brian Massumi (London: Athlone, 1988), 95.

24. Jay, *Downcast Eyes*, 265.

25. John Shepherd, *Music as Social Text* (Cambridge: Polity Press, 1991), 156.

26. Walter Murch, foreword to Chion, *Audio-Vision*, vii ff.

27. Albrecht Riethmüller, "Wunschbild: Beethoven als Chauvinist," *Archiv für Musikwissenschaft* 58, no. 2 (2001): 101.

28. Vida T. Johnson and Graham Petrie, "Tarkovsky," in *Five Filmmakers: Tarkovsky, Forman, Polanski, Szabó, Makavejev*, ed. Daniel J. Goulding (Bloomington: Indiana University Press, 1994), 27.

29. Maya Turovskaya, *Tarkovsky: Cinema as Poetry*, trans. Natasha Ward (Boston: Faber and Faber, 1989), 119.

30. Daniel J. Goulding, "Makavejev," in *Five Filmmakers*, 217.

31. For a complementary reading of this scene, see Petr Král (trans. Kevin Windle), "Pages from the Past: Tarkovsky, or the Burning House, Part III," *Slavic and East European Performance: Drama, Theatre, Film* 16, no. 2 (Spring 1996): 50.

32. The scant references to music are the one qualification to the otherwise finely nuanced analysis of Tarkovsky's soundtracks in Andrea Truppin, "And Then There Was Sound: The Films of Andrei Tarkovsky," in *Sound Theory / Sound Practice*, ed. Rick Altman (London: Routledge, 1992), 235–48. In particular my own analysis diverges from hers with regard to the function and source of music at the conclusion of *Stalker:* "The train roars by, obscenely blaring strains of orchestral music and filling the previously tranquil room with violence" (248).

33. But here as elsewhere Truppin's warning holds: "Ambiguity in sound stems not only from the inability to ascertain a sound's source, but also from uncertainty as to who, if anyone, in the diegesis is hearing the sound and in what state of mind" (ibid., 239).

34. Wolfgang Thiel, former East German author of a major book on film music (*Filmmusik in Geschichte und Gegenwart* [Berlin: Henschel, 1981]), gives this salutary reminder in relation to Tarkovsky's *The Mirror* (1974), where the final sequence is accompanied by the entry of the choir in Bach's *St. John Passion:* "Through the voice of Bach, Tarkovsky confesses who for him is the actual 'ruler over all lands' and the ruler throughout history. The entry of the choral section is unmistakably from offstage/offscreen. But in the given social context, sacred music only had ideological validity as a functionally secularized heritage of material culture." See Wolfgang Thiel, "Versiegelte Klänge, Gedanken zur musikalischen Konzeption in den Filmen von Andrej Tarkowski," in *Film und Musik*, ed. Regina Schlagnitweit and Gottfried Schlemmer (Vienna: Synema, 2001), 126.

35. See Andrey Tarkovsky, *Sculpting in Time: Reflections on the Cinema*, trans. Kitty Hunter-Blair (Austin: University of Texas Press, 1989), 204–206.

4. A Wagnerian German Requiem

1. Anton Kaes, "Holocaust and the End of History: Postmodern Historiography in Cinema," in *Probing the Limits of Representation: Nazism and the "Final Solution,"* ed. Saul Friedländer (Cambridge: Harvard University Press, 1992), 209.

2. Among the more panoramic approaches to music, see Russell A. Berman, "Of Fantastic and Magical Worlds," in *New German Filmmakers*, ed. Klaus Phillips (New York: Ungar, 1984), 374–76. The only really detailed account I have come across is that of Hans R. Vaget, "Syberberg's *Our Hitler:* Wagnerianism and Alienation," *Massachusetts Review* 23 (Winter 1982): 593–612. In particular Syberberg's use of the *Rienzi* Overture and the Prelude to act 1 of *Parsifal*, as well as his integration of aspects of the *Ring*, find insightful treatment here.

3. The connotations of Wagner under the Nazis extend beyond German borders. To give just one example, when an SA officer in Visconti's *The Damned* gives a drunken rendition of Wagner's "Liebestod," the extramusical associations are clear.

4. Carolyn Abbate, *Unsung Voices: Opera and Musical Narrative in the Nineteenth Century* (Princeton, N.J.: Princeton University Press, 1991), 13.

5. See Hans-Jürgen Syberberg, *Hitler, ein Film aus Deutschland* (Reinbek: Rowohlt, 1978), 154: "Die deutsche Frage ist die Kunst" [The issue for Germany is art]. Quoted by Stephen Brockmann, "Syberberg's Germany," *German Quarterly* 69, no. 1 (Winter 1996): 55. Brockmann describes Syberberg's films as "embodiments of a reactionary German idealism" (59). If *reactionary* were replaced by *utopian*, Syberberg would probably agree to what he would regard as an accolade. A German view aptly puts it thus: "Like a true Romantic, Syberberg laments art's loss of a center, and like the early German Romantics, he wants to create a new center for art with a new mythology of artifice. It is to be a center that art can develop to completion. Syberberg links up with modernism's project of an aesthetic revolution arising from the spirit of myth. But the German quest for paradise lost (Ludwig II and Karl May) always finishes up in imitation paradises, in individual mythologies bordering on madness." Bernd Kiefer, "Kulturmontage im Posthistoire: Zur Filmästhetik von Hans-Jürgen Syberberg," in *Montage im Theater und Film*, ed. Horst Fritz (Tübingen: Francke, 1993), 239.

6. Syberberg, *Hitler: A Film from Germany*, 9. Future references to this script in the body of the text are to *Hitler*, plus a page number.

7. Rudy Koshar, "*Hitler: A Film from Germany:* Cinema, History, and Structures of Feeling," in *Revisioning History: Film and the Construction of a New Past*, ed. Robert Rosenstone (Princeton, N.J.: Princeton University Press, 1995), 158.

8. But also Arnold Fanck's film *Der heilige Berg*. See Manfred Schneider, "Der ungeheure Blick des Kinos auf die Welt: Die Wissensmächte Musik und Film in Wagner/Syberbergs *Parsifal*," *Merkur* 38 (1984): 892. This combination locates Syberberg as not just reclaiming German myths from the Nazis but Germanicizing myths from Hollywood and international cinema.

9. I cannot agree with Paul Coates's claims that "nothing is made . . . of the crystal ball in *Citizen Kane* as a parallel to Syberberg's own crystal ball snow scene-opening" and, more generally, that "except in rare cases . . . the combinations [of 'endlessly variable signs'] are not meaningful." See Paul Coates, *The Gorgon's Gaze: German Cinema, Expressionism, and the Image of Horror* (Cambridge: Cambridge University Press, 1991), 122, 118.

10. This is featured with strong gender implications in Sanders-Brahms's *Germany Pale Mother*. Directly before her house is destroyed in a bombing raid, Lene nurses baby Anna as the historical broadcast fills the room, its semblance of invincible German military power cruelly at odds with the air-raid siren that interrupts Lene's listening.

11. Kiefer, "Kulturmontage im Posthistoire," 240, addresses the dramatic structure compatible with this: "Syberberg takes montage to be cultural montage, namely, the work involved in recalling what has been forgotten and suppressed in human memory, stored in pictures and sounds."

12. Roland Barthes, "Rhetoric of the Image," in *Image/Music/Text*, trans. Stephen Heath (New York: Hill and Wang, 1977), 44.

13. Jay, *Downcast Eyes*, 444.

14. Lacan's term *suture* is usually used to address the viewer's interaction with the screen image and the stitching process that creates an illusion of unity. Yet again the sense of hearing is downplayed, whereas in examples like this— historical "rightness" through invoking technology contemporary with the event, rather than a pristine quality—it clearly has great potential.

15. Late January 2004 this site listed just two Wagner works whose appearances in films made double figures, with the *Lohengrin* Bridal Chorus scoring forty-nine hits and the Ride of the Valkyries next at twelve.

16. David Huckvale, "The Composing Machine: Wagner and Popular Culture," in *A Night in at the Opera*, ed. Jeremy Tambling (London: Libbey, 1994), 135.

17. See Slavoj Žižek, "There Is No Sexual Relationship," in *Gaze and Voice as Love Objects*, ed. Renata Salecl and Slavoj Žižek (Durham, N.C.: Duke University Press, 1996), 221–23. Žižek traces Wagnerian features of Hollywood classicism that include "the invisibility of the apparatus that produces music," "emotions translated by music," and "narrative cueing" (222).

18. This achievement plus the kind of amalgam discussed above defuses, I feel, Rudy Koshar's objection that "the constant linking of Wagnerian music and Germanic myth with Hitler and the rise of Nazism" is "hackneyed." See Koshar, *"Hitler: A Film from Germany,"* 167.

19. On Wagner and nineteenth-century socialism, see Frank Trommler, "The Social Politics of Musical Redemption."

20. A brilliant meshing of the personal with the political occurs in a film directed by Jiří Menzel in 1966: "Liszt's *Les Préludes*, abused in the Third Reich through introducing radio announcements from the eastern front in pompous fashion, is used as a Nazi emblem in the film *Closely Watched Trains*, set in occupied Czechoslovakia. The music takes on a dimension of comedy when unexpectedly used to poke fun in heroic vein at the finally consummated love of the touchingly young Resistance fighter who had considered himself to be impotent. The special announcement (*Sondermeldung*) about the hero on the eastern front provokes laughter, but also alerts the viewer to ambivalence, because the music retains its dreadful political overtones. It functions as a metaphor for the subsequent slaying of the boy; the generally prevailing proximity of the categories of comedy and tragedy is evident here." See de la Motte-Haber and Emons, *Filmmusik*, 208–09.

21. An instructive instance of this and other Germanic works used before the Nazi era is Murnau's first Hollywood film, *Sunrise* (1927). *Les Préludes* features at the beginning, in a long lead-up to the grand chords that subse-

quently became Nazified. At that point we see a train at Central Station, and thereafter "natural sounds" take over from a continuation of the Liszt. The music functions purely dramatically, matching a snatch of *Till Eulenspiegel's Merry Pranks* when something rakish happens, or excerpts from Wagner's *Siegfried Idyll* when we see the first full domestic scene with mother, father, and child.

22. McClary, *Feminine Endings*, 128.

23. For example, Coates, *The Gorgon's Gaze*, 119; Kaes, *From Hitler to Heimat*, 70.

24. *Hitler*, 18: "[H]ere, at the end of these seven hours of the Hitler-Germany Tragedy, joy despite everything is still possible. . . . Not embracing the world in this kiss of the entire world, with joy, but entering the black hole of the future, full of melancholy."

25. Susan Sontag, "Syberberg's Hitler," in *Syberberg: A Filmmaker from Germany*, ed. Heather Stewart (Watford: BFI, 1992), 22 (originally published in *Under the Sign of Saturn*, 1979).

26. Paul Robinson, ed., *Ludwig van Beethoven, Fidelio* (Cambridge: Cambridge University Press, 1996), 159.

27. Ibid., 158.

28. Edward W. Said, "From Silence to Sound and Back Again: Music, Literature, and History," *Raritan* 17, no. 2 (Fall 1997): 6.

29. Dennis, *Beethoven in German Politics*, 162–63.

30. Emanuelle Senici and Anya Suschitzky, "Conference Report: 'Representations of Gender and Sexuality in Opera' September 14–17, 1995, State University of New York at Stony Brook," *Journal of Musicological Research* 15, no. 4 (1995): 278.

31. Compare Dennis, *Beethoven in German Politics*, 27: "But the famous trumpet call announcing salvation at the hands of an aristocratic redeemer complicates reception of this "rescue opera" as a piece of revolutionary propaganda."

32. Compare Ernst Bloch's interpretation of the trumpet signal in *Das Prinzip Hoffnung*.

33. James Webster, "The Form of the Finale of Beethoven's 9th Symphony," in *Beethoven Forum I*, ed. Lewis Lockwood and James Webster (Lincoln: University of Nebraska Press, 1992), 46, 50, and 61.

34. Ulrich Kurowski, "Was ist ein deutscher Film?" summarized in Kaes, *From Hitler to Heimat*, 44.

5. Alexander Kluge's Songs without Words

1. Oskar Negt and Alexander Kluge, *Public Sphere and Experience: Toward an Analysis of the Bourgeois and Proletarian Public Sphere*, foreword by Miriam Hansen, trans. Peter Labanyi et al. (Minnesota: University of Minnesota Press, 1993), 34.

2. See chap. 2, endnote 31.

3. Eric Rentschler, "Remembering Not to Forget: A Retrospective Reading of Kluge's *Brutality in Stone*," *New German Critique* 49 (Winter 1990): 39; Kaes, *From Hitler to Heimat*, 132; Omer Bartov, "War, Memory, and Repression: Alexander Kluge and the Politics of Representation in Postwar Germany," in *Murder in Our Midst: The Holocaust, Industrial Killing, and Representation* (New York: Oxford University Press, 1996), 139–52.

4. Godard went one step further: "Making a film today about the concentration camps is dishonest. It should have been made in 1943. The only person to have succeeded in making such a film recently is Alain Resnais, because he didn't make his film on the camps themselves, but on the memory of them." Quoted by Brown, *Overtones and Undertones*, 34.

5. "Das Politische als Intensität alltäglicher Gefühle: Rede bei der Verleihung des Fontane-Preises für Literatur in der Berliner Akademie der Künste," in Alexander Kluge, *Theodor Fontane, Heinrich von Kleist, und Anna Wilde: Zur Grammatik der Zeit* (Berlin: Wagenbach, 1987), 16.

6. For a rich, panoramic analysis of this film, see Timothy Corrigan, *New German Film: The Displaced Image*, rev. ed. (Bloomington: Indiana University Press, 1994), 12–17.

7. *Germany in Autumn* drew an audience within Germany approaching the 400,000 mark. Peter C. Lutze, *Alexander Kluge: The Last Modernist* (Detroit: Wayne State University Press, 1998), 226n16.

8. Margarete Myers Feinstein, "Deutschland über alles? The National Anthem Debate in the Federal Republic of Germany," *Central European History* 33, no. 4 (December 2000): 507.

9. Alan E. Steinweis, *Art, Ideology, and Economics in Nazi Germany: The Reich Chambers of Music, Theater, and the Visual Arts* (Chapel Hill: University of North Carolina Press, 1993), 166.

10. Banned by the Allies in 1945, the "Deutschlandlied" set to Haydn's melody was reinstated in 1952 as the official anthem of the fledgling West German state—a restoration only made possible by Austria having deemed the same melody no longer suitable for its national anthem in 1946! But the officially sanctioned verse for state occasions was the third, beginning "Einigkeit und Recht und Freiheit," "unity, justice, and freedom," its first abstract noun, of course, also open to particular interpretation during the Cold War., See Ragozat, *Die Nationalhymnen der Welt*, 55ff.

11. Feinstein, "Deutschland über alles?" 508.

12. Numbers of scenes refer to Alexander Kluge, *Die Patriotin: Texte/Bilder 1–6* (Frankfurt: Zweitausendeins, 1979). Subsequent page references in brackets are to this edition. The texts far exceed a script in their commentaries and speculations. Remaining gaps in the music are unlikely to affect a cinema audience's response, the examples having been run past a couple of musicologists. Nonetheless, I would welcome identification from readers.

13. Kaes, *From Hitler to Heimat*, 110. Kluge's central image is no mere whim of the director, as indicated in the article "Baggern im Mittelalter," *Die Zeit*

(Auslandsausgabe) 52 (December 27, 1996): 17. The summary of the article reads: "In Cologne archaeology has become a sport of the people. It is conducted by researchers and thieves."

14. A detailed analysis of Kluge's short film *Porträt einer Bewährung* (*Proven Competence Portrayed*, 1964) is to be found in Rudolf Hohlweg, "Musik für Film—Film für Musik: Annäherung an Herzog, Kluge, Straub," in *Herzog/Kluge/Straub*, ed. Peter W. Jansen and Wolfram Schütte (Munich: Hanser, 1976), 57–61. It is preceded (55–57) by a valuable close analysis of the opening of the feature film *Die Artisten in der Zirkuskuppel: ratlos* (*Artists under the Big Top*, 1968). The opening sequence of *Die Macht der Gefühle* (*The Power of Emotion*, 1983), especially the effect of the *Parsifal* Prelude (117), receives perceptive treatment in Lutze, *Alexander Kluge*, 116–31, while Caryl Flinn's *The New German Cinema*, 138ff., devotes a chapter to the film.

15. John Whiteclay Chambers II and David Culbert, *World War II: Film and History* (New York: Oxford University Press, 1996), 152. This quotation is also addressed to *Germany, Pale Mother* and *Hitler: A Film from Germany*. My modification in the text applies at least as much to Syberberg.

16. Quoted in Rey Chow, *Primitive Passions: Visuality, Sexuality, Ethnography and Contemporary Chinese Cinema* (New York: Columbia University Press, 1995), 93.

17. Even here, in this detail which seemingly belongs to post-1960s West German life, Kluge establishes a continuity in passing. In scenes 75ff., "The relationship of a love story to history," Fred Tacke and his wife pack their cases, while on honeymoon in Rome. Hers, he assures her, will be fetched by the "Fremdarbeiter" [the foreign (captive) laborer]. The same continuity is present in Reitz's *Heimat I*, with POWs as farm laborers.

18. John O'Kane, "History, Performance, Counter-Cinema—'Die Patriotin,'" *Screen* 26, no. 6 (November/December 1985): 8.

19. Agawu, "The Challenge of Semiotics," 143.

20. "Identity, the category of patriots. The word *patriot* stems from father-society. The French Revolution patriarchs call themselves patriots. From there the word was taken up by the Prussian reformers against the usurper, Napoleon. For roughly 150 years the word has been in the private possession of the political Right. The word is not used by Gaby Teichert herself." Kluge, *Die Patriotin*, 342.

21. Albrecht Dümling, "Eisler's Music for Resnais' *Night and Fog* (1955): A Musical Counterpoint to the Cinematic Portrayal of Terror," *Historical Journal of Film, Radio, and Television* 18, no. 4 (1998): 575–84 [accessed online].

22. Thomas Elsaesser, "New German Cinema and History: The Case of Alexander Kluge," in *The German Cinema Book*, ed. Tim Bergfelder, Erica Carter, and Deniz Göktürk (London: BFI, 2002), 185.

23. As noted by Kaes, *From Hitler to Heimat*, 240n12, Kluge's own assessment of his work was that ice, in its relationship to history, was an image central to

Die Patriotin. It seems even this road, at the level of more formal analysis, leads to Stalingrad.

24. My thanks to Deborah Crisp for pointing me in the direction of Skryabin and locating many of these pieces.

25. Especially in Rückert's Barbarossa poem (*Zeitgedichte*, 1814–15).

26. At least this holds for Kluge's audience/viewers in the late 1970s. But this is yet another example with historical offshoots. Goebbels "endorsed research in historical musicology only when it could serve propagandistic ends. Herbert Gerigk, for example, received support to write a biography of Sibelius in 1942 on the strength of its potential to help reinforce the 'Nordic ties' between Germany and Finland." Pamela M. Potter, "Musicology under Hitler: New Sources in Context," *Journal of the American Musicological Society* 49, no. 1 (Spring 1996): 81.

27. A BBC ban on *Finlandia* curiously remained in force until May 18, 1945, despite the armistice signed in September 1944 by Finland and the Soviet Union. See Robert Mackay, "Being Beastly to the Germans: Music, Censorship, and the BBC in World War II," *Historical Journal of Film, Radio, and Television* 20, no. 4 (October 2000): 519.

28. Howard Pollack, "Samuel Barber, Jean Sibelius, and the Making of an American Romantic," *Musical Quarterly* 84, no. 2 (Summer 2000): 183. See also Pamela M. Potter, *Most German of the Arts*, 134: "In its quest to accumulate a comprehensive knowledge of the Germanic race, the 'Ahnenerbe' defined Germanic music as broadly as possible, including all aspects of Nordic musical culture, past and present. Bose's first project for the SS was a research trip to Finland in summer 1936 to evaluate folk music materials."

29. Kaes, *From Hitler to Heimat*, 113.

30. At least this was the standard version of history at the time Kluge's film was made. For modifications to this version in the last decade, see John Erickson, "Barbarossa June 1941: Who Attacked Whom?" *History Today* 51, no. 7 (July 2001): 11–17.

31. See Kluge, *Die Patriotin*, 301: "Complete comprehension of films is conceptual imperialism, a colonisation of objects. If I have understood everything, something has been emptied. We have to make films which are totally opposed to this colonisation of the consciousness." One source he seems to have had in mind with these frames was a radio broadcast of the Haydn version on May 8, 1945. This was authorized by the Dönitz government; at midnight that night, hostilities officially ceased. Such a source could hardly be deduced from the film. See ibid., 433.

32. "Tausend Jahre fiel der Tau. / Morgen bleibt er aus. / Sterne treten ungenau / In ein neues Haus." [For a thousand years the dew fell / Tomorrow there will be none. / Stars enter a new house without precision.]

33. In this my view differs from that of Caryl Flinn: "And it is clear that Beethoven's Germanic 'patriotism' is at best illusory in *Die Patriotin*, nothing more than a crutch." See Caryl Flinn, "Strategies of Remembrance," 123.

188

Rather than a crutch it strikes me, to stay with the film's imagery, as part of the "Zusammenhang" formulated by the Knee.

34. Inspired by the famous Leipzig New Year's Eve concerts under Nikisch, Berlin also adopted the Ninth for the same occasion during the years 1927–32. It was performed at the Volksbühne by orchestras including the Berlin Philharmonic. See Ingeborg Allihn, *Musikstädte der Welt: Berlin* (Berlin: Laaber, 1991), 56. See also Karl Christian Führer, "A Medium of Modernity? Broadcasting in Weimar Germany, 1923–1932," *Journal of Modern History* 69, no. 4 (December 1997): 748: "Nearly all political parties welcomed the educational efforts of Weimar broadcasting. This is especially true of the Social Democrats, who enthusiastically believed that a common knowledge of works by Beethoven or Schiller would promote general enlightenment."

35. Utopian this may still be, but it is not the vague utopianism attributed to this Beethoven entry and indeed to the film as a whole by Rainer Rother, *Die Gegenwart der Geschichte: Ein Versuch über Film und zeitgenössische Literatur* (Stuttgart: Metzler, 1990), 94–95.

36. See the coauthors' introduction to Negt and Kluge, *Public Sphere and Experience*, xliii. See also the related views of Adorno, summarized and then quoted in the following: "Beethoven's works, genuinely revolutionary in their time, have come in a later period to function as elements of bourgeois ideology, expressing the ideal of the free individual and harmonious community in a society which is in reality totalitarian . . . 'a music's social function may diverge from the social meaning it embodies.'" Peter J. Martin, *Sounds and Society: Themes in the Sociology of Music* (Manchester: Manchester University Press, 1995), 91.

37. Stuart Liebman, "On New German Cinema, Art, Enlightenment, and the Public Sphere: An Interview with Alexander Kluge," *October* 46 (Fall 1988): 27.

38. Anton Kaes, "German Cultural History and the Study of Film: Ten Theses and a Postscript," *New German Critique* 65 (Spring/Summer 1995): 55.

6. Fassbinder's Compromised Request Concert

1. Andreas Huyssen, *After the Great Divide* (Bloomington: Indiana University Press, 1986), 197–98.

2. Thomas Elsaesser, "Primary Identification and the Historical Subject: Fassbinder and Germany," in *Narrative, Apparatus, Ideology: A Film Theory Reader*, ed. Philip Rosen (New York: Columbia University Press, 1986), 540, 548.

3. David Denby quoted by Philip Reed, "Aschenbach Becomes Mahler: Thomas Mann as Film," in *Benjamin Britten: Death in Venice*, ed. Donald Mitchell (Cambridge: Cambridge University Press, 1987), 181.

4. The same holds true of a very different satire, John Ruane's use of the Adagietto in his *Death in Brunswick* (1990). (Brunswick is a suburb of Mel-

bourne.) Here it is the favorite music of the mother of the mother-fixated central figure, and he puts on a recording in a scene when he offers her a fatal drink, all this done in outrageously lurid, self-satirical style (unlike Fassbinder's in this film).

5. Bernd Sponheuer traces offshoots of a Romantic philosophy of art in the prostration of the German "Bildungsbürgertum" before the altar of culture-as-religion. Ostensibly remote from political concerns, this paved the way for the aestheticization of politics, with devastating consequences. See Bernd Sponheuer, "Musik, Faschismus, Ideologie: Heuristische Überlegungen," *Die Musikforschung* 46, no. 3 (1993): 241–53. I rephrase part of p. 246 above. Sponheuer also poses the question, which his article indirectly answers, as to "how Beethoven's work . . . could be submitted to a reinterpretation in the sense of Fascism with so relatively few complications" (241). This situation led to filmmaker Wim Wenders's rejection of what he saw as an ideologically tainted musical tradition (see p. 136).

6. Eugen Hadamovsky, head of the Reich Radio until he was removed in April 1942, regarded Hitler and Beethoven as twin "high points of our spiritual heritage." See Dennis, *Beethoven in German Politics*, 142.

7. To this point this section draws on part of my more extensive analysis of "Narrative, Sound, and Film," 188–89.

8. Many Fassbinder films combine quotations from composers like Beethoven and Mahler with an original score by Peer Raben. The mapping of the soundtrack was a combined decision by director and composer, though apparently Fassbinder had major input into this film. See "Peer Raben: Work without End," 29–39. See also Hans Günther Pflaum and R. W. Fassbinder, *Das bißchen Realität, das ich brauche: Wie Filme entstehen* (Munich: Spangenberg, 1976), 121–28. The degree of involvement of the director is conveyed by the following: "As a rule, composer and director decide in tandem those places of the film where the music will be inserted. Both make concrete suggestions, and then decisions are usually made at the stage of mixing" (128).

9. The sanctioning of the profile would seem to be complete in a film of 2003. Sönke Wortmann's *Das Wunder von Bern* [*The Miracle of Bern*] celebrates the same soccer game with nostalgia.

10. McClary, *Feminine Endings*, 128.

11. Thomas Elsaesser, "Tales of Sound and Fury: Observations on the Family Melodrama," in *Film Theory and Criticism: Introductory Readings*, ed. Gerald Mast et al. (New York: Oxford University Press, 1992), 523.

12. The melos of melodrama is largely neglected in connection with Fassbinder. An exception is Caryl Flinn's treatment of the important topic of "Music and the Melodramatic Past of New German Cinema," in *Melodrama: Stage, Picture, Screen*, ed. Jacky Bratton et al. (London: BFI, 1994), 106–18. In relation to some of the following examples, she reaches conclusions that differ from mine.

13. My thanks for this telling point to an anonymous reader commissioned by Indiana University Press.

14. Flinn, "Music and the Melodramatic Past," 115. But while I agree with Flinn here, the argument mounted around the same Mahler symphony in *Lili Marleen* shows where we differ when she claims: "Even without access to Raben's or Fassbinder's intentions, it is difficult to imagine their selection of music here [Mahler] as much else but parodic." See Flinn, "Strategies of Remembrance," 133. A mythical rather than a more culturally specific referentiality also holds for the use of Mahler's Eighth in the epilogue of *Berlin Alexanderplatz*. See Andreas Rost, "Kinostunden der wahren Empfindung: Herzog, Wenders, Fassbinder, und der Neue deutsche Film," in *Positionen deutscher Filmgeschichte*, ed. Michael Schaudig (Munich: diskurs film, 1996), 407–408.

15. Hans Günther Pflaum, *Rainer Werner Fassbinder: Bilder und Dokumente* (Munich: Spangenberg, 1992), 76.

16. Potter, *Most German of the Arts*, 49.

17. See especially Saul Friedländer, *Reflections of Nazism: An Essay on Kitsch and Death*, trans. Thomas Weyr (Bloomington: Indiana University Press, 1993); Janusz Bodek, *Die Fassbinder-Kontroversen: Entstehung und Wirkung eines literarischen Textes* (Frankfurt/Main: Lang, 1991), 213–26; Coates, *The Gorgon's Gaze*, 135–40.

18. See the section "Popular Entertainment and the Fate of High Culture," in Potter, *Most German of the Arts*, 25ff.

19. At least the copy used, Roxy-Film 1980: the MIA video replaces this with a sort of sepia print of an undefined town with a couple of spires sticking up that could be Zurich.

20. See Flinn, "Strategies of Remembrance," 136: "The film finally suggests the irreducibility of music to fixed functions, objects, or desires of any sort."

21. When in quotation marks, the title refers to the song; when italicized, it refers to the film.

22. Less vacillating, and certainly less well known, the BBC exercised a comparable policy: "While it is true that there was no blanket ban on German music, within days of the start of the war music programming was being subjected to a 'racial' filter. By July 1940 a formal blacklist of 'alien' composers was in operation, enduring with minor modifications for the duration of the war." Mackay, "Being Beastly to the Germans," 513–14.

23. Thomas Elsaesser, "Subject Positions, Speaking Positions: From *Holocaust, Our Hitler*, and *Heimat* to *Shoah* and *Schindler's List*," in *The Persistence of History: Cinema, Television, and the Modern Event*, ed. Vivian Sobchack (London: Routledge, 1996), 164.

24. Fred Ritzel and Jens Thiele, "Ansätze einer interdisziplinären Filmanalyse am Beispiel *Lili Marleen* (R. W. Fassbinder, BRD 1980)," *Filmanalyse interdisziplinär* (special volume of *LiLi*) 15 (1988): 114.

25. Erik Levi, "Music and National Socialism: The Politicisation of Criticism,

Composition, and Performance," in *The Nazification of Art: Art, Design, Music, Architecture, and Film in the Third Reich,* ed. Brandon Taylor and Wilfried van der Will (Winchester: Winchester School of Art Press, 1990), 165.

26. "Not only musicians but all Germans are involved in the fate of German music, for in no other art does the race of Bach, Beethoven, and Bruckner tower over all others to the same degree as in music." In *Zeitschrift für Musik,* October 1939, 1030, quoted in Josef Wulf, *Kultur im Dritten Reich: Musik* (Frankfurt/Main: Ullstein, 1989), 323. See also Benjamin Marcus Korstvedt, "Anton Bruckner in the Third Reich and After: An Essay on Ideology and Bruckner Reception," *Musical Quarterly* 80, no. 1 (Spring 1996): 138–39. For more on music programming in the Third Reich, see Potter, *Most German of the Arts,* 26.

27. See Linda Schulte-Sasse, *Entertaining the Third Reich* (Durham, N.C.: Duke University Press, 1996), 297. Highly suggestive in the current context is her description of the "Beethoven" scene in *Wunschkonzert,* the "epiphanous ecstasy" of the audience, the way "'high' Culture becomes a collective mirror, though the film unwittingly reveals this Culture as ideology," and above all the way "'Beethoven' freezes time in a tableau of listeners with their heads dutifully cocked in attention, as if to ironize the 'contemplative' reception of art" (296). Fassbinder mirror images each of these descriptions in "low" culture, but also transgresses the national unambiguity, the "common German cultural heritage" (296) binding the listeners.

28. Ritzel and Thiele, "Ansätze einer interdisziplinären Filmanalyse," 127, point out a musical reference to Fassbinder's own reworking of Döblin's novel with a self-quotation by Raben of his music (the "Waldmusik") for the other work. As so often with Fassbinder, the issue of referentiality becomes very involved indeed. Beyond self-advertisement of his own version of his idol's work, Fassbinder finds a blueprint for his own artistic procedure in this film of transforming a given biography.

29. Most notably in his play *Der Müll, die Stadt, und der Tod* (*The Garbage, the City, and Death*), written in 1975, performed once in Germany to a closed audience in 1985, but also in his unrealized plan to serialize Freytag's novel *Soll und Haben.*

30. UFA, already a famous production company in the 1920s, fell under the aegis of the Propaganda Ministry in 1933, the year of the Nazi takeover.

31. Karen Jaehne, review of *Lili Marleen* in *Film Quarterly* 35, no. 2 (Winter 1981–82): 46.

32. Royal S. Brown, "Film Music: The Good, the Bad, and the Ugly," *Cinéaste* 21, no. 1–2 (February 1995): 64.

33. On hardening policies on jazz in the Third Reich, see Michael Kater, "Forbidden Fruit? Jazz in the Third Reich," *American Historical Review* 94, no. 1 (February 1989): 11–43, and more extensively in his *Different Drummers: Jazz in the Culture of Nazi Germany* (New York: Oxford University Press, 1992).

34. Dennis, *Beethoven in German Politics*, 168.

35. In Kluge's film it, or rather its outgrowth in the Holocaust, is nonetheless there from the outset at the acoustic level. Hitler is also seen fleetingly a single time. At the end of a sequence where the voiceover comments on a figure enacting an absurdly ecstatic goosestep, it moralizes about how Knees are not meant to walk. The inversion of history from above and history from below is total.

36. Friedländer, *Reflections of Nazism*, 17.

37. Schulte-Sasse, *Entertaining the Third Reich*, 291. This seemed to have a musical corollary. In a chapter examining twelve Nazi-era films about ten composers, Guido Heldt concludes: "The gods from the pantheon of German music are missing. There is no Beethoven, Wagner, or Bruckner." Guido Heldt, "Hardly Heroes: Composers as a Subject in National Socialist Cinema," *Music and Nazism: Art under Tyranny, 1933-1945*, eds. Michael H. Kater and Albrecht Riethmüller (Laaber: Laaber, 2003), 116.

38. Wolfgang Benz, "The Ritual and Stage Management of National Socialism: Techniques of Domination and the Public Sphere," in *The Attractions of Fascism*, ed. John Milfull (New York: Berg, 1990), 287.

39. Edward W. Said, *Musical Elaborations* (London: Vintage, 1992), 70.

40. See Michael Meyer, *The Politics of Music in the Third Reich* (New York: Peter Lang, 1993), 59n98.

41. See Albrecht Riethmüller, "Musik, die 'deutscheste' Kunst," in *Verfemte Musik: Komponisten in den Diktaturen unseres Jahrhunderts*, ed. Joachim Braun et al. (Frankfurt/Main: Peter Lang, 1995), 91–103.

42. Potter, "Musicology under Hitler," 105.

43. Deleuze and Guattari, *A Thousand Plateaus*, 302. For what they understand by "deterritorialized," we have merely to invert the terms in the following: "territorialized, in other words, regulated by matters of expression rather than by stimuli in the exterior milieu" (332).

44. See Hans Vaget, "National and Universal," in *Music and German National Identity*, ed. Celia Applegate and Pamela Potter (Chicago: University of Chicago Press, 2002), 173: "This nationalistic habit of mind induced most Germans to believe that the perceived hegemony of German music somehow justified and, in the last analysis, legitimized Germany's push for comparable political hegemony. This sort of reasoning found its most influential articulation in the work of Houston Stewart Chamberlain and was fundamental to Nazi *Weltanschauung.*"

45. Ritzel and Thiele, "Ansätze einer interdisziplinären Filmanalyse," 127.

46. Michael Chanan, *Musica Practica: The Social Practice of Western Music from Gregorian Chant to Postmodernism* (London: Verso, 1994), 40.

47. For further nineteenth-century musical settings, see Herbert Lindenberger, "Closing Up *Faust:* The Final Lines According to Schumann, Liszt, and

Mahler," in *Interpreting Goethe's Faust Today*, ed. Jane K. Brown et al. (Columbia: Camden House, 1994), 123–32.

48. For all the changes rung by Raben in the course of his variations, this remains the basic register of his arrangements of the song. The historical Lale Andersen, on the other hand, fell foul of a 1943 restriction on jazz in the Sudetenland and was interrupted in the course of a performance by Hitler Youth squads. See Kater, "Forbidden Fruit?" 29.

49. See Meyer, *The Politics of Music*, 75. See also Steinweis, *Art, Ideology, and Economics*, 120–26, for the historical chapter of what he calls "A Jewish Chamber" (120).

50. Meyer, *The Politics of Music*, 76. See also Fred K. Prieberg, *Musik im NS-Staat* (Frankfurt/Main: Fischer Taschenbuchverlag, 1982), 84, 102.

51. Steinweis, *Art, Ideology, and Economics*, 120.

52. David Bathrick, "Inscribing History, Prohibiting and Producing Desire: Fassbinder's *Lili Marleen*," *New German Critique* 63 (Fall 1994): 48.

53. This "guest" appearance is the most vehement critique of Furtwängler in Ronald Harwood's play *Taking Sides* (1995), the basis for Szabó's recent film (see p. 48), just about the only barb that is not returned upon his attackers by the character of the conductor.

54. Bathrick, "Inscribing History," 43.

55. Dennis, *Beethoven in German Politics*, 168; Buch, *Beethoven's Ninth*, 205.

56. Bathrick, "Inscribing History," 53.

57. And where again there is a historical parallel in the high art realm. See Levi, "Music and National Socialism," 173–74, for the effect of the Führer's judgment on that of critics of Werner Egk's *Peer Gynt*, premiered in Berlin in 1938.

58. Elsaesser, *Fassbinder's Germany*, 293.

7. The Great Eclecticism of the Filmmaker Werner Herzog

1. For example, the historical straitjacketing of Büchner's Woyzeck in Herzog's period piece film seems to exclude any referentiality to Herzog's Germany. This, too, is belatedly in flux, with the final line of Herzog's *Invincible* (2001). In 1932 a bespectacled Talmud student asks, "What do we have to fear from the Nazis in Berlin in this remote Polish village?"

2. Robert Phillip Kolker and Peter Beicken, *The Films of Wim Wenders: Cinema as Vision and Desire* (Cambridge: Cambridge University Press, 1993), 12–13.

3. Here in discussion with Andreas Rost in 1985, cited in "Kinostunden der wahren Empfindung," 373.

4. See Holly Rogers, "Fitzcarraldo's Search for Aguirre: Music and Text in the Amazonian Films of Werner Herzog," *Journal of the Royal Musical Association* 129, no. 1 (Spring 2004): 77–99. While I disagree with some comments

on narrative and historical strategies, "the filmic relationship between music, text, and image" (Abstract, 99) is really illuminated.

5. Details are taken from the third program in the series *Filmkunst: Gespräche mit Werner Herzog*, transmitted by Austrian television (ÖRF) on January 10, 1992. My thanks to Franz Kuna for facilitating this.

6. In his analysis of the stagecraft of Büchner's play, Michael Ewans makes a persuasive case for these sounds being heard by Woyzeck alone in stage productions. See Michael Ewans, *Georg Büchner's "Woyzeck": Translation and Theatrical Commentary* (New York: P. Lang, 1989), 77.

7. For identifying just which Beethoven movement is being used here, my thanks to Michael Morley.

8. In a 1989 German film, Jörg Graser's *Abrahams Gold* (*Abraham's Gold*), the same music appears at the end as two figures stand by a graveside, one expressing the wish that it might have been "a beautiful burial." The body is that of a fourteen-year-old victim of this society, primarily of her unrepentant Nazi grandfather who has raised her. But to broaden the thrust of his accusation, the filmmaker brings in this music at the very point where the script simply has to allude to Büchner's play, and where his own film now alludes to Herzog's and its frame of reference. This acoustic equivalent of point of view—yet again it becomes clear how inadequate our vocabulary is for terms in the domain of the soundtrack—is a very powerful narrative gloss. At the same time a mise-en-abîme effect is created akin to that of *In a Year of Thirteen Moons* vis-à-vis *Death in Venice* (see p. 111).

9. Werner Herzog, *Fitzcarraldo: Erzählung* (Munich: Hanser, 1982).

10. For this information, and for refinement of my points, my thanks to Deborah Crisp.

11. See Deborah Crisp and Roger Hillman, "Verdi and Schoenberg in Bertolucci's 'The Spider's Stratagem,'" *Music and Letters* 82, no. 2 (2001): 251–67.

12. Katie Trumpener, "On the Road: Labor, Ethnicity, and the New 'New German Cinema' in the Age of the Multinational," *Public Culture* 2, no. 1 (Fall 1989): 20.

13. See also David Huckvale, "The Composing Machine," 136–37.

14. In his 1976 film *La Soufrière*, about a volcano that confounded seismological forecasts and failed to erupt, Herzog uses Siegfried's funeral march above the words "report on an inevitable catastrophe that did not take place." Here then the overtones are sardonic, a debunking of Wagnerian mythological grandeur, while simultaneously the music still effectively builds up the mood of the film. See also the following verdict on the effect achieved: "With *La Soufrière* Herzog uses classical music as an empty swell, an outrageous insult, a sardonic commentary. . . . In the Herzog film, the musical score accompanies inanimate objects, feels more like an afterthought, a post-production overlay, and so is doubly ironic, since the satire is frankly a beautiful much ado about nothing." William van Wert, "Last Words: Observations on a New Lan-

guage," in *The Films of Werner Herzog: Between Mirage and History*, ed. Timothy Corrigan (New York: Methuen, 1986), 70.

15. When in Mozart's *Magic Flute* a priest doubts Tamino's capacity to endure the ordeals, since he is a prince, the high priest replies: "Mehr, er ist ein Mensch," "He is a (full) human."

---

8. Pivot Chords

1. See Deborah Crisp and Roger Hillman, "Verdi in Postwar Italian Cinema," in *Opera and Cinema*, ed. Jeongwon Joe and Rose M. Theresa (New York: Routledge, 2002), 157–78.

2. Compare a German historian's view: "Thus did the Italian bourgeoisie keep on hanging on to the dream of a unified Italy, inspired by the great operas of Guiseppe Verdi, whose *Trovatore* or *Sicilian Vespers* brought barely concealed appeals to revolt against the occupier, and were understood by the Italian public as demonstrations of revitalized Italian national culture." Hagen Schulze, *Staat und Nation in der europäischen Geschichte* (Munich: C. H. Beck, 1995), 225.

3. An exception is Graham Bruce, "The Sounds of the Risorgimento Music in Visconti's Historical Drama *Senso*," in *Screening the Past: The Sixth Australian History and Film Conference Papers*, ed. John Benson et al. (Melbourne, 1993), 265. But his examination is confined to the level of narrative, not of ideology.

4. Claretta Tonetti, *Luchino Visconti* (London: Columbus Books, 1987), 61.

5. Wilhelm Furtwängler, "Anton Bruckner: Vortrag gehalten anlässlich des Festes der Deutschen Bruckner-Gesellschaft in Wien 1939," in *Johannes Brahms/Anton Bruckner* (Stuttgart: Reklam, 1963), 31.

6. Gilliam, "The Annexation of Anton Bruckner," 598.

7. For an intriguing gap in the text, not least (when considered alongside *Senso*) because at a Bruckner concert we only get to hear Verdi, see Caryl Flinn's discussion of Schroeter's *Bomber Pilot* in Flinn, *The New German Cinema*, 251–52.

8. Quoted in Gilliam, "The Annexation of Anton Bruckner," 592.

9. Compare Christa Brüstle's report of Michael H.Kater's paper at the conference "Bruckner-Probleme" (Berlin, October 7–9, 1996) in *Die Musikforschung* 50, no. 3 (1997): 336.

10. H. C. Robbins Landon, "The Baffling Case of Anton Bruckner," *High Fidelity*, February 1963, 48. Furtwängler's more "inside" view (*Johannes Brahms*, 35) confirms this.

11. Paul Stefan as quoted in Fabian R. Lovisa, *Musikkritik im Nationalsozialismus: Die Rolle deutschsprachiger Musikzeitschriften, 1920–1945* (Berlin: Laaber, 1993), 78.

12. See the following dialogue, after the Furtwängler recording is placed on the

turntable, in Ronald Harwood's play *Taking Sides* (1995), with the conductor being tormented by the crassly triumphalist U.S. Major Arnold:

ARNOLD: You know the last time it was played on these air waves?
FURTWÄNGLER: How should I know such a thing?
ARNOLD: Well then, I'll tell you. The last time this music was played on these air waves was after they announced that your pal Adolf had blown his brains out. Listen to it.
(*They listen.*)
Did they pick little K's [von Karajan's] recording? Did they pick some other band leader? No, they picked you and why? Because you and nobody else represented them so beautifully. When the Devil died they wanted his band leader to play the funeral march. You were *everything* to them. (Ronald Harwood, *Plays: Two* [London: Faber and Faber, 1995], 62–63)

13. Hans Weigel, *O du mein Österreich* (Munich: Artemis, 1976), 16.

14. See, e.g., Angela Dalle Vacche, *The Body in the Mirror: Shapes of History in Italian Cinema* (Princeton, N.J.: Princeton University Press, 1992), 135–36, 145; Mira Liehm, *Passion and Defiance: Film in Italy from 1942 to the Present* (Berkeley: University of California Press, 1984), 150; Tonetti, *Luchino Visconti,* 69.

15. Dalle Vacche, *The Body in the Mirror,* 121.

16. See Russell A. Berman, "Piedmont as Prussia: The Italian Model and German Unification," in *Cultural Studies of Modern Germany: History, Representation, and Nationhood* (Madison: University of Wisconsin Press, 1993), 73–88, for "the German account of Italian nationhood" (73).

17. See Henry Bacon, *Visconti: Explorations of Beauty and Decay* (Cambridge: Cambridge University Press, 1998), 139–87.

18. To adapt the title of Kaja Silverman's book, *The Acoustic Mirror: The Female Voice in Psychoanalysis and Cinema* (Bloomington: Indiana University Press, 1988).

19. A coda to Visconti's handling of his musical forces is perhaps to be seen, as later in *Death in Venice,* in the performance of Austrian music on the soundtrack by an Italian orchestra. Bruckner is estranged from his Austrian roots, particularly in a use of rubato which almost cranks down the orchestra at one point.

Conclusion

1. In Mieke Bal's introduction to *The Practice of Cultural Analysis: Exposing Interdisciplinary Interpretation* (Stanford, Calif.: Stanford University Press, 1999), 10–11.

2. Gilbert, "Ich habe von einem Esel gelernt," 63.

3. Lisa Saltzman, *Anselm Kiefer and Art after Auschwitz* (Cambridge: Cambridge University Press, 1999), 10.

4. Bal, *The Practice of Cultural Analysis*, 331.

5. See Roger Hillman, "Beethoven, Mahler, and the New German Cinema," *Musicology Australia* 20 (1997): 84–93.

6. Bal, *The Practice of Cultural Analysis*, 337. See also Rob Kroes, *If You've Seen One, You've Seen the Mall: Europeans and American Mass Culture* (Urbana: University of Illinois Press, 1996), 43–44: "In contrast to Americans, Europeans tend to pride themselves on a firm sense of cultural hierarchy, the sense of high versus low, of the sublime versus the vulgar. . . . The European cultural landscape, these critics tell us, has undergone a ruthless flattening in America."

7. Michael H. Kater, "Music: Performance and Politics in Twentieth-Century Germany" (review article), *Central European History* 29, no. 1 (1996): 93.

8. Silberman, "What Is German in the German Cinema?" 313.

9. Jonathan Harvey, *The Music of Stockhausen: An Introduction* (London: Faber and Faber, 1975), 101.

10. Leon Botstein, "Memory and Nostalgia as Music-Historical Categories," *Musical Quarterly* 84, no. 4 (Winter 2000): 532.

11. For the origins of this, see Na'ama Sheffi, trans. Martha Grenzeback, "Cultural Manipulation: Richard Wagner and Richard Strauss in Israel in the 1950s," *Journal of Contemporary History* 34, no. 4 (October 1999): 619–39.

12. Herbert Lindenberger, *Opera in History: From Monteverdi to Cage* (Stanford, Calif.: Stanford University Press, 1998), 158–59.

Select Bibliography

Film and Music/the Soundtrack

Boltz, Marilyn G. "Musical Soundtracks as a Schematic Influence on the Cognitive Processing of Filmed Events." *Musical Perception* 18, no. 4 (Summer 2001): 427–54.

Brösske, Gabriele. " . . . a language we all understand: Zur Analyse und Funktion von Filmmusik." In *Strategien der Filmanalyse* (= *Münchner Beiträge zur Filmphilologie* 1), ed. L. Bauer et al., 9–23. Munich: diskurs film, 1987.

Brown, Royal S. "Film and Classical Music." In *Film and the Arts in Symbiosis: A Resource Guide,* ed. Gary R. Edgerton, 165–215. New York: Greenwood, 1988.

———. *Overtones and Undertones: Reading Film Music.* Berkeley: University of California Press, 1994.

———. "Film Music: The Good, the Bad, and the Ugly." *Cinéaste* 21, nos. 1/2 (February 1995): 62–67.

Bruce, Graham. "The Sounds of the Risorgimento Music in Visconti's Historical Drama *Senso.*" In *Screening the Past: The Sixth Australian History and Film Conference Papers,* ed. John Benson et al. Melbourne, 1993.

Buhler, James, Caryl Flinn, and David Neumeyer, eds. *Music and Cinema.* Hanover, N.H.: Wesleyan University Press, 2000.

Burnand, David, and Benedict Sarnaker. "The Articulation of National Identity through Film Music." *National Identities* 1, no. 1 (March 1999): 7–13.

199

Burt, George. *The Art of Film Music.* Boston: Northeastern University Press, 1994.

Chion, Michel. *Audio-Vision: Sound on Screen.* Trans. Claudia Gorbman. New York: Columbia University Press, 1994.

———. *The Voice in Cinema.* Trans. Claudia Gorbman. New York: Columbia University Press, 1999.

Clancy, Jack. "Music in the Films of Peter Weir." *Journal of Australian Studies* 41 (1994): 24–34.

Cohen, Annabel J. "Associationism and Musical Soundtrack Phenomena." *Contemporary Music Review* 9, nos. 1/2 (1993): 163–78.

Cook, Nicholas. *Analysing Musical Multimedia.* New York: Oxford University Press, 2000.

Crisp, Deborah, and Roger Hillman. "Verdi and Schoenberg in Bertolucci's 'The Spider's Stratagem.'" *Music and Letters* 82, no. 2 (2001): 251–67.

———. "Verdi in Postwar Italian Cinema." In *Opera and Cinema,* ed. Jeongwon Joe and Rose M. Theresa, 157–78. New York: Routledge, 2002.

Flinn, Caryl. *Strains of Utopia: Gender, Nostalgia, and Hollywood Film Music.* Princeton, N.J.: Princeton University Press, 1992.

———. "Music and the Melodramatic Past of New German Cinema." In *Melodrama: Stage, Picture, Screen,* ed. Jacky Bratton, Jim Cook, and Christine Gledhill, 106–18. London: BFI, 1994.

———. "The Legacy of Modernism: Peer Raben, Film Music, and Political After Shock." In *Cinesonic: The World of Sound in Film,* ed. Philip Brophy, 171–88. North Ryde, NSW: Australian Film Television and Radio School, 1999.

———. "Strategies of Remembrance: Music and History in the New German Cinema." In *Music and Cinema,* ed. James Buhler, Caryl Flinn, and David Neumeyer, 118–41. Hanover, N.H.: Wesleyan University Press, 2000.

———. *The New German Cinema: Music, History, and the Matter of Style.* Berkeley: University of California Press, 2004.

Gorbman, Claudia. *Unheard Melodies: Narrative Film Music.* Bloomington: Indiana University Press, 1987.

———. "The State of Film Music Criticism." *Cinéaste* 21, nos. 1/2 (1995): 72–75.

———. "Drums along the LA River: Scoring the Indian." In *Cinesonic: Cinema and the Sound of Music.* ed. Philip Brophy, 97–115. North Ryde, NSW: Australian Film Television and Radio School, 2000.

Hohlweg, Rudolf. "Musik für Film—Film für Musik: Annäherung an Herzog, Kluge, Straub." In *Herzog/Kluge/Straub,* ed. Peter W. Jansen and Wolfram Schütte, 45–68. Munich: Hanser, 1976.

Kalinak, Kathryn. *Settling the Score: Music and the Classical Hollywood Film*. Madison: University of Wisconsin Press, 1992.

Kassabian, Anahid. *Hearing Film: Tracking Identifications in Contemporary Hollywood Film Music*. New York: Routledge, 2001.

Lack, Russell. "Arthouse Cinema and Classical Music." *Twenty-four Frames Under: A Buried History of Film Music*, 296–309. London: Quartet Books, 1997.

Larson, Randall D. *Musique fantastique: A Survey of Film Music in the Fantastic Cinema*. Metuchen, N.J.: Scarecrow, 1985.

Levinson, Jerrold. "Film Music and Narrative Agency." In *Post-Theory: Reconstructing Film Studies*, ed. David Bordwell and Noël Carroll, 248–82. Madison: University of Wisconsin Press, 1996.

Lorenz, Juliane, ed. "Peer Raben: Work without End." In *Chaos as Usual: Conversations about Rainer Werner Fassbinder*, trans. Christa Armstrong and Maria Pelikan, 29–39. New York: Applause, 1997.

Motte-Haber, Helga de la, and Hans Emons. *Filmmusik: Eine systematische Beschreibung*. Munich: Hanser, 1980.

Nasta, Dominique. *Meaning in Film: Relevant Structures in Soundtrack and Narrative*. Berne: Lang, 1991.

Rauchfleisch, Udo. *Musik schöpfen, Musik hören: Ein psychologischer Zugang*. Göttingen and Zurich: Vandenhoeck und Ruprecht, 1996.

Reed, Philip. "Aschenbach Becomes Mahler: Thomas Mann as Film." In *Benjamin Britten: Death in Venice*, ed. Donald Mitchell, 178–83. Cambridge: Cambridge University Press, 1987.

Schneider, Norbert Jürgen. *Handbuch Filmmusik I: Musikdramaturgie im Neuen Deutschen Film*. 2d ed. Munich: Oelschläger, 1990.

Stilwell, Robynn J. "'I just put a drone under him . . . ': Collage and Subversion in the Score of 'Die Hard.'" *Music and Letters* 78, no. 4 (November 1997): 551–80.

Symes, Colin. "Beating up the Classics: Aspects of a Compact Discourse." *Popular Music* 16, no. 1 (January 1997): 81–95.

Žižek, Slavoj. "There Is No Sexual Relationship." In *Gaze and Voice as Love Objects*, ed. Renate Saleci and Slavoj Žižek, 208–49. Durham, N.C.: Duke University Press, 1996.

Music and Culture

Abbate, Carolyn. *Unsung Voices: Opera and Musical Narrative in the Nineteenth Century*. Princeton, N.J.: Princeton University Press, 1991.

Agawu, V. Kofi. *Playing with Signs: A Semiotic Interpretation of Classic Music*. Princeton, N.J.: Princeton University Press, 1991.

———. "The Challenge of Semiotics." In *Rethinking Music*, ed. Nicholas

Cook and Mark Everist, 138–60. Oxford: Oxford University Press, 2001.

Allihn, Ingeborg. *Musikstädte der Welt: Berlin.* Laaber: Laaber, 1991.

Applegate, Celia, and Pamela Potter, eds. *Music and German National Identity.* Chicago: University of Chicago Press, 2002.

Barthes, Roland. "Rhetoric of the Image." In *Image/Music/Text.* Trans. Stephen Heath. New York: Hill and Wang, 1977.

Botstein, Leon. "Memory and Nostalgia as Music-Historical Categories." *Musical Quarterly* 84, no. 4 (Winter 2000): 531–36.

Buch, Esteban. *Beethoven's Ninth: A Political History.* Trans. Richard Miller. Chicago: University of Chicago Press, 2003.

Carroll-Phelan, Berenice, and Peter J. Hampson. "Multiple Components of the Perception of Musical Sequences: A Cognitive Neuroscience Analysis and Some Implications for Auditory Imagery." *Music Perception* 13, no. 4 (Summer 1996): 517–61.

Chanan, Michael. *Musica Practica: The Social Practice of Western Music from Gregorian Chant to Postmodernism.* London: Verso, 1994.

Clark, Caryl. "Forging Identity: Beethoven's 'Ode' as European Anthem." *Critical Inquiry* 23 (Summer 1997): 789–807.

Cohen, Annabel J. "Introduction to the Special Volume on the Psychology of Film Music." *Psychomusicology: A Journal of Research in Music Cognition* 13, nos. 1/2 (Spring/Fall 1994).

Cook, Nicholas. *Beethoven Symphony No 9.* New York: Cambridge University Press, 1993.

deBellis, Mark. *Music and Conceptualization.* Cambridge: Cambridge University Press, 1995.

Dennis, David B. *Beethoven in German Politics, 1870–1989.* New Haven, Conn.: Yale University Press, 1996.

Dümling, Albrecht. "Eisler's Music for Resnais' *Night and Fog* (1955): A Musical Counterpoint to the Cinematic Portrayal of Terror." *Historical Journal of Film, Radio and Television* 18, no. 4 (1998): 575–84.

Eichhorn, Andreas. *Beethovens Neunte Symphonie: Die Geschichte ihrer Aufführung und Rezeption.* Kassel: Bärenreiter, 1993.

Feinstein, Margarete Myers. "Deutschland über alles? The National Anthem Debate in the Federal Republic of Germany." *Central European History* 33, no. 4 (December 2000): 505–31.

Furtwängler, Wilhelm. "Anton Bruckner: Vortrag gehalten anlässlich des Festes der Deutschen Bruckner-Gesellschaft in Wien 1939." In *Johannes Brahms/Anton Bruckner.* Stuttgart: Reklam, 1963.

Gilbert, Michael. "'Ich habe von einem Esel gelernt': Eisler Pro und Contra Schönberg." In *High and Low Cultures: German Attempts at Media-*

tion, ed. Reinhold Grimm and Jost Hermand, 59–74. Madison: University of Wisconsin Press, 1994.

Gilliam, Bryan. "The Annexation of Anton Bruckner: Nazi Revisionism and the Politics of Appropriation." *Musical Quarterly* 78, no. 3 (Fall 1994): 584–604.

Green, Lucy. *Music on Deaf Ears: Musical Meaning, Ideology, and Education.* Manchester: Manchester University Press, 1988.

Harvey, Jonathan. *The Music of Stockhausen: An Introduction.* London: Faber and Faber, 1975.

Heldt, Guido. "Hardly Heroes: Composers as a Subject in National Socialist Cinema." In *Music and Nazism: Art under Tyranny, 1933–1945*, ed. Michael H. Kater and Albrecht Riethmüller, 114–36. Laaber: Laaber, 2003.

Heyman, Barbara B. *Samuel Barber: The Composer and His Music.* New York: Oxford University Press, 1992.

Higgins, Kathleen. *The Music of Our Lives.* Philadelphia: Temple University Press, 1991.

Hillman, Roger. "Beethoven, Mahler, and the New German Cinema." *Musicology Australia* 20 (1997): 84–93.

Huckvale, David. "The Composing Machine: Wagner and Popular Culture." In *A Night in at the Opera*, ed. Jeremy Tambling, 113–43. London: Libbey, 1994.

Kater, Michael. "Forbidden Fruit? Jazz in the Third Reich." *American Historical Review* 94, no. 1 (February 1989): 11–43.

———. *Different Drummers: Jazz in the Culture of Nazi Germany.* New York: Oxford University Press, 1992.

———. "Music: Performance and Politics in Twentieth-Century Germany" (review article). *Central European History* 29, no. 1 (1996): 93–106.

Kater, Michael H., and Albrecht Riethmüller, eds. *Music and Nazism: Art under Tyranny, 1933–1945.* Laaber: Laaber, 2003.

Korstvedt, Benjamin Marcus. "Anton Bruckner in the Third Reich and After: An Essay on Ideology and Bruckner Reception." *Musical Quarterly* 80, no. 1 (Spring 1996): 132–60.

Kramer, Lawrence. *Music as Cultural Practice, 1800–1900.* Berkeley: University of California Press, 1990.

———. *Classical Music and Postmodern Knowledge.* Berkeley: University of California Press, 1995.

———. *Musical Meaning: Toward a Critical History.* Berkeley: University of California Press, 2002.

Levi, Erik. "Music and National Socialism: The Politicisation of Criticism, Composition, and Performance." In *The Nazification of Art: Art,*

Design, Music, Architecture, and Film in the Third Reich, ed. Brandon Taylor and Wilfried van der Will, 158–82. Winchester: Winchester School of Art Press, 1990.

Lidov, David. "Music." In *Encyclopedic Dictionary of Semiotics*, 2nd ed., ed. Thomas A. Sebeok, 577–87. Berlin: Mouton de Gruyter, 1994.

Lindenberger, Herbert. "Closing up *Faust:* The Final Lines According to Schumann, Liszt, and Mahler." In *Interpreting Goethe's Faust Today*, ed. Jane K. Brown et al., 123–32. Columbia: Camden House, 1994.

———. *Opera in History: From Monteverdi to Cage.* Stanford, Calif.: Stanford University Press, 1998.

Lovisa, Fabian R. *Musikkritik im Nationalsozialismus: Die Rolle deutschsprachiger Musikzeitschriften, 1920–1945.* Laaber: Laaber, 1993.

Mackay, Robert. "Being Beastly to the Germans: Music, Censorship, and the BBC in World War II." *Historical Journal of Film, Radio, and Television* 20, no. 4 (October 2000): 513–25.

Martin, Peter J. *Sounds and Society: Themes in the Sociology of Music.* Manchester: Manchester University Press, 1995.

McClary, Susan. *Feminine Endings: Music, Gender, and Sexuality.* Minneapolis: University of Minnesota Press, 1991.

Meyer, Michael. *The Politics of Music in the Third Reich.* New York: Peter Lang, 1993.

Pollack, Howard. "Samuel Barber, Jean Sibelius, and the Making of an American Romantic." *Musical Quarterly* 84, no. 2 (Summer 2000): 175–205.

Potter, Pamela M. "Musicology under Hitler: New Sources in Context." *Journal of the American Musicological Society* 49, no. 1 (Spring 1996): 70–113.

———. *Most German of the Arts: Musicology and Society from the Weimar Republic to the End of Hitler's Reich.* New Haven, Conn.: Yale University Press, 1998.

———. "Musical Life in Berlin from Weimar to Hitler." In *Music and Nazism: Art under Tyranny, 1933–1945*, ed. Michael H. Kater and Albrecht Riethmüller, 90–101. Laaber: Laaber, 2003.

Prieberg, Fred K. *Musik im NS-Staat.* Frankfurt/Main: Fischer Taschenbuchverlag, 1982.

Ragozat, Ulrich. *Die Nationalhymnen der Welt: Ein kulturgeschichtliches Lexikon.* Freiburg: Herder, 1982.

Riethmüller, Albrecht. "Musik, die 'deutscheste' Kunst." In *Verfemte Musik: Komponisten in den Diktaturen unseres Jahrhunderts*, ed. Joachim Braun et al., 91–103. Frankfurt/Main: Peter Lang, 1995.

———. "Wunschbild: Beethoven als Chauvinist." *Archiv für Musikwissenschaft* 58, no. 2 (2001): 91–109.

Robinson, Paul, ed. *Ludwig van Beethoven, Fidelio.* Cambridge: Cambridge University Press, 1996.
Said, Edward W. *Musical Elaborations.* London: Vintage, 1992.
———. "From Silence to Sound and Back Again: Music, Literature, and History." *Raritan* 17, no. 2 (Fall 1997): 1–21.
Schröder, Heribert. "Beethoven im Dritten Reich: Eine Materialsammlung." In *Beethoven und die Nachwelt: Materialien zur Wirkungsgeschichte Beethovens,* ed. Helmut Loos, 187–221. Bonn: Beethoven-Haus, 1986.
Senici, Emanuelle, and Anya Suschitzky. "Conference Report: 'Representations of Gender and Sexuality in Opera' September 14–17, 1995, State University of New York at Stony Brook." *Journal of Musicological Research* 15, no. 4 (1995).
Sheffi, Na'ama. "Cultural Manipulation: Richard Wagner and Richard Strauss in Israel in the 1950s." Trans. Martha Grenzeback. *Journal of Contemporary History* 34, no. 4 (October 1999): 619–39.
Shepherd, John. *Music as Social Text.* Cambridge: Polity Press, 1991.
Shepherd, John, and Peter Wicke. *Music and Cultural Theory.* Cambridge: Polity Press, 1997.
Shirakawa, Sam H. *The Devil's Music Master: The Controversial Life and Career of Wilhelm Furtwängler.* New York: Oxford University Press, 1992.
Solie, Ruth. "Beethoven as Secular Humanist: Ideology and the Ninth Symphony in Nineteenth-Century Criticism." In *Explorations in Music, the Arts, and Ideas: Essays in Honor of Leonard B. Meyer,* ed. Eugene Narmour and Ruth Solie, 1–42. Stuyvesant: Pentagon, 1988.
Sponheuer, Bernd. "Musik, Faschismus, Ideologie: Heuristische Überlegungen." *Die Musikforschung* 46, no. 3 (1993): 241–53.
———. "Reconstructing the Ideal Types of the 'German' in Music." In *Music and German National Identity,* ed. Celia Applegate and Pamela Potter, 36–58. Chicago: University of Chicago Press, 2002.
Steinweis, Alan E. *Art, Ideology, and Economics in Nazi Germany: The Reich Chambers of Music, Theater, and the Visual Arts.* Chapel Hill: University of North Carolina Press, 1993.
Swain, Joseph P. "The Range of Musical Semantics." *Journal of Aesthetics and Art Criticism* 54, no. 2 (Spring 1996): 135–52.
Taruskin, Richard. "Resisting the Ninth." *Nineteenth Century Music* 12 (1989): 241–56.
Treitler, Leo. *Music and the Historical Imagination.* Cambridge: Harvard University Press, 1989.
Trommler, Frank. "The Social Politics of Musical Redemption." In *Re-Reading Wagner,* ed. Reinhold Grimm and Jost Hermand, 119–35. Madison: University of Wisconsin Press, 1993.

Webster, James. "The Form of the Finale of Beethoven's 9th Symphony." In *Beethoven Forum I*, ed. Lewis Lockwood and James Webster, 25–62. Lincoln: University of Nebraska Press, 1992.

Wulf, Josef. *Kultur im Dritten Reich: Musik*. Frankfurt/Main: Ullstein, 1989.

German Cinema

Bartov, Omer. "War, Memory, and Repression: Alexander Kluge and the Politics of Representation in Postwar Germany." In *Murder in Our Midst: The Holocaust, Industrial Killing, and Representation*, 139–52. New York: Oxford University Press, 1996.

Bathrick, David. "Inscribing History, Prohibiting and Producing Desire: Fassbinder's *Lili Marleen*." *New German Critique* 63 (Fall 1994): 35–53.

Berman, Russell A. "Of Fantastic and Magical Worlds." In *New German Filmmakers*, ed. Klaus Phillips, 359–78. New York: Ungar, 1984.

Bodek, Janusz. *Die Fassbinder-Kontroversen: Entstehung und Wirkung eines literarischen Textes*. Frankfurt/Main: Lang, 1991.

Brockmann, Stephen. "Syberberg's Germany." *German Quarterly* 69, no. 1 (Winter 1996): 48–62.

Coates, Paul. *The Gorgon's Gaze: German Cinema, Expressionism, and the Image of Horror*. Cambridge: Cambridge University Press, 1991.

Corrigan, Timothy. *New German Film: The Displaced Image*. Rev. ed. Bloomington: Indiana University Press, 1994.

Elsaesser, Thomas. "Primary Identification and the Historical Subject: Fassbinder and Germany." In *Narrative, Apparatus, Ideology: A Film Theory Reader*, ed. Philip Rosen, 535–49. New York: Columbia University Press, 1986.

———. *New German Cinema: A History*. New Brunswick, N.J.: Rutgers University Press, 1989.

———. *Fassbinder's Germany: History Identity Subject*. Amsterdam: Amsterdam University Press, 1996.

———. "Subject Positions, Speaking Positions: From *Holocaust, Our Hitler*, and *Heimat* to *Shoah* and *Schindler's List*." In *The Persistence of History: Cinema, Television, and the Modern Event*, ed. Vivian Sobchack, 145–83. New York: Routledge, 1996.

———. "New German Cinema and History: The Case of Alexander Kluge." In *The German Cinema Book*, ed. Tim Bergfelder, Erica Carter, and Deniz Göktürk. London: BFI, 2002.

Herzog, Werner. *Fitzcarraldo: Erzählung*. Munich: Hanser, 1982.

Hillman, Roger. "Narrative, Sound, and Film: Fassbinder's 'The Marriage of Maria Braun.'" In *Fields of Vision: Essays in Film Studies, Visual Anthropology, and Photography*, ed. Leslie Devereaux and Roger Hillman, 181–95. Berkeley: University of California Press, 1995.

———. "Germany after Unification: Views from Abroad." *Film Historia* 7, no. 2 (1997): 103–12.

Kaes, Anton. *From Hitler to Heimat: The Return of History as Film*. Cambridge: Harvard University Press, 1989.

———. "How German Is It? Probleme beim Schreiben einer nationalen Filmgeschichte." *Filmkunst* 148 (1995): 54–63.

———. "German Cultural History and the Study of Film: Ten Theses and a Postscript." *New German Critique* 65 (Spring/Summer 1995): 47–58.

Kiefer, Bernd. "Kulturmontage im Posthistoire. Zur Filmästhetik von Hans-Jürgen Syberberg." In *Montage im Theater und Film*, ed. Horst Fritz, 229–47. Tübingen: Francke, 1993.

Kluge, Alexander. *Die Patriotin: Texte/Bilder 1–6*. Frankfurt: Zweitausendeins, 1979.

Koepnik, Lutz. *The Dark Mirror: German Cinema between Hitler and Hollywood*. Berkeley: University of California Press.

Koshar, Rudy. "*Hitler: A Film from Germany*: Cinema, History, and Structures of Feeling." In *Revisioning History: Film and the Construction of a New Past*, ed. Robert A. Rosenstone, 155–73. Princeton, N.J.: Princeton University Press, 1995

Liebman, Stuart. "On New German Cinema, Art, Enlightenment, and the Public Sphere: An Interview with Alexander Kluge." *October* 46 (Fall 1988): 23–59.

Lutze, Peter C. *Alexander Kluge: The Last Modernist*. Detroit: Wayne State University Press, 1998.

Meurer, Hans Joachim. *Cinema and Divided Identity in a Divided Germany, 1979–1989: The Split Screen*. Lewiston, Me.: Edwin Mellen, 2000.

Moeller, Hans-Bernhard. "Zur deutschen Filmkomödie der Generation nach 1968." *Monatshefte* 93, no. 2 (Summer 2001): 196–208.

Negt, Oskar, and Alexander Kluge. *Public Sphere and Experience: Toward an Analysis of the Bourgeois and Proletarian Public Sphere*. Foreword by Miriam Hansen. Trans. Peter Labanyi et al. Minneapolis: University of Minnesota Press, 1993.

O'Kane, John. "History, Performance, Counter-Cinema—'Die Patriotin.'" *Screen* 26, no. 6 (November–December 1985): 2–17.

Pflaum, Hans Günther. *Rainer Werner Fassbinder: Bilder und Dokumente*. Munich: Spangenberg, 1992.

Pflaum, Hans Günther, and R. W. Fassbinder. *Das bißchen Realität, das ich brauche: Wie Filme entstehen*. Munich: Spangenberg, 1976.

Rentschler, Eric. "Remembering Not to Forget: A Retrospective Reading of Kluge's *Brutality in Stone.*" *New German Critique* 49 (Winter 1990): 23–41.

———. "From New German Cinema to Post-Wall Cinema of Consensus." In *Cinema and Nation*, ed. Mette Hjort and Scott Mackenzie, 260–77. London: Routledge, 2000.

Ritzel, Fred, and Jens Thiele. "Ansätze einer interdisziplinären Filmanalyse am Beispiel 'Lili Marleen' (R. W. Fassbinder, BRD 1980)." *Filmanalyse interdisziplinär* (special volume of *LiLi*) 15 (1988): 109–32.

Rogers, Holly. "Fitzcarraldo's Search for Aguirre: Music and Text in the Amazonian Films of Werner Herzog," *Journal of the Royal Musical Association* 129, no. 1 (Spring 2004): 77–99.

Rost, Andreas. "Kinostunden der wahren Empfindung: Herzog, Wenders, Fassbinder, und der Neue deutsche Film." In *Positionen deutscher Filmgeschichte*, ed. Michael Schaudig, 367–408. Munich: diskurs film, 1996.

Rother, Rainer. *Die Gegenwart der Geschichte: Ein Versuch über Film und zeitgenössische Literatur.* Stuttgart: Metzler, 1990.

Schneider, Manfred. "Der ungeheure Blick des Kinos auf die Welt: Die Wissensmächte Musik und Film in Wagner/Syberbergs 'Parsifal.'" *Merkur* 38 (1984): 882–92.

Schulte-Sasse, Linda. *Entertaining the Third Reich.* Durham, N.C.: Duke University Press, 1996.

Silberman, Marc. "Interview with Helke Sander: Open Forms." In *Gender and German Cinema: Feminist Interventions*, vol. 1: *Gender and Representation in New German Cinema*, ed. Sandra Frieden et al., 163–65. Providence: Berg, 1993.

———. "What Is German in the German Cinema?" *Film History* 8 (1996): 297–315.

Sontag, Susan. "Syberberg's Hitler." In *Syberberg: A Filmmaker from Germany*, ed. Heather Stewart, 13–25. Watford: BFI, 1992.

Syberberg, Hans-Jürgen. *Hitler, ein Film aus Deutschland.* Reinbek: Rowohlt, 1978.

———. *Hitler: A Film from Germany.* Preface by Susan Sontag, trans. Joachim Neugroschl. New York: Farrar Straus Giroux, 1982.

Trumpener, Katie. "On the Road: Labor, Ethnicity and the New 'New German Cinema' in the Age of the Multinational." *Public Culture* 2, no. 1 (Fall 1989): 20–30.

Vaget, Hans R. "Syberberg's *Our Hitler:* Wagnerianism and Alienation." *Massachusetts Review* 23 (Winter 1982): 593–612.

———. "National and Universal." In *Music and German National Identity*, ed. Celia Applegate and Pamela Potter, 155–77. Chicago: University of Chicago Press, 2002.

van Wert, William. "Last Words: Observations on a New Language." In *The Films of Werner Herzog: Between Mirage and History*, ed. Timothy Corrigan, 51–71. New York: Methuen, 1986.

German History and Cultural History

Benz, Wolfgang. "The Ritual and Stage Management of National Socialism: Techniques of Domination and the Public Sphere." In *The Attractions of Fascism*, ed. John Milfull, 273–88. New York: Berg, 1990.

Berman, Russell A. "Piedmont as Prussia: The Italian Model and German Unification." In *Cultural Studies of Modern Germany: History, Representation, and Nationhood*, 73–88. Madison: University of Wisconsin Press, 1993.

Burns, Rob, and Wilfried van der Will. "Americanization and National Identity." In *German Cultural Studies: An Introduction*, ed. Rob Burns, 310–23. Oxford: Oxford University Press, 1995.

Elias, Norbert. *The Germans: Power Struggles and the Development of Habitus in the Nineteenth and Twentieth Centuries*. Ed. Michael Schröter, trans. Eric Dunning and Stephen Mennell. New York: Columbia University Press, 1996.

Erickson, John. "Barbarossa June 1941: Who Attacked Whom?" *History Today* 51, no. 7 (July 2001): 11–17.

Friedländer, Saul. *Reflections of Nazism: An Essay on Kitsch and Death*. Trans. Thomas Weyr. Bloomington: Indiana University Press, 1993.

Führer, Karl Christian. "A Medium of Modernity? Broadcasting in Weimar Germany, 1923–1932." *Journal of Modern History* 69, no. 4 (December 1997): 722–53.

Fulbrook, Mary. *German National Identity after the Holocaust*. Cambridge: Polity Press, 1999.

Giesen, Bernhard. *Intellectuals and the German Nation: Collective Identity in an Axial Age*. Trans. Nicholas Levis and Amos Weisz. Cambridge: Cambridge University Press, 1998.

Hahn, Silke. "Vom *zerrissenen Deutschland* zur *vereinigten Republik*: Zur Sprachgeschichte der 'deutschen Frage.'" In *Kontroverse Begriffe: Geschichte des öffentlichen Sprachgebrauchs in der Bundesrepublik Deutschland*, ed. Georg Stötzel and Martin Wengeler, 285–353. Berlin: Walter de Gruyter, 1995.

Jäckel, Eberhard. *Das deutsche Jahrhundert: Eine historische Bilanz*. Stuttgart: Deutsche Verlags-Anstalt, 1996.

Mushaben, Joyce Marie. *From Post-War to Post-Wall Generations: Changing Attitudes toward the National Question and NATO in the Federal Republic of Germany*. Boulder, Colo.: Westview Press, 1998.

Parkes, Stuart. *Understanding Contemporary Germany*. London: Routledge, 1997.

Phillips, Donald G. *Post-National Patriotism and the Feasibility of Post-National Community in United Germany*. Westport, Conn.: Praeger, 2000.

Reichel, Peter. "Culture and Politics in Nazi Germany." In *Political Culture in Germany*, ed. Dirk Berg-Schlosser and Ralf Rytlewski, 60–77. New York: St Martin's Press, 1993.

Schröder, Richard. *Deutschland schwierig Vaterland: Für eine neue politische Kultur*. 3rd ed. Freiburg: Herder, 1995.

Schulze, Hagen, *Staat und Nation in der europäischen Geschichte*. Munich: C. H. Beck, 1995.

Sheehan, James J. "National History and National Identity in the New Germany." In *European Cultures: Studies in Literature and the Arts*, vol. 1: *1870/71–1989/90 German Unifications and the Change of Literary Discourse*, ed. Walter Pape, 25–36. Berlin and New York: W. de Gruyter, 1993.

van der Will, Wilfried. "Culture and the Organization of National Socialist Ideology, 1933 to 1945." In *German Cultural Studies: An Introduction*, ed. Rob Burns, 101–45. Oxford: Oxford University Press, 1995.

Verheyen, Dirk. *The German Question: A Cultural, Historical, and Geopolitical Exploration*. Boulder, Colo.: Westview Press, 1999.

Weidenfeld, Werner. *Nachdenken über Deutschland: Materialien zur politischen Kultur der Deutschen Frage*. Köln: Wissenschaft und Politik, 1985.

Other Works Cited

Assmann, Jan. *Das kulturelle Gedächtnis*. Munich: Beck, 2000.

Bacon, Henry. *Visconti: Explorations of Beauty and Decay*. Cambridge: Cambridge University Press, 1998.

Bakhtin, M. M. *The Dialogic Imagination: Four Essays*. Ed. Michael Holquist, trans. Caryl Emerson and Michael Holquist. Austin: University of Texas Press, 1981.

Bal, Mieke, ed. *The Practice of Cultural Analysis: Exposing Interdisciplinary Interpretation*. Stanford, Calif.: Stanford University Press, 1999.

Benjamin, Walter. "A Berlin Chronicle." In *Selected Writings*, vol. 2: *1927–1934*, ed. Michael W. Jennings et al., trans. Rodney Livingstone et al. Cambridge: Harvard University Press, 1999.

Bowler, Anne. "Methodological Dilemmas in the Sociology of Art." In *The Sociology of Culture: Emerging Theoretical Perspectives*, ed. Diana Crane, 247–66. Oxford: Blackwell, 1994.

Chambers, John Whiteclay, II, and David Culbert. *World War II: Film and History*. New York: Oxford University Press, 1996.

Chow, Rey. *Primitive Passions: Visuality, Sexuality, Ethnography, and Contemporary Chinese Cinema*. New York: Columbia University Press, 1995.

Dalle Vacche, Angela. *The Body in the Mirror: Shapes of History in Italian Cinema*. Princeton, N.J.: Princeton University Press, 1992.

Dear, I. C. B., gen. ed. *The Oxford Companion to World War II*. Oxford, New York: Oxford University Press, 1995.

Deleuze, Gilles, and Félix Guattari. *A Thousand Plateaus: Capitalism and Schizophrenia*. Trans. and foreword by Brian Massumi. London: Athlone, 1988.

Eley, Geoff, and Ronald Grigor, eds. *Becoming National: A Reader*. New York: Oxford University Press, 1996.

Elsaesser, Thomas. "Tales of Sound and Fury: Observations on the Family Melodrama." In *Film Theory and Criticism: Introductory Readings*, ed. Gerald Mast et al., 512–35. New York: Oxford University Press, 1992.

Ewans, Michael. *Georg Büchner's "Woyzeck": Translation and Theatrical Commentary*. New York: P. Lang, 1989.

Goulding, Daniel J., ed. *Five Filmmakers: Tarkovsky, Forman, Polanski, Szabó, Makavejev*. Bloomington: Indiana University Press, 1994.

Harwood, Ronald. *Plays: Two*. London: Faber and Faber, 1995.

Huyssen, Andreas. *After the Great Divide*. Bloomington: Indiana University Press, 1986.

Jay, Martin. *Downcast Eyes: The Denigration of Vision in Twentieth-Century French Thought*. Berkeley: University of California Press, 1993.

Johnson, Vida T., and Graham Petrie. "Tarkovsky." In *Five Filmmakers: Tarkovsky, Forman, Polanski, Szabó, Makavejev*, ed. Daniel J. Goulding, 1–49. Bloomington: Indiana University Press, 1994.

Kaes, Anton. "Holocaust and the End of History: Postmodern Historiography in Cinema." In *Probing the Limits of Representation: Nazism and the "Final Solution,"* ed. Saul Friedländer, 206–22. Cambridge, Mass.: Harvard University Press, 1992

Kolker, Robert Phillip, and Peter Beicken. *The Films of Wim Wenders: Cinema as Vision and Desire*. Cambridge: Cambridge University Press, 1993.

Král, Petr. "Pages from the Past: Tarkovsky, or the Burning House, Part III." Trans. Kevin Windle. *Slavic and East European Performance: Drama, Theatre, Film* 16, no. 2 (Spring 1996): 50–56.

Kroes, Rob. *If You've Seen One, You've Seen the Mall: Europeans and American Mass Culture*. Urbana: University of Illinois Press, 1996.

Landon, H. C. Robbins. "The Baffling Case of Anton Bruckner." *High Fidelity*, February 1963, 48.

Liehm, Mira. *Passion and Defiance: Film in Italy from 1942 to the Present*. Berkeley: University of California Press, 1984.

Morley, Dave, and Kevin Robins. "No Place Like *Heimat*: Images of

Home(land) in European Culture." In *Space and Place: Theories of Identity and Location,* ed. Erica Carter, James Donald, and Judith Squires, 3–32. London: Lawrence and Wishart, 1993.

Picht, Robert. "Disturbed Identities: Social and Cultural Mutations in Contemporary Europe." In *European Identity and the Search for Legitimacy,* ed. Soledad García, 81–94. London: Pinter, 1993.

Rosenstone, Robert. *Visions of the Past: The Challenge of Film to Our Idea of History.* Cambridge: Harvard University Press, 1995.

Saltzman, Lisa. *Anselm Kiefer and Art after Auschwitz.* Cambridge: Cambridge University Press, 1999.

Silverman, Kaja. *The Acoustic Mirror: The Female Voice in Psychoanalysis and Cinema.* Bloomington: Indiana University Press, 1988.

Stam, Robert, Robert Burgoyne, and Sandy Flitterman-Lewis, eds. *New Vocabularies in Film Semiotics: Structuralism, Post-Structuralism, and Beyond.* London: Routledge, 1992.

Tarkovsky, Andrey. *Sculpting in Time: Reflections on the Cinema.* Trans. Kitty Hunter-Blair. Austin: University of Texas Press, 1989.

Thiel, Wolfgang. "Versiegelte Klänge, Gedanken zur musikalischen Konzeption in den Filmen von Andrej Tarkowski." In *Film und Musik,* ed. Regina Schlagnitweit and Gottfried Schlemmer, 125–35. Vienna: Synema, 2001.

Tonetti, Claretta. *Luchino Visconti.* London: Columbus Books, 1987.

Truppin, Andrea. "And Then There Was Sound: The Films of Andrei Tarkovsky." In *Sound Theory / Sound Practice,* ed. Rick Altman, 235–48. London: Routledge, 1992.

Turovskaya, Maya. *Tarkovsky: Cinema as Poetry.* Trans. Natasha Ward. Boston: Faber and Faber, 1989.

Weigel, Hans. *O du mein Österreich.* Munich: Artemis, 1976.

Wolf, Eric R. *Envisioning Power: Ideologies of Dominance and Crisis.* Berkeley: University of California Press, 1999.

Index

213

Index

214

Index

215

Index

217

ROGER HILLMAN heads the Film Studies Program and convenes the German Studies Program at the Australian National University (Canberra).